PRACTICAL GARDEN DESIGN

BY THE SAME AUTHOR

Terrace and Courtyard Gardens
Grow it and Cook it (with Kate Crosby)

Practical
Garden Design

Denis Wood

with a foreword by
Graham Stuart Thomas, OBE, VMH

London
J. M. Dent & Sons Ltd

First published 1976

© Text, Denis Wood, 1976

All rights reserved. No part of this
publication may be reproduced, stored
in a retrieval system, or transmitted,
in any form or by any means, electronic,
mechanical, photocopying, recording or
otherwise, without the prior permission
of J. M. Dent & Sons Ltd.

Made in Great Britain
at the Aldine Press · Letchworth · Herts
for
J. M. DENT & SONS LTD
Aldine House · Albemarle Street · London

This book is set in 10 on 11 point Times New Roman 327

ISBN 0 460 04167 3

Contents

Plates

Plates

20. Picket or palisade fence in white-painted wood. *Photograph by courtesy of Messrs Larch-Lap Ltd.*

21. Practical single hunting and handgate.

22. Double white-painted hunting gate.

23. White obelisk. *Photograph by courtesy of Messrs Chilstone Garden Ornaments.*

24. Queen Victoria's dog Bosco at Frogmore.

25. Draped reclining figure by Henry Moore in a landscape designed by Lanning Roper. By courtesy of Sir Robert Sainsbury. *Photograph by Sidney W. Newbery.*

26. Bronze horse by Elizabeth Frink, in a landscape.

27. Elms near Chilton Foliat. By courtesy of the Princess Rupert Loewenstein.

28. Radiating steps at Buckhurst Park. By courtesy of Peter Palumbo Esq.

29. Pleached hornbeam alley at Great Bedwyn. Designed by Lanning Roper. By courtesy of Alistair Buchanan Esq.

30. Block steps in brick at Great Bedwyn. Designed by Lanning Roper. By courtesy of Alistair Buchanan Esq.

31. Roses over a gateway at Croft Castle. A National Trust property.

32. 'March Sunshine' daffodils naturalized in grass.

ILLUSTRATIONS IN TEXT

Foreword

by Graham Stuart Thomas, OBE, VMH

I feel that the title for this book should have been *Practical Garden Design seen through an Artist's Eye*. It has always amazed me during many years' friendship with Denis Wood that he has continually fused these two extremes—the practical and the artistic. Anyone who remembers the many exhibits put up by his firm at Chelsea Show in the fifties and sixties of this century will have realized that he has always combined these two qualities, so rarely found in equal abundance in an individual. And of course he has spent a long life in designing gardens and helping people with them, whether it is the mixing of concrete or preparing the soil to receive some new and treasured plant. So we find in this book a brain equally capable of explaining metricated modern gardening while the eye, the ear and the nose are calling us back all the time to some of life's fundamentals, the beauty of flowers, shadows, bird song and music, while fragrance greets us at every turn of the path. A fragrance of the memory, too, because for all the progress there is in modern garden design, at the back of the mind of each of us there is the escape route to the ancient traditions of English gardening—the simple flowers, fruits and the cobbled path.

Garden design is a subject of which one never reaches the end and about which the last word will never be written. Today garden design is not just the prerogative of the rich, employing a garden staff, but the pursuit and recreation of most households. Denis Wood loves gardens and plants, and our supposedly insuperable problems are melted away by the warmth of his approach to this age-old embellishment of our homes, and his thoughtful advice.

Acknowledgments

I thank my friend, W. T. M. Williams, a former colleague, for the drawings illustrating points of garden design and technical details; and 'all other my benefactors': Graham Stuart Thomas for suggesting I should attempt the book, Janice Robertson and Pamela Watson for continuing encouragement and guidance, and Mr Colin Allsebrook of Allsebrook Surveys for his assistance in matters of water supply, irrigation, fountains and waterfalls; Mr D. Pilkington of Hozelock Limited, Mr M. D. Squire of Wright Rain and Mr D. J. Tennant of John Blake Limited, makers of the Hydram. Mr J. D. Oakley of Penguin Swimming Pools Limited gave me useful practical advice.

I also thank Mr J. B. Stirrat of the Forestry Commission at Reading for the benefit of his experience on the density of planting hardwoods.

My thanks are also due to the Editors of *Country Life*, the *Daily Telegraph* and *The Spectator* for permission to draw upon articles written for their papers.

My thanks are also due to former colleagues in William Wood & Son Limited, Joyce Edmonds, William Brett and Neville Parsons; and very far from least those ladies who have so valiantly undertaken the typing, Ursula Bieri, Veronique Crowley and Shirley Wills.

FOR PHOENIX

Introduction

This book is concerned with the art of the possible in garden design, to study the hard facts of climate and terrain, to establish as it were the syntax before beginning to compose the poem or the piece of prose which the garden is to become. It begins with a look at prevailing local conditions of climate—rainfall, temperature, wind—and soil conditions and examines ways of exploiting or combating these. The twenty-one plans, with their commentaries, are intended progressively to be an exposition of the application to design of practical considerations.

Because, in Britain certainly, almost all the *raison d'être* of a garden is the cultivation of plants, I have dwelt in some detail on foundation planting—this being an integral and indispensable part of the designs. Secondary planting, being in the nature of decoration, is a matter of strong individual preferences and prejudices, and I have therefore not gone deeply into this except to provide short basic lists of some plants that may help an entire beginner at least to make a start, until he has gained the experience to alter and expand at his own judgment.

Some of the design plans indicate spaces for growing vegetables or full-scale kitchen gardens not only because these are natural in gardens worthy of the name, but also because a garden provides the opportunity of creating a self-supporting independent unit, an attractive concept at the present time, producing vegetables at home, conserving water falling within one's own ring fence, re-cycling what would otherwise be waste material, keeping bees for honey and to ensure pollination of fruit trees, runner beans and other plants, and possibly even embarking again on keeping hens.

The space occupied simply by a house itself takes up only a small proportion of a whole building plot or area of land that is now probably one's most valuable possession. It would seem well therefore to exploit this very expensive piece of property to the greatest possible degree by making it not only beautiful, but also useful, combining both in the manner of a French *potager*.

Measurements are given in imperial units and metric units in accordance with the International System (SI), which is explained in British Standard No. 3763 and in the British Standards Institution leaflet 'The use of SI units PD 5686'. This explains the use of millimetres, metres and kilometres only for measurements of length. The centimetre, although recognized, is not a preferred sub-multiple of the metre.

Chapter 1

Climate and Terrain

This chapter is concerned with the preliminary reconnaissance and appreciation of physical conditions prevailing in an existing garden or the place where a new one is to be made, and the consideration of ways in which these conditions can be exploited or ameliorated.

SUNLIGHT

Plants need direct sunlight on their foliage to carry on the process of photosynthesis by which, through the agency of chlorophyll in the leaves and green parts, carbon dioxide and oxygen from water and air are made into sugar and starches, indispensable food materials for animals and men. Some plants (referred to later) prosper best in conditions of partial shade, but the great majority, including many vegetables, need positions with full exposure to sunlight—notably some from Mediterranean regions such as *Cistus*, lavender, rosemary, nerines and *Amaryllis belladonna*, which need not only the actinic effect of sunlight, but also its baking heat.

The opposite of light is shade, and it is fortunate that there are plants which require this: most rhododendrons and camellias, hydrangeas, lilies, hostas, euphorbias, hellebores and ferns. Many ground-cover plants endure a good deal of shade: ivy, periwinkle, wild strawberries, lily of the valley and cyclamens, among many others. Where shade conditions are constant, it is wise to recognize the fact and to confine the planting to shade-tolerant plants, rather than try to make sun-loving plants grow there. There is no kind of grass that will thrive in deep shade; see Chapter 5. In lawns grass will grow better either under trees that cast a light shade, such as birches, robinias and gleditsias, or under mature trees that have either shed their lower branches or possess the habit of beginning branching high up; the 'Tree of Heaven' and the tulip tree are examples. By contrast, to give cool shade on hot summer days there are limes, particularly when planted in alleys, cedars, catalpas and some mature weeping trees, notably the weeping elm. Old apple trees give the best of both worlds, soft green grass to lie on, and dappled shade in which to read.

SUN HEAT

The sun, source of light, is also the source of heat, another essential factor in plant growth, the optimum temperature for which in temperate regions is between 23.8 and 29.4° C, 75 and 85° F, temperatures reached from time to time in Britain but seldom, if ever, maintained for any period. For example, the mean *maximum* air temperature at Kew in July is 26.9° C, 80.4° F, but the mean air temperature for the same month is 17.6° C, 63.7° F. Plants do not grow at earth temperatures below 5.6° C, 42° F, and the mean at Kew does not reach

15

this until March, and drops below it again in December, so that little or no growth occurs there out of doors in unprotected positions during the three months December, January, February.

This indicates the advantage of obtaining as much light and heat as can possibly be arranged. But exposure to the light and heat of the sun ought not also to incur exposure to the wandering wind from all its quarters. Wind is not only a destroyer of peace, but the arch-thief of heat. It is because of it that we create localized micro-climates with cloches, frames and greenhouses able to retain the radiant heat of the sun which, but for them, would be diluted and dispersed. Different expedients are devised to baffle the damaging wind; for example, planting against a wall where a buffer effect of wind creates calm conditions against the wall face. Walls also absorb heat in the daytime and give it back at night, so that a south-facing mellow brick wall may be the most congenial place in the garden for plants on the wrong side of tenderness, and for fruit such as peaches and figs which would be less likely to ripen in the open garden. Temporary rigging of hurdles, screens of hessian or old sacks to protect newly planted trees, even a net hung in front of peach blossom, will slow down the movement of the air by acting like a cellular vest, and will often just hold a temperature high enough to give protection against all but the severest frost. An imaginative disposal of hedges inside a garden also reduces the movement of air and even a low box hedge round vegetable beds can make a difference by foiling at ground level the machinations of the wind. Slatted fences to gardens by the sea are put up not only because solid ones would get blown down, but also because a solid barrier creates calm conditions in its lee for only about three times its height, and beyond that causes severe turbulence from down draughts. By contrast, a slatted fence or hedge, by filtering the wind, considerably reduces its speed for a distance at least six times its height. This property is employed on a large scale in the planting of shelter belts of trees to windward, described in Chapter 3.

Precipitation is another factor; heavy rain resulting in waterlogged conditions of soil above poor drainage lowers the temperature and slows down plant growth; and to dig in and bury snow causes cold soil conditions for a very long time. Temperature can also be dramatically and disastrously lowered by radiation frosts. These usually occur in spring and at night in conditions of clear sky, when the heat won from the sun in the daytime is radiated out with no local cloud or mist to hold it back. This can cause freezing temperatures and consequently heavier air at ground level; where this occurs on slopes, the cold, heavy, freezing air will slide down the hillside until it reaches the bottom of the valley, or is held up by a barrier such as a wall or hedge. It is when this happens that a frost pocket forms; the freezing air, not being able to drain away down to a valley, builds up against the barrier and can destroy early potatoes and even reach to the height of blossom of trees. This can be countered, when a garden stands a little way up sloping ground, by providing effective frost drainage below.

WATER SUPPLY AND IRRIGATION

It will be seen that films of water round particles of soil are as important to the roots of growing plants as are air and food materials; these are normally provided for in a good soil structure, but they are dependent upon an adequate supply of water from the surface, very largely from rain. The flora of any district has, by the process of survival of the fittest, adapted itself to prevailing rainfall and soil characteristics in so far as water-holding and water-transmission are concerned. In a garden the situation is different, for we are not always concerned with the survival of the fittest; on the contrary, it may be that we expend time and trouble in cosseting plants that are unfit to survive without our unnatural ministrations.

Established trees and shrubs seldom need extra water but newly planted material, in particular evergreens and vegetables, must have water given to them when they need it and not just when it happens to come down in the meteorological lottery at the whim of the clerk of the weather. Therefore an adequate supply must be on hand in the six critical months April to September, during which, in the east and south of England, more water is lost by transpiration/evaporation than falls as rain, the deficiency being equivalent to between 102 and 152 mm, 4–6 in, of rain. Even simply to restore this deficiency may not always be adequate to keep vegetables such as lettuce and spinach growing quickly enough to make them tender. For this reason the calculations in Appendix A are based on the provision of the equivalent of 152 mm, 6 in, of rain.

In many small gardens a main will supply enough water for supplementary irrigation, but where the garden is large, and if the water supply is poor or likely to be turned off in drought, it is worth investigating auxiliary supplies.

Primary sources include wells, bore holes, ponds, streams and collection from roof gutters. It is in any case an attractive concept to make use of and not to waste water that lies under, or falls within, our own ring fence, and after all there were times when gardeners and growers managed very well without the main.

A well is a hole dug down to a water-bearing soil stratum and is large enough in diameter for a man to descend and excavate with manual tools. The top few feet and any lower sections that are liable to collapse are lined with concrete rings, or in older wells with bricks or stones, this lining being known as steining. The rest of the hole is often left unlined, if the walls are self-supporting. A bore hole is much smaller, too small for a man to descend, about 305 mm, 1 ft, in diameter, excavated by machine and drawn upon by a submersible pump. A tube well is a pipe with a perforated and pointed bottom section and is driven into the ground. It is usually no bigger than 51 mm, 2 in, in diameter, and is only of practical use in soil strata such as valley gravel, where the water level is not more than 3.7 m, 12 ft, or so below ground, so that a suction pump can be used, the hole being too small to take a submersible pump.

A lake or a pond that remains reasonably full of water throughout the whole year is a valuable primary source, and so is a stream that does not dry up—its usefulness can sometimes be extended by putting in a dam and opening up a pool. From all these, water can be pumped either directly to the point of irrigation or to intermediate staging tanks which, if sufficiently high above the point of discharge (such as tanks in the roof of a house or small water towers), can exert a reasonable gravity head of water, provided that the pipelines to the discharge point are of a diameter large enough to create minimal internal pipe friction. A staging tank can also be filled by a ram which, although it cannot by itself exert enough pressure to operate sprinklers or irrigation jets, by its continuous day and night operation can accumulate in tanks over a period a surprisingly large amount of water for subsequent distribution by pump. In addition, staging tanks can be filled by rainwater falling upon roofs; the volume of this is surprising, as will be seen in Appendix A. Static tanks are much less expensive to make now that water-retaining sheets of a membrane such as butyl rubber can be used to line excavated areas. Rainwater from roofs, whether or not it is intended to run it into sizeable storage tanks, ought to be collected first in waterbutts at each point of discharge of a down pipe, allowing the overflow from these to run on into larger tanks (see Appendix A). These waterbutts are useful to dip watering-cans into for supplies of soft water at atmospheric temperature for newly planted-out vegetables and flowering plants.

Whenever the supply from a main is inadequate or non-existent, water will in most cases have to be pumped from one or more of the primary sources referred to above, to the points of irrigation. The rare exceptions are when an adequate gravity head can be obtained from a raised tank, as already referred to.

In very small gardens a simple hand pump to fill watering-cans may be all that is needed, but usually pumping has to be done by power—electricity when the length of cable run is acceptable, otherwise by petrol-driven motor. The pump chosen must have the necessary characteristics to raise the water from the well or other source, and to push it probably partly uphill to the discharge point and, on the way, to overcome friction in the pipeline. There are many advantages in a submersible pump; the whole unit, pump and waterproofed electric motor, is suspended in the well, bore hole or tank, and no difficulties of priming the pump or dampness in the motor are encountered; it is also almost noiseless in operation. Alternatively, dry-motor or surface pumps can be installed outside the source; these pumps, unless they are below water level (which can sometimes occur in the case of an ornamental pool on a terrace, with the pump installed in a cellar in the house), have first to exert a suction lift before the water is propelled along its delivery piping. Another disadvantage of dry-motor pumps is that the electric motors are liable to suffer from condensation, and they ought never to be installed in chambers below ground level. These are matters which may be easily resolved by a pumping engineer, who will also advise if it is necessary to apply for a licence to extract ground water from a bore hole.

WATER SUPPLY, FOUNTAINS AND FALLS

Fountains and waterfalls are almost always operated by recirculating water in pools or lakes, and no question of a separate source arises as it does for water expended for irrigation (there are rare examples where a fountain jet is worked by gravity from a lake high up in mountains or a nearby hillside, as at Geneva or Chatsworth). Fountains can be powerful jets or gently tinkling droplets, the latter being preferred by a fish population. Usually these water delights are produced by pumps that draw from the lowest pool and deliver through pipes to jets or sprays. No demands are made for large quantities of water, because once the system has been filled the only extra water needed will be what is required to replenish loss due to splashing and evaporation. A submersible pump can be installed in the pool itself, sometimes immediately under the jet it is to operate; but it is often better to locate the pump in a wet sump outside the pool and connected directly to it, where it can be reached easily, or else in a sump in the pool and near to its edge. In either case some form of strainer of ample dimensions is needed to catch leaves to prevent them from settling upon and blocking the smaller inlet strainer on the pump itself. It is necessary for the wet sump to be large enough to hold ample water so that the pump will not be 'on-air' when water is out on circulation, raising the levels in the pools to create the cascades.

Circulating water over a cascade or through a jet aerates it and makes it sparkle. In planning the pipe system it is desirable to put the pump at the opposite end of the pool to the discharge in order to circulate all the water, and as far as possible avoid stagnant areas. The same considerations regarding characteristics of pumps and friction in pipes arise as in irrigation, but the pressures involved tend to be less and the volumes greater. It is useful to fit a regulating valve near the pump where it can be reached easily and used to adjust the force of the water flow, making it possible to reduce the height of tall jets in windy weather, because wind, drift and splash from water falling back into the pool must be considered. A yardstick rule is to limit the height of jets to about two-thirds of their lateral distance from the nearest edge of the pool. Jets of comparatively large diameter, even if they are not forced to great height, are more satisfying than thin spray jets, fancy Prince of Wales' Feather patterns, etc.—a fat 16 mm, $\frac{5}{8}$ in, jet, only 1.5–1.8 m, 5–6 ft, high is much more impressive than a number of small 2–3 mm, $\frac{1}{16}-\frac{1}{8}$ in, sprays.

The rate of discharge from jets and the frictional loss of 'head' through piping are referred to at Appendix A.

DRAINAGE

Plants need water to take up nutrients in solution and also to maintain turgidity in their structures, because without sufficient water pressure from below, leaves and/or whole plants will wilt or collapse. This water they obtain from moisture films around soil particles in the pore spaces, but plant root systems, and some of the bacteria and fungi that assist in the process of assimilation, also need oxygen from the atmosphere circulating in the pore spaces. If, therefore, the supply of water from above through rain or irrigation, or from below in a water table, is copious enough to fill up these pore spaces, air will be driven out and excluded from the plant roots, which will be drowned. In fact, the supply and removal of water must be in equilibrium.

In many cases, provided that the topsoil has a good structure and the under soil is reasonably free draining, and if, further, there is a gentle slope on the ground, there will be good natural drainage. But if the ground is flat it may be necessary to put in some sort of artificial drainage to maintain the soil in friable condition. Field drainage aims at controlling the water table at a desired level, usually about 914 mm, 3 ft, below the surface, and it works by collecting soil water from below as the water table rises after continued rainfall. Its efficiency must depend upon porous soil allowing rainwater to drain into levels below the drains and build up a water table. An old guide for the depth and spacing apart of agricultural drainage pipes in open soils, is that a drain will collect water from soil on either side of it to a distance equal to five or six times its depth.[1] As a guide in open soils, drains at a depth of 914 mm, 3 ft, would be 9.1 m, 30 ft, apart; in medium soils 7.6 m, 25 ft; and in clay soils 3.7 m, 12 ft. At a depth of 610 mm, 2 ft, the distances would be: in open soils 6.1 m, 20 ft, apart, in medium soils 4.6 m, 15 ft, apart, and in clay soils 2.7 m, 9 ft, apart. And at a depth of 457 mm, 18 in: in open soils 1.5 m, 5 ft, apart, in medium soils 1.2 m, 4 ft, apart, and in clay soils 610 mm, 2 ft, apart.

Field drains will work by hydrostatic pressure even if laid dead level, but much better results are obtained if they are laid to a slope. A fall of 1 in 100 is effective, although at such a shallow gradient care must be taken to ensure that the drain trench is evenly graded and has no mini-switchback characteristics. For layout diagrams and sections of field drains see Appendix E.

On stiff clay soils, provided that there is a natural fall on the ground, mole-

[1] H. H. Nicholson, in *The Principles of Field Drainage* (Cambridge University Press 1942), considers that drains should be put in wider apart than indicated in this rule of thumb.

draining, although it may have to be repeated in from five to ten years, is a much less expensive process. The mole, shaped like the nose of a shell and fixed to a steel blade, is inserted into the ground in a hole dug at the upper end, and then drawn down by winch to the lower end. A part of the success in this system lies in the slit that the blade makes, which allows water to run into the channel left by the mole. The process can only be used when there is a fall on the ground, because the mole has to be drawn down at a constant level below the surface.

On really recalcitrant clay soils and over small areas, the topsoil may be excavated and put to one side, and a 'carpet', 305–457 mm, 12–18 in, deep, of coarse drainage material, clinker, brick or stone, laid down and the soil replaced. It is essential that the drainage layer should be tapped by drains leading away to lower levels, otherwise the clinker carpet will become a tank. The success of this operation must also depend upon the replaced topsoil being permeable.

In very serious conditions, methods such as those employed for sports grounds might be necessary. Here the upper 102 mm, 4 in, or so become severely impeded, partly because of compaction by heavy rolling and partly also because of the surface being kicked up and poached in goal-mouths, creating mud, fine particles in suspension, which block up the natural drainage capillaries in the soil. In these cases the drain, instead of collecting water only on its upward passage from the water table, has to collect as much water as possible on its way down. The drains are put fairly close together at a depth of perhaps only 305–457 mm, 12–18 in, with a porous layer above each drain in contact with the topsoil. In the case of sports grounds extreme measures such as frequent deep slitting and spiking have to be undertaken to get the water through the impeded top layer, and even on garden lawns that lie hopelessly waterlogged, this process of spiking and slitting can be useful.

A French drain consists of a tile drain laid in a trench near the surface and covered with shingle that goes right up to the level of the grass or topsoil, and therefore traps surface water and prevents it from going on further down the slope.

It is necessary to provide a means of disposal for water collected at the out-fall of a drainage system. This is often a ditch, which must be kept cleaned and from time to time 'bottomed' to remove accumulated silt and sludge. If there is no ditch and it is impossible to make one, a sump can be constructed provided that free draining subsoil, gravel or chalk, is encountered at the bottom. A sump is a large hole which may measure upwards of 1.8 m by 1.8 m by 1.8 m, 6 ft by 6 ft by 6 ft, and is filled with coarse ballast. If it is impossible to make a serviceable sump and permission cannot be obtained to run water into a local authority's storm-water or sewage system, the only course left is to create a bog garden or a pond at the lowest part of the garden.

Once an efficient drainage system has been installed, it is necessary to keep a watch on the moisture content of the soil with a view to irrigation in dry periods.

SOIL

The soil is something far more than a medium into which roots proliferate to provide anchorage for plants. It consists of mineral particles, the detritus of rocks and, when in good condition, water, air, material of organic origin known as humus and a teeming population of micro-organisms. All of these are responsible for the structure of the soil. A good soil structure contains pores through which atmospheric oxygen and water can reach the roots and through which again, in lower layers, water is drained away.

Humus plays many parts in the fertility of the soil. One is concerned with drainage in that it exerts a crumb-forming action by cementing together small particles to make larger ones with spaces between. Humus also promotes soil drainage by attracting worms, which, in their upward journeys from lower levels, leave behind them channels for drainage and the penetration of roots. Another of its functions is to provide lodging and food for those micro-organisms which co-operate with the root hairs of plants in taking up nutrients from the soil. Humus is also a complete fertilizer, resulting as it does from the decomposition of leaves and other vegetative parts of plants, of animal droppings, urine and the dead bodies of animals and insects. It is a product of nature's slow re-cycling process; such a tempo can be accepted on large organic farms when whole fields can be left for relatively long periods before being cropped again, but in the intensive cultivation of gardens, and particularly small gardens, the process is too slow, and instead of leaving it entirely to nature humus has to be obtained by making compost. This is done by filling bins with garden 'arisings', grass cuttings, outer leaves of lettuces, cabbages, etc., and also much kitchen waste such as tea leaves, egg-shells, potato peelings, orange peelings, fish-bones and lobster shells. A description of a compost bin and a method of making compost are given in Appendix B. The process of composting will result in the production of humus described by Sir Albert Howard, in *An Agricultural Testament* (OUP 1940), as 'a complex residue of partly oxidized vegetable and animal matter together with the substances synthesized by the fungi and bacteria which break down these wastes'. Gardeners are much inclined to look for what they think are short cuts by rushing to sodium nitrate or ammonium sulphate, much as a hypochondriac will reach for the whisky or the pill box, but by far the best way to plan for fertility in the soil is to maintain a correct balance of plant nutrients and traceele-ments by organic means.

Many garden soils contain a reserve of micro-organisms sufficient to build up a fertile soil of good structure if fresh compost is put on, and supplies of it are periodically renewed, to replace the food materials taken away either as vegetables or parts of flowering plants cut down or as leaves swept away. If, on the other hand, the soil intended for cultivation is found to contain practically no humus, having been exhausted by over-intensive cultivation or by a proportion of the topsoil having been blown away because of inadequate shelter, it will be necessary to start the process of humus formation in the ground by digging in animal manure at a nominal rate of 0.8 m³ to 20.9 m², 1 cu. yd to 25 sq. yds. In the absence of animal manure the reconstitution of fertility can begin by forking in hoof-and-horn meal and bonemeal, each at the rate of 57 g per 0.8 m². 2 oz. per sq. yd.

Apart from these occasions it is better not to dig soil, especially kitchen gardens and beds where crops are changed from year to year, as for bedding plants, and also to avoid as much as possible the treading of the soil, to prevent compaction and sealing up of the ventilating and draining capillaries. In fact, after soil has been deeply dug it may take a year or two for it to regain a satisfactory structure through the presence of humus, the activities of worms, baking and cracking in hot weather and fracture in hard frost.

A depth of 457 mm, 18 in, of fertile topsoil is desirable for shrubs, roses and herbaceous plants. Such depth will often be found to exist already in many gardens, but where this is not so it will be necessary to depart from the precept of leaving soil undisturbed and to dig down to the required depth, discarding subsoil, adding fresh compost or animal manure, as indicated above, and bringing in fresh topsoil to establish the required depth.

Soil acidity and alkalinity are measured in terms of hydrogen-ion concentration, expressed as pH. pH 7.0 is neutral, pH 6.0 is slightly acid, pH 8.0 is alkaline. Most plants, including trees and vegetables, are content in neutral or very slightly acid soils, pH 6.0 to 6.5. Plants that will not grow in alkaline conditions, that is when lime is present, are known as calcifuges. The best known of these are members of the Ericaceae Family: rhododendrons [1] and azaleas (but not *Arbutus*), also camellias, enkianthus, hamamelis, liquidambar, *Photinia villosa* and others. Certain fruit trees and vegetables also enjoy mild acidity, strawberries, raspberries and potatoes among them. Plants which demand alkaline conditions (calcicoles), that is a pH of above 7.0, include many of the Cruciferae Family, particularly the Brassicae, cabbages and broccoli, also wallflowers and sweet rocket.

It is wiser to accept the existing pH in the soil than to try to alter it to grow special plants, such as rhododendrons and camellias. Dosings and dopings may be effective for a short time, but there is nearly always an inward-moving seepage of water from the surrounding soil. Tricks can be played by laying a sheet of polythene in a trench or in a wide excavated area, and filling this with peat and acid topsoil, but there will have to be drainage holes in the polythene to prevent the rooting medium becoming waterlogged, and infiltration from below by water containing lime is possible if the localized water table rises after heavy rain. In any case polythene sheeting is not a durable material in the long run. Someone determined to cultivate calcifuge plants in gardens of alkaline soil would do best to make raised beds. The principle of these is to build up retaining walls and to fill behind them with an acid soil mixture. The whole system will then be above ordinary soil level and independent of localized fluctuation in the water table. The retaining walls can be from 305 mm, 1 ft, upwards in height and made of bricks or sleepers; Valerie Finnis uses the latter. [2] Apart from providing acid soil conditions above ground level, raised beds are useful for the cultivation of rock plants—alpines—which generally require sharper drainage than is encountered at ordinary ground level. For this purpose Valerie Finnis uses a growing medium of 50 per cent loam, 25 per cent peat and 25 per cent flint grit (5 mm, $\frac{3}{16}$ in, gauge). For calcifuges Miss Finnis raises the height of the beds to that of two sleepers, lining them with thick polythene sheeting and filling the compartments with two parts of acid loam and one part of peat.

Minor alterations to soil acidity and alkalinity can be effected by the application of chemicals. It is, for example, a simple matter to increase the pH of soil by adding lime as calcium carbonate, calcium hydroxide or dolomite limestone; the last contains also some of the magnesium required by many plants. To decrease the pH is more difficult and the measures taken are usually only temporarily effective. One reason for the success of the old lawn sand, which contained ammonium sulphate and ferrous sulphate, was that the ammonium sulphate induced an acid condition in the top 25 mm, 1 in, or so, of soil—an acid condition in which grasses generally succeed better than weeds, in particular clover, which usually require alkaline soils: but it creates what has been called a 'droughted out' surface in lawns, and in cultivated soils it militates against a good crumb structure. Magnesium sulphate (Epsom Salts) can also render lime unavailable by producing calcium sulphate and magnesium carbonate. Alumin-

---

[1] *Rhododendron ponticum* and hybrids grafted on to *ponticum* stock will grow in soil at a pH of 6.0, but most of the rhododendron species will not tolerate soils with a pH above 5.5 and generally will do best in the range pH 5.0 to 5.5.

[2] *Journal of the Royal Horticultural Society*, vol. xcviii, June 1973.

ium sulphate is successful in making acid conditions in soil where hydrangeas are required to be blue. In general, though, attempts to create an acid soil are usually temporary because rainfall leaches out the chemicals.

It is far better to keep the planting of the garden in key with the surrounding landscape. On the dry acid soils of parts of Surrey the acid-loving heathers, brooms, pines and birches and, in partial shade, the hardier rhododendrons are successful. On lusher acid soils, as in the western counties of England and the south-west of Ireland and Scotland, tenderer and more recondite rhododendron species, camellias and all the proud retinue of enkianthus, liquidambar, and hamamelis can be grown. But there are major compensations for those who garden on chalk: beech woods with wild cherries at their edges, for instance; and, bringing to mind the ancient trackways over the chalk downs, yew, flashing whitebeams, the wayfaring tree, nearly all the viburnums, 'Old Man's Beard' and, surprisingly, *Arbutus*.

ASPECT

The best position is one on shallow rising ground and far enough up from the bottom to allow radiation frosts to drain away, and with protection from the north and east, either by planted shelter belts or, better, by continuation of the rising ground, which for entire perfection would curve a little like a protecting arm, if necessary, and where finance permits, being modelled in this way. Large trees planted to give shelter on hillsides are so planted that when fully grown they are below the rim of the hilltop; indeed, it is a good principle that everything that is high—not only trees but also pylons and the cooling towers of power stations— is 'contained' by higher land behind.

GRADIENT

As well as protecting a garden from radiant frosts and vastly simplifying its drainage, a falling prospect is attractive, giving a commanding view, laying open the landscape, providing opportunities for terraces and steps, and perhaps a pool in its natural expected place at the lowest part of the garden. The opposite state of affairs, in which the ground rises away from the house, is far more difficult to deal with. Too often a louring, threatening impression is imposed. The way to alleviate this is to push the slope as far away as can be managed in the length of the garden, even at the expense of creating a steeper bank at the far end. The precious flat, or apparently flat, area close to the house will at least give breathing space before facing up to the 'cliff' at the end. This cliff can have a general gradient as steep as 1 in 3, which is an easily mowable slope, and if the garden is of some size can be terraced on its way to the top. A garden of this sort is shown in Figure 9.

Transverse slopes are the least attractive, and can be the most difficult. The eye can appreciate and be content with, or at least become accustomed to, slopes *en face* on a longitudinal axis, whether falling or rising, but serious discontent sets in with a tilted horizon. The only way to resolve this is to carry out terracing, if necessary on a massive scale, so that the greatest part of the garden seen from the house is level from side to side, and the horizon restored to familiar horizontality. An example of this is seen in Figure 10.

Alterations to levels have to be carried out within the boundaries of the property, something which may be easier in longitudinal cases than in transverse ones. Where there is enough room, the variations can best be taken care of by grass banks, which can have quite sharp rakes; for example, a slope of 1 in 3 will reconcile a 1.5 m, 5 ft, difference in levels within a horizontal distance of 4.6. m, 15 ft, and even steeper slopes can be mown with a Flymo. Planting beds can be finished to a rake of 1 in 10 and so can woodland spinneys on the boundaries; the disposal of drainage water away from neighbours' gardens should be borne in mind (see page 20). If there is not enough room for banks, it will be necessary to build walls on or close to the boundaries, vertical retaining walls in materials to match the house and the district, stone or brick in formal surroundings, dry walling where such walls are seen in nearby fields, Jack-and-Jill style in Devon and Cornwall, or whitened cob walls by the sea.

Only a small part of these observations will be useful to many who occupy a ready-made garden, or indeed to one who has acquired a piece of land with all the garden to do, and a house already built at the whim of a previous owner or developer. But perhaps some of the principles suggested will prove to be useful in making alterations. That rare and enviable bird who can choose in what part of the country he will build his house and make his garden, will take note of Sir George Sitwell's [1] ironic conclusion that

> we should abandon the struggle to make nature beautiful round the house and should rather move the house to where nature is beautiful. It is only part of the garden which lies within the boundary walls, and a great scheme planned for dull or commonplace surroundings is a faulty conception, as if one were to propose to build half a house or to paint half a picture. The garden must be considered not as a thing by itself, but as a gallery of foregrounds designed to set off the soft hues of the distance; it is nature which should call the tune and the melody is to be found in the prospect of blue hill or shimmering lake, or mystery-haunted plain, in the aerial perspective of great trees beyond the boundary, in the green cliffs of leafy woodland which wall us in on either hand. It may be argued further that real beauty is neither in garden nor landscape, but in the relation of both to the individual, that what we are seeking is not only a scenic setting for pool and fountain and parterre, but a background for life.

[1] *On the Making of Gardens* (Charles Scribner's Sons, New York; Duckworth & Co. Ltd, London), 1951.

Chapter 2

Design in Detail

When the practical assets and liabilities, actual and potential, of a garden plot have been examined, it will be possible to make a start on design in detail.

Of the twenty-one plans in the following pages, some are of real gardens, some have been "idealized" and others are entirely imaginary in order to illustrate particular points of design. It is not suggested that any one of them would or should be adopted in its entirety. They are all intended to indicate ways of exploiting "capabilities", or overcoming disadvantages of aspect, climate, gradient or the shape of the piece of land.

Garden plans are generally drawn on sheets of paper measuring up to 914 mm by 610 mm, 3 ft by 2 ft, at metric scales of 1 : 50, 1 : 100, 1 : 200 etc. corresponding approximately to the familiar imperial scales of $\frac{1}{4}$ in, $\frac{1}{8}$ in, $\frac{1}{16}$ in on the paper representing 1 ft on the ground. Such scales cannot be applied to plans of the size of a page in a book; therefore, for each of the garden plans illustrated in the following pages, a special scale has been worked out, and printed below each design. It will be found most convenient to use dividers to interpret the dimensions, opening them to correspond with points between which a dimension is to be established, and then laying them along the scale below to obtain an approximate measurement—and approximate it must be at such small scales.

Nearly all the designs are substantially geometric because curves and bulges are extravagant of space in limited areas, while geometric shapes are usually simpler to maintain; but a gardener so minded could if he wished introduce waves and wiggles by bending or twisting the lines of many of the designs.

A caveat may be entered against tricky, clever gardens sometimes seen at flower-shows, planted with an undue proportion of plants in flower at that time, often rhododendrons and azaleas, and intended, one imagines, more to show off the designer's ingenuity than to provide a comfortable, all-the-year-round environment. Clever gardens can too easily be too clever by half, and as the seasons change, and the owner's taste matures, come to be seen for the impostors they are, pert and ill-mannered.

The importance of available water supply has been stressed in Chapter 1 and Appendix A. In the following plans water points are indicated thus: ⓦ

Some of the first examples on a small scale of domestic gardens intended to produce vegetables and flowers for a family are still to be seen. Figure 1 shows a pair of farm labourers' cottages at the side of one of the fields of a farm in the foothills of the Chilterns, on a plot extending back 22.9 m, 75 ft, from the lane. Each has a road frontage of 12.8 m, 42 ft, giving gardens of about 25 m², 300 sq. yds, a sixteenth of an acre or ten poles, commonly now regarded as a standard for allotment gardens and the size also that was recommended by the then Ministry of Food in the successful 'Dig for Victory' campaign in the Second

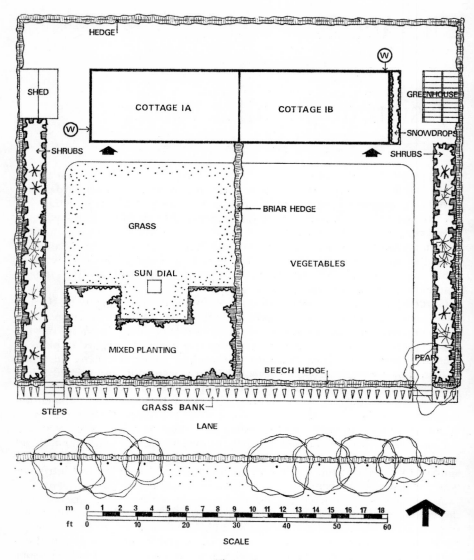

Figure 1

World War. It is also the size of the Royal Horticultural Society's model vegetable garden at Wisley, near Ripley in Surrey, an area which, as the Society states, if 'properly cropped and maintained should supply all the vegetables needed by a large family with the exception of items such as asparagus and mushrooms'. The field slopes gently down to the cottages, whose gardens follow the southward slope to a bank of rough grass and wild flowers above the lane. Flights of four rough stone steps lead up through the bank to gravel paths, 1.2 m, 4 ft, wide, running to the front door at the outside corner of each cottage. The gardens are bounded on all four sides by beech hedges, which flourish in the chalky Chiltern country.

26

In the garden of one of these cottages, 1A, vegetables are no longer cultivated, the front garden having been made over to lawn and flower beds. These latter are stuffed chiefly with old-fashioned flowers; for some reason cottage garden flowers seem infallibly to grow happily together, either because of an innate sense of colour and design in the cottagers or because the simpler, less emphatic flowers mix more easily together than later, more sophisticated plants which have to be placed in carefully thought-out groups. The owners, although they spend time in the flower tents of local shows, cannot afford to buy new plants such as phlox, delphiniums, irises and roses, but have to make do with what they are given and what they can raise for themselves from packets of seed sown in the open. The result is a haphazard arrangement of such perennials as campanulas (*C. pyramidalis* and *persicifolia*), candytuft, columbines, *Delphinium belladonna*, gaillardia, geum, hollyhocks (which re-seed themselves) and lychnis; biennials, or those plants now generally treated as such—forget-me-nots, sweet williams, Canterbury bells, and sweet rocket; annuals—larkspurs, nasturtiums, mignonette, zinnias and, in some years, sweet peas.

In the other cottage, 1B, the garden is still largely devoted to vegetables which keep the family during the year. The crops are systematically 'rotated', the ground occupied by peas, beans, onions, leeks, lettuces, tomatoes, spinach and celery being followed in the next year by potatoes, carrots, beetroots, parsnips and swedes and, in the third year, by brassicas, which will require lime—cabbages, Brussels sprouts, cauliflowers, kale and the different kinds of broccoli. Room is made for a few flowers—in a bed against the house where wallflowers are planted in October, to be followed by stocks for the summer. In this case the stocks are what used to be known as Gethsemane or Jerusalem stocks, a kind of Brompton stock, mauve-pink, nearly all single and strongly scented. Seed of these has long disappeared from nurserymen's lists, but the cottagers save it from year to year. To the right of the path from the lane to the front door is a wider bed planted each year with what may be available from seeds saved at home or with plants given by neighbours, polyanthuses, sweet williams, hollyhocks, pansies, Canterbury bells, pinks, pot marigolds and one or two of the old hybrid perpetual roses, 'Ulrich Brunner', 'Général Jacqueminot' and 'Mrs John Laing', obtained as they became obsolete and were discarded from larger gardens in the neighbourhood. At the end of this bed there is a large bush of *Daphne mezereum*, flowering in March, strongly scented and growing with Madonna lilies, often associated with cottage gardens because they seem to thrive best in these humble surroundings.

By the gate to the road is a tall pear tree and along the boundary with the other cottage is a row of sweet briars trained to make a sort of hedge. This is *Rosa rubiginosa*, once known also as eglantine, a name which derived from the French *l'aiglante*, the prickly one. Honeysuckle has also been called Eglantine, but this is wrong. The old English name for honeysuckle is woodbine, the native *Lonicera periclymenum*, which hangs over the porch of this cottage.

Alongside the cottage at the end of the path from the lane is a small greenhouse about 3m by 2.4 m, 10 ft by 8 ft, made by the occupant, who is handyman about the farm. Here early cabbages and cauliflowers can be started off, half a dozen tomato plants grown along one side, and cuttings made of geraniums which spend most of the year in the front windows. There is an oil heater to keep out the frost at critical times, but for the most part this greenhouse is used as a cold house.

Against the wall of the house on the east side there is a narrow bed 381 mm,

27

15 in, wide, of snowdrops only; these are enchanting for a few weeks early in the year; in cottage gardens of this sort there is often no money to spare for a calculated succession of plants. Here we see a primitive simplicity and contentment with humble things, which have a curiously spare attraction often overlooked in the complicated sophistication of present-day planting design.

Figure 2 shows a weekend cottage in a piece of land measuring about 12.2 m by 21.3 m, 40 ft by 70 ft, standing by itself 7.6 m, 25 ft, back from a gravel road across common land. The real garden is at the front of the house, which faces south-west, and is about the same size as those of the cottagers already described and was once probably used for vegetables, but it has now, with the cottage itself, been entirely altered: 'tarted up by the gentry', as they say in the Dog and Pot in the village a quarter of a mile away. The front boundary is a 1.2 m, 4 ft, high white palisade or picket fence with a gate in the middle leading directly by a stone paved path to the front door. There are panels of grass on either side of the path and, beyond these, beds 2.4 m, 8 ft, wide for planting. Against the front wall of the house a narrow bed 610 mm, 2 ft, wide is planted with many scented plants, some permanent lavender and rosemary and seasonal infillings of wallflowers, tobacco plants and heliotrope. Immediately in front of this bed is a wide paved cross path on to which chairs can be put out in the summer. There are times, however, when the repeated backward and forward canterings of the pony club become monotonous (although the manure is useful, stealthily collected at dusk), so a retreat has been made to a small enclosed garden area at the back, partly paved and partly lawn. Here it is possible to sit out in peace, unobserved by passers-by on the common. Against the pink-washed brick wall is a narrow bed for plants bought from the garden centre for the summer, some zonal and scented geraniums, marigolds and petunias, varied from year to year. Permanent climbers on this wall are *Hydrangea petiolaris*, *Jasminum officinale*, *Campsis radicans* and *Passiflora caerulea*, a blue passion flower. The shed holds the folding table and chairs in the winter. In this little back courtyard there are tubs filled with polyanthuses for spring and trailing geraniums for summer. The herbs grown in the herb garden are basil, chives, fennel, marjoram, mint, parsley, sage, thyme and tarragon, all these bought in peat pots at the local garden centre. Rosemary, as has already been seen, is planted on the other side of the house by the front door.

For the most part the cottage is unoccupied from Friday to Monday, and the owners do not wish to spend a high proportion of their limited time away from the town in run-of-the-mill gardening. For this reason they have chosen, for the two beds at either side of the front, plants which need practically no attention from year to year: *Osmanthus delavayi*, *Viburnum* × *burkwoodii*, *Hypericum* 'Hidcote', the small *Philadelphus* 'Manteau d'Hermine', *Potentilla* 'Elisabeth' can all be left entirely alone for ten years, as also can *Senecio laxifolius* and *Phlomis fruticosa*. But *Buddleia alternifolia* needs to be pruned each July and hybrid tea and hybrid polyantha roses, needed for their continuous flowering contribution, also have to be pruned annually. There are also some herbaceous plants which need not be staked and seldom need to be lifted and divided, among them some of the scented double Chinese peonies in red, white, pink and lilac-pink colours, and white or pink Japanese anemones, monkshood and dittany. In the bed facing north-west are hellebores, hostas, *Skimmia japonica* 'Fragrans' and *Sarcococca humilis*, which need practically no attention over a long period.

The small lawns can be mown in half an hour with such a machine as a

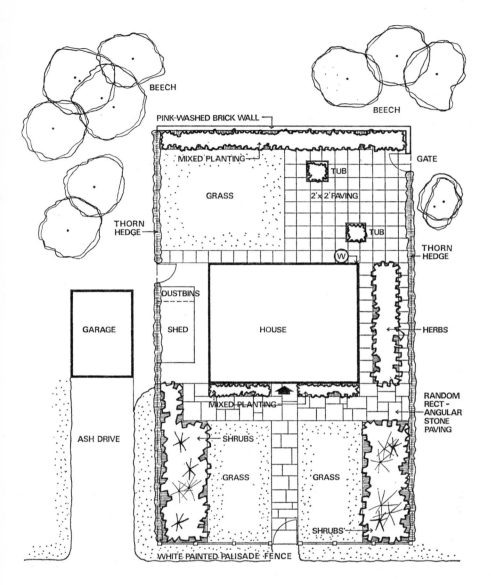

BEECH

BEECH

PINK-WASHED BRICK WALL

MIXED PLANTING

GATE

TUB

2' x 2' PAVING

GRASS

THORN
HEDGE

TUB

W

THORN
HEDGE

DUSTBINS

SHED

HOUSE

HERBS

GARAGE

MIXED PLANTING

RANDOM
RECT-
ANGULAR
STONE
PAVING

ASH DRIVE

SHRUBS

GRASS

GRASS

SHRUBS

WHITE PAINTED PALISADE FENCE

LANE

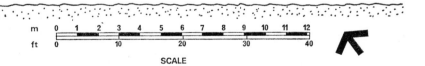

m	0	1	2	3	4	5	6	7	8	9	10	11	12
ft	0			10			20			30			40

SCALE

Figure 2

305–356 mm, 12–14 in, electrically driven mains cable machine. It would be a reasonable estimate, therefore, to assume that the maintenance time throughout the thirty growing weeks from the middle of March to the middle of October would be no more than thirty hours, made up as follows:

Lawn mowing, twenty-five times	12½ hours
Hoeing weeds in April, May, June, July, August, September, October, 1 hour each time	7 hours
Pruning and tidying in March and October, 2 hours each time	4 hours
Removing old spring bedding and planting summer bedding, May	2 hours
Removing old summer bedding and planting spring bedding, October	2 hours
Fertilizing lawn, twice April and June	2 hours
Total	29½ hours

A garage has been put up alongside on common land, with a rough ash drive leading to it. A car has to be reversed on to an area of the common, where the land has been firmed by rolling in clinkers, through which the grass and weeds have grown.

A permanent resident with more time on his hands would plant this garden rather differently and an eccentric owner, appreciating that parts of the cottage are very old, might go to the lengths of including only plants that were cultivated in English gardens in the seventeenth century. With John Parkinson [1] taking the place of Debrett, the garden could become a self-conscious exercise in that anything 'not in Parkinson' would be snobbishly excluded. The deprivation would not be great, for the beds could contain a mixture of columbines, scabious, campanulas (*Campanula pyramidalis*, the great or steeple bell-flower) and the old double red and double white cottage peonies, *Paeonia officinalis*, natives of Europe with a harsh smell (unlike the sweetly scented Chinese peonies deriving from *P. lactiflora* and introduced later); and with these a number of plants that we now think of as biennials—Canterbury bells, foxgloves, wall-gilliflowers, pansies, primroses, and cowslips. There could also be 'Crown Imperials', the white lily, *L. candidum*, and the 'Convally Lily' (lily of the valley) in company with the true black hellebore, or Christmas rose, *Daphne mezereum* and irises— the white 'flower-de-luce', *Iris florentina*, which may have been the model of the shape at least for the fleur-de-lis; and that fine plant that Parkinson calls the great 'Dalmation Flowerdeluce', which is probably what we know as *Iris pallida dalmatica*. Besides all these the garden could include many roses; the English white rose known to us now as *Rosa alba semiplena*, the 'White Rose of York'; the English red rose, *R. gallica officinalis*, known also as the Provins rose; and Parkinson's *Rosa provincialis sive Hollandica Damascena* 'which some call Centifolia Batavica incarnata' (this is what we know as a cabbage rose, or 'Rose of Provence'); the true 'York and Lancaster', *R. damascena versicolor*, in which the white petals have pale pink markings contrasting only slightly with the general whiteness, unlike those of 'Rosa Mundi', *R. gallica versicolor*, whose petals are markedly striped and blotched and which is not in Parkinson.

[1] *Paradisi in Sole Paradisus Terrestris*, 1629. The reprint of 1904 published by Methuen is available in libraries.

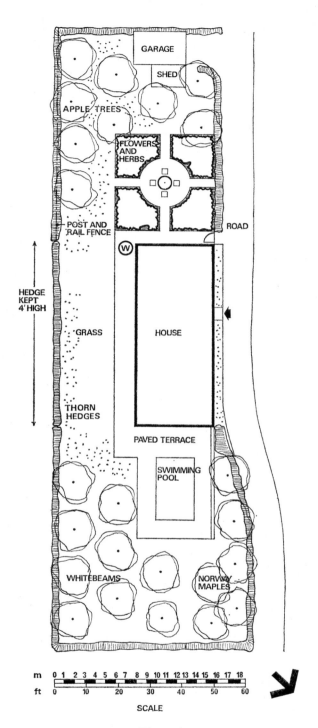

GARAGE

SHED

APPLE TREES

FLOWERS
AND
HERBS

POST AND
RAIL FENCE

ROAD

(W)

HEDGE
KEPT
4' HIGH

GRASS

HOUSE

THORN
HEDGES

PAVED TERRACE

SWIMMING
POOL

WHITEBEAMS

NORWAY
MAPLES

m   0 1 2 3 4 5 6 7 8 9 10 11 12 13 14 15 16 17 18
ft   0   10   20   30   40   50   60

SCALE

Figure 3

There would be no perpetual roses or tall delphiniums or even phlox to disturb the quiet colour of this gentle planting, preserving something of the atmosphere of things past.

Figure 3 shows a garden of rather less than a quarter of an acre measuring about 61 m by 15.2 m, 200 ft by 50 ft, about 919.7 m², 1100 sq. yds. The garden side of the house faces south-east.

This is another weekend country cottage, originally two labourers' cottages at the edge of a cornfield, standing within 1 m, 3 ft, of the road. The very small depth of the garden behind the house was presumably decided on by the farmer when he sold the cottages, in order to project as little as possible into his field. He may have thought that the plot ought to be somewhere near a quarter of an acre, and for this reason allowed a length of as much as 61 m, 200 ft, along the roadside.

Before the garden was designed the prospect from the windows of the sitting-rooms appeared to be one of cornfields stretching to eternity through 180°. The first requirement seemed to be to induce a sense of enclosure in scale with the dimensions of the cottage. This was done by, as it were, boxing in one side by whitebeams planted quincuncially 4.6 m, 15ft, apart which, when they had settled in and grown a little together after a few years, created a much more comfortable feeling, and the other side by apple trees. In front of the house a paved path 1.8 m, 6 ft, wide separates it from the narrow lawn running to a post and rail fence at the edge of the field. A thorn hedge was planted on either wing of the garden inside the post and rail fence. It is intended that on the flanks this hedge shall in time reach from 1.8 m to 2.4 m, 6 ft to 8 ft, in height to assist as a wind filter, but for 18.3 m, 60 ft, in the middle the height of the hedge will be kept at 1.2 m, 4 ft, because the view across the cornfield to the far-off hills is pleasant.

To the left, the north-east, there is room for a small swimming bath 6.1 m by 3.7 m, 20 ft by 12 ft, with a paved surround 1.8 m, 6 ft, wide on three sides and 3 m, 10 ft, wide between the pool and the side of the house. A new brick wall 2.4 m, 8 ft, high is built at the outer edge of the paving on the north-west side to give protection from northerly winds. A solid barrier such as this will create calm conditions in its lee for a distance of three times the height of the barrier, in this case 7.3 m, 24 ft, but beyond that considerable down-draughts will occur. To prevent this a screen of Norway maples is planted between the protective wall and the road; the trees have now reached a height of 6.1 m, 20 ft. This screen greatly reduces turbulence and makes the whole pool area habitable in nearly all conditions of wind in which the occupants would wish to swim.

At the other end of the cottage is a small garden of flowers and herbs. In its centre is a clear paved circle 4.9 m, 16 ft, in diameter, with a table in the middle, around which chairs can be drawn for suppers on fine evenings with benefit of a southern aspect.

Beyond this little garden are a garage and tool shed.

The garden in Figure 4 is 1786 m², rather under half an acre, is level and faces south-west and south-east, measuring 36.6 m, 120 ft, frontage by 48.8 m, 160 ft, depth. This is a seventeenth- and eighteenth-century cottage alongside a road in a small village. The boundary to the road is a low brick wall 1.5 m, 5 ft, high. The garage opens directly on to the road and is separated from the house by a passage, 2.4 m, 8 ft, wide. Behind the garage is a very old potting shed. Entrance to the house is normally by a handgate from the road side and along a path which turns through a right angle to lead straight to the front door. To the right

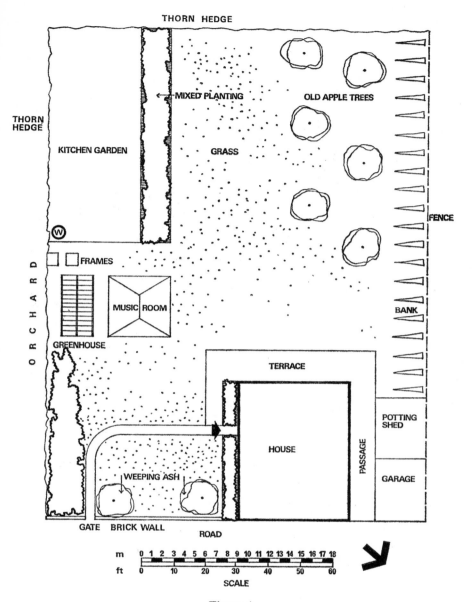

THORN HEDGE

THORN HEDGE

←—MIXED PLANTING

OLD APPLE TREES

KITCHEN GARDEN

GRASS

FENCE

W

FRAMES

MUSIC ROOM

BANK

GREENHOUSE

O R C H A R D

TERRACE

POTTING SHED

HOUSE

PASSAGE

GARAGE

WEEPING ASH

GATE   BRICK WALL

ROAD

m 0 1 2 3 4 5 6 7 8 9 10 11 12 13 14 15 16 17 18
ft 0   10   20   30   40   50   60
SCALE

Figure 4

of this path is a small lawn and two weeping ash trees near the boundary. In this area alongside the boundary the grass is allowed to grow long and is planted with drifts of daffodils and winter aconites. The native English iris, *I. foetidissima*, was also found growing in this part of the garden. Beyond this is the music room, a brick and tiled building, 6.1 m, 20 ft, square, which must be nearly as old as the cottage. It is large enough for a small string band and harpsichord and, in the summer, is sometimes used for concerts where players can have the benefit

33

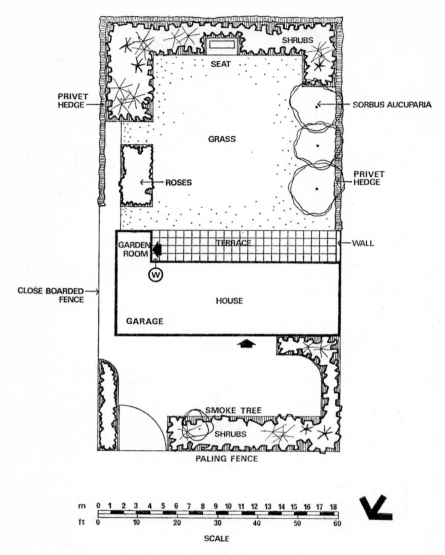

PRIVET HEDGE

SORBUS AUCUPARIA

SHRUBS

SEAT

GRASS

PRIVET HEDGE

ROSES

TERRACE

WALL

GARDEN ROOM

W

CLOSE BOARDED FENCE

HOUSE

GARAGE

SMOKE TREE

SHRUBS

PALING FENCE

m 0 1 2 3 4 5 6 7 8 9 10 11 12 13 14 15 16 17 18

ft 0   10   20   30   40   50   60

SCALE

Figure 5

of electric light to read their scores while the small audience lies on the grass to listen to Vivaldi floating out from the glowing lantern of light. Beside the music room is a greenhouse and beyond this some frames and beyond that again the kitchen garden about 251 m², 300 sq. yds. This is to an extent screened from the house by the 3m, 10 ft, wide bed of mixed planting, some of which still consists of lupins which the new owners had not the heart to take away. Beyond this mixed border is a grass space, about 251 m², 300 sq. yds, where small children play, and beyond this again six very old apple trees, pruned now for their outline rather than their fruit. The boundary to the north-west is a sloping bank planted with daffodils and still holds a few of the old cottage peonies, leading down from a dilapidated wooden fence separating the garden from a footpath (not shown on plan) leading to woods. The boundaries to the south-west and south-east are thorn hedges against a surrounding orchard.

Figure 5 shows a garden for a detached suburban house on a level plot in a cold climate. The frontage is 18.3 m, 60 ft, to the road and the depth is 35 m, 115 ft, giving an area for the whole plot of rather over 640 m², 766 sq. yds. The front door faces north-west and the main axis of the garden behind looks towards the south-east.

Here the provision of a garage necessitates enough space between the entrance from the road and the garage itself to allow for cars to be reversed on to a small forecourt in front of the house so as to be able to drive out on to the road head first. A depth of 9.1 m, 30 ft, is required for this. The boundaries on either side and at the back of the house consist of developer's black chain-link wire fences, 1.2 m, 4 ft, high, against which privet hedges are planted. Inside the front fence, borders are provided for shrubs, hardy in a cold climate, such as the evergreen *Lonicera pileata, Euonymus japonicus robustus, Mahonia aquifolium* and yew; deciduous shrubs and trees, the Scotch laburnum (*Laburnum alpinum*), sycamore (*Acer pseudoplatanus*), mountain ash (*Sorbus aucuparia*), birch (*Betula pendula*), thorn (*Crataegus monogyna*), the smoke tree (*Cotinus coggyria*), and the snowball tree (*Viburnum opulus*).

In this family there might be four children, therefore as large a lawn area as would seem reasonable has been provided for, about 168 m², 200 sq. yds, equal to scarcely half the size of a tennis court, small enough in all conscience, but a safe place for children and dogs if a side gate is provided and kept locked. To one side there is a bed for roses facing between south and south-west, and at the far end a 2.4 m, 8 ft, wide mixed border of shrubs, roses and herbaceous plants hardy in northern latitudes, with a recess for a seat.

The house has been designed with a garden room projecting at right angles on to the northern end of the 3 m, 10 ft, wide terrace. This has its own door into the garden through which to go out and to return to change shoes or wellingtons, dry the dog after its walk and generally minimize the amount of garden brought into the house. This little arm to the north makes a protecting wall at the end of the terrace and gives some shelter. The door into it can be made to look inviting and relieve an otherwise blank wall.

Answers to a questionnaire sent out by the Royal Horticultural Society in 1972 indicated that a great majority of Fellows had gardens of a quarter of an acre or less. A quarter of an acre provides and makes possible a reasonably spacious lawn, more flowers, many shrubs, several trees, a small greenhouse, space for compost bins and for burning, a larger tool shed, spare ground and some sort of prospect, together with a small front garden, a garage and a front forecourt to permit a car to be turned before being driven out on to the road.

In Figures 6, 7 and 8 the plot size and shape and the type and position of the house are exactly the same, the three plans showing different ways of dealing with the same area. The plots have a frontage of 27.3 m, 90 ft, and a depth of 38 m, 125 ft, giving 1045 m², 1250 sq. yds, which is about a quarter of an acre. The front door faces east, and the long axis of the garden behind runs towards the west. The house and garage are set 11.6 m, 38 ft, back from the road, providing a fairly comfortable forecourt to enable a car to be driven straight into the garage and reversed back in front of the house before being driven out. It is a

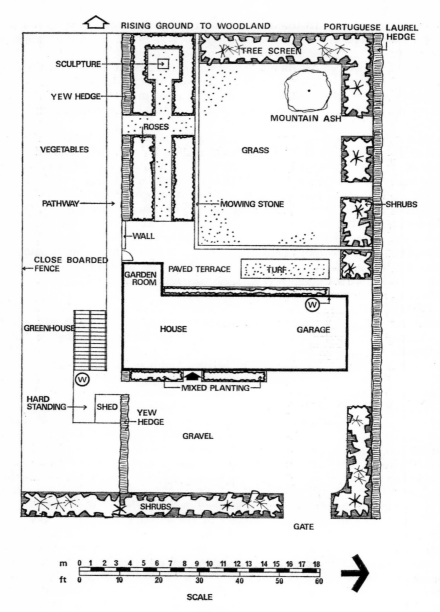

RISING GROUND TO WOODLAND

PORTUGUESE LAUREL HEDGE

SCULPTURE

YEW HEDGE

ROSES

VEGETABLES

GRASS

TREE SCREEN

MOUNTAIN ASH

PATHWAY

MOWING STONE

SHRUBS

WALL

CLOSE BOARDED FENCE

PAVED TERRACE

TURF

GARDEN ROOM

GREENHOUSE

HOUSE

GARAGE

HARD STANDING

SHED

YEW HEDGE

MIXED PLANTING

GRAVEL

SHRUBS

GATE

m 0 1 2 3 4 5 6 7 8 9 10 11 12 13 14 15 16 17 18
ft 0   10   20   30   40   50   60

SCALE

Figure 6

rectangular plot in a row of houses on level ground. At the further end of the garden are more two-storey houses, beyond which the land rises to a wood, 457 m, 500 yds away. A screen of trees in the garden conceals or at least 'breaks up' the view of the houses and takes the eye on to woodland on rising ground beyond.

In garden No. 6 the terrace, 3 m, 10 ft, wide on average, is returned at one end to give a paved area facing towards the south and south-west. There is a small

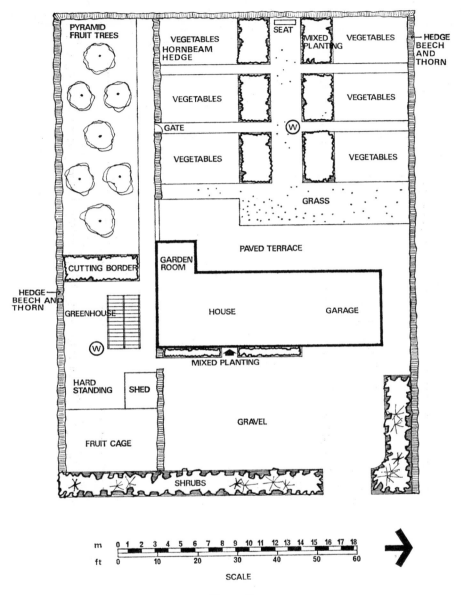

Figure 7

vegetable garden of about 117 m², 140 sq. yds (less than half the prescribed standard ¹), together with a small greenhouse and potting shed. These have been put near the house in order that the length of electric cable for heating and lighting the greenhouse should be as short as possible. To the left of the plan, towards the west, there is a small formal garden with rectangular beds for mixed planting on either side of a 1.2 m, 4 ft, grass path terminating in a white figure.

¹ See page 25.

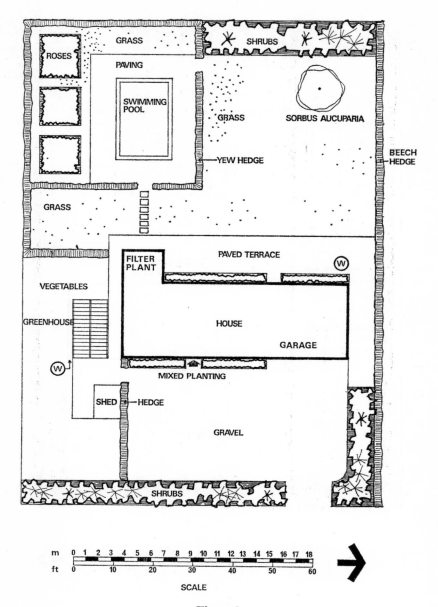

Figure 8

The tree at the north-west corner is a mountain ash, which has an ultimate height of about 7.6 m, 25 ft, and is in scale with the size of this garden. Against the front boundary is a mixed shrub bed.

The raised narrow border 381 m, 15 in, high and 610 mm, 2 ft, wide between the house and the front forecourt is planted with *Sarcococca humilis*, seldom if ever exceeding 610 mm, 2 ft, in height and having pointed leaves rather like those of butcher's broom, and small, white, very strongly scented flowers in the dead of winter; mixed with this is another evergreen, *Viburnum davidii*, which in time will achieve a height of 914 mm to 1.2 m, 3 to 4 ft, with an equivalent spread and spill out over the edge of the bed.

Garden No. 7 shows that another way of treating the same plot would be to make an approach towards a French *potager* to make the garden productive of vegetables in a framework of flowers and shrubs. Leading on from the middle point of the terrace is a grass path making a strong central axis. On either side of this are beds for mixed planting, and beyond these on each side are three kitchen garden plots, making altogether about 167 m², 200 sq. yds, of kitchen garden. In this plan the gate from the side path to the terrace (in Figure 6) is moved farther up to give access to the kitchen garden beds. The greenhouse and the potting shed remain.

In Figure 8 the arrangements in front of the house are the same as in Nos. 6 and 7, but at the back towards the west a swimming bath 6.1 m by 3.7 m, 20 ft by 12 ft, is provided. This is enclosed by a 1.8 m, 6 ft, yew hedge extended to enclose also a small geometrically arranged garden for roses. The garden room in figures 6 and 7 now houses the filtration and heating plant and from this stepping stones lead across the grass to an opening in the yew hedge enclosing the pool. To the right of this yew hedge and the pool complex is a small lawn about 210 m², 250 sq. yds, again with a mountain ash in the north-western corner. Across the far end is a bed 2.4 m, 8 ft, deep for shrubs or mixed planting.

Figure 9 shows a garden measuring 24 m by 44 m, 78 ft by 145 ft, the land rising away from the house towards the south-east. A steep bank falling towards a house is always disturbing and can be formidable. The best way to treat such conditions is to push the bank away as far as possible, even at the expense of increasing the angle of slope. This is done in this case by making an apparently flat grass extension to the terrace 6.1 m, 20 ft, wide, before a grass bank rising at a gradient of 1 in 3 (which is easily mowable by all types of mowing machine), and from the top of this bank on to the end of the garden providing for a rise of 3 m, 10 ft. The so-called flat previously referred to will, in fact, have a slope of 610 mm, 2 ft, towards the terrace, but this will not be noticeable. At the front edge of the terrace a French drain [1] is constructed to make certain that all water going down from the higher ground above is trapped and taken away before it can reach the terrace, which itself has a slope of 25 m in 3 m, 1 inch in 10 ft, away from the house towards the drain. Beyond the top of the grass bank the land continues to rise at a slope of 1 in 4 for a distance of 12.2 m, 40 ft, to the south-eastern boundary which is, therefore, 4.3 m, 14 ft, above terrace level. This garden ends in a mini-copse of mixed woodland, oak, beech and lime, which would entirely shut in the horizon if a gap had not been cut in the middle to give a dramatic view of the sky. Beds 2.4–3 m, 8–10 ft, wide are made to the left of the house to hold roses and grey-foliaged plants. The narrower bed against the house is wide enough, 1.5 m, 5 ft, to accommodate more than the usual scented-leaved mixture. The level of the garden beyond the top of the grass bank follows that of the surrounding land. Below this, banks 3.7 m, 12 ft, wide on either side have had to be made to accommodate the descent of 610 mm, 2 ft, these banks being at a slope of rather more than 1 in 4, as far down as the line of the terrace, where short retaining walls are needed until the ground flattens out at the level of the house platform.

[1] See Appendix E.

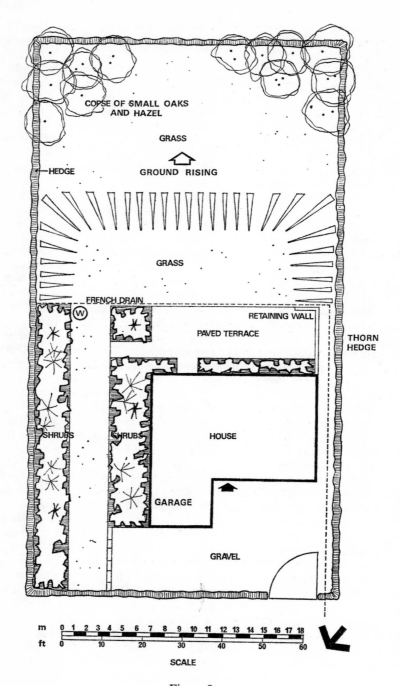

COPSE OF SMALL OAKS AND HAZEL

GRASS

GROUND RISING

HEDGE

GRASS

FRENCH DRAIN

W

RETAINING WALL

PAVED TERRACE

THORN HEDGE

SHRUBS

SHRUBS

HOUSE

GARAGE

GRAVEL

m   0 1 2 3 4 5 6 7 8 9 10 11 12 13 14 15 16 17 18
ft   0   10   20   30   40   50   60

SCALE

Figure 9

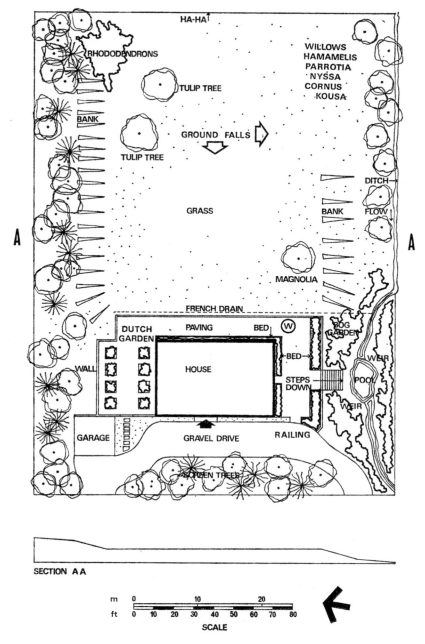

Figure 10

Figure 10 shows a garden with a pronounced transverse slope from north to south. The size is about 4100 m², slightly over one acre, 54.9 m, 180 ft, frontage by 76.2 m, 250 ft, depth. The house is detached and faces west. There are two entrances along the frontage, with the garage opposite the northern entrance, and a screen of trees, birches and Austrian pines, between the two drive gates. A long screen of trees to the north is similarly planted. The slope from north to south is 3.7 m, 12 ft, 1 in 15. The screen of trees to the north is planted on the natural slope at this gradient, continuing on along a bank 4.6 m, 15 ft, wide at 1 in 3. Below this the main lawn falls for 32 m, 105 ft, towards the south at a gradient of 1 in 100. Beyond this is a grass bank 4.6 m, 15 ft, wide, gradient 1 in 3, and beyond this again the natural fall of the ground towards the ditch on the southern boundary is regained. There is also a fall of 610 mm, 2 ft, from east to west along the ditch and also along the main lawn from the ha-ha to the terrace. The terrace has a parapet wall 610 mm, 2 ft, high at its outer edge. Below this a French drain collects water running down the slope and conducts it to the ditch at the southern boundary. The large grass lawn measures 32 m by 47 m, 105 ft by 155 ft, an area of about 1504 m², 1800 sq. yds.

To the left of the lawn, part of the sloping bank is taken up with rhododendrons. On the opposite side, to the right (south) at the foot of the grass bank is planted a number of trees suitable for damp, rather acid soils, willows, *Parrotia, Nyssa*, liquidambar and *Hamamelis*. Towards the line of the house, the ditch is diverted to run over a weir into a small pool and out over an overflow weir in a curving line back to the original line of the ditch. All round the pool is a bog garden from which ten steps lead up to the south terrace, which is 4.6 m, 15 ft, wide excluding two beds, one close to the house, the other against the retaining wall, 1.2 m, 4 ft, wide. These beds are planted with polyanthuses followed by summer flowers. There is a railing at the top of the retaining wall returning on both sides down the steps. On the opposite side of the house to the north is a small Dutch garden with rectangular beds set into paving for tulips followed by summer flowering plants.

Figure 11 shows a garden with a transverse longitudinal slope away from the house. The size is 1952 m², nearly half an acre, 30.5 m, 100 ft, frontage by 64 m, 210 ft, deep. The garden lies to the south-east of the house.

The long narrow shape of this plot gives a reason for making a strong central axis with enclosed gardens opening off it. There is an overall slope of about 1.2 m, 4 ft, from the edge of the house terrace to the boundary at the south-east, a gradient of 1 in 31, which is reconciled in the following manner. Four steps from the terrace to the first lawn take up 610 mm, 2 ft, then there is a slope of 152 mm, 6 in, across the lawn (12.2 m, 40 ft, wide), a gradient of 1 in 80. Then two steps down, taking up 305 mm, 1 ft, to the enclosed gardens on either side of the *tapis vert*—'green carpet'—along the 11 m, 36 ft, length of which is again a slope of 152 mm, 6 in, a slightly sharper gradient of 1 in 72. Beyond this is the *potager*, which is kept level not only to arrest the visible downward progression but to regain the original level along the line where the next property begins.

The drainage arrangements are as follows: a slope of 51 mm, 2 in, across the terrace, which is 4.6 m, 15 ft, wide, in order to ensure that water runs away from the foundations of the house. From the front edge of the terrace, water runs into a narrow bed, 610 mm, 2 ft, wide above the retaining wall and through 'weep-holes' in the retaining wall to a French drain (see Appendix E), conducting the water to the right of the drawing, then turning down through the shrub border at the side, picking up on its way drainage from the next terrace and running into a sump which could be 1.8 m, 6 ft, square and the same depth, if at this depth a connection would be made either to chalk or to free-draining gravel. If the sub-soil were clay this sump might overflow and it would be necessary to make arrangements with a neighbour or the local council for way-leave

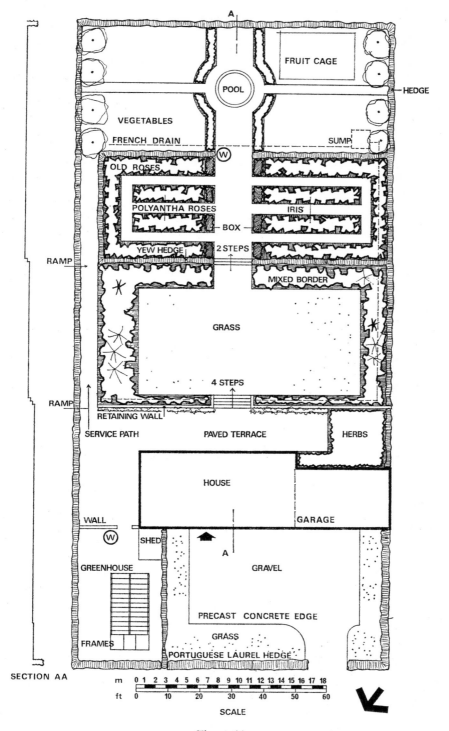

A

FRUIT CAGE

HEDGE

POOL

VEGETABLES

FRENCH DRAIN

SUMP

OLD ROSES

POLYANTHA ROSES

IRIS

BOX

YEW HEDGE

2 STEPS

RAMP

MIXED BORDER

GRASS

4 STEPS

RAMP

RETAINING WALL

SERVICE PATH

PAVED TERRACE

HERBS

HOUSE

GARAGE

WALL

W

SHED

A

GREENHOUSE

GRAVEL

PRECAST CONCRETE EDGE

GRASS

FRAMES

PORTUGUESE LAUREL HEDGE

SECTION AA

m 0 1 2 3 4 5 6 7 8 9 10 11 12 13 14 15 16 17 18

ft 0   10   20   30   40   50   60

SCALE

Figure 11

to take the surplus from the sump to a permitted place of disposal, probably a ditch or a road gutter.

The lawn measures about 21.3 m by 10.6 m, 70 ft by 35 ft, about 226 m², 272 sq. yds. In the beds of shrubs, 3 m, 10 ft, wide on either side the planting is confined to a few of the summer-flowering magnolias, *M. sinensis* and *wilsonii*, lilacs, *Philadelphus* and Rugosa roses, with an irregular edging of *Viburnum davidii*. The planting in the two mixed beds on either side of the steps and facing towards the house consists of five myrtles on each side against the yew hedge and, in front of this, a mixture of the deciduous *Potentilla* 'Elisabeth' and the ever-grey *Phlomis fruticosa*. The yew hedge behind is 1.8 m, 6 ft, high to conceal the two hidden gardens. One of these, the one to the right, is planted with blue irises only in the middle beds and a mixture of white *Anemone* × *hybrida* 'Honorine Jobert' and lilac-pink scented peonies in the three beds round the sides. In the corresponding garden on the other side of the *tapis vert*, the middle beds are planted with hybrid tea and hybrid polyantha roses for picking, with a fair proportion of grey foliage, largely *Ballota pseudodictamnus*, a plant not reliably hardy outside the south of England and often grown each year in a greenhouse. In the beds along the outside there are 'old' shrub roses—Hybrid Musks 'Moonlight' and 'Pax', the common pink Moss, the Gallica 'Tuscany', the Bourbon rose 'Souvenir de la Malmaison', *R. alba* 'Koenigin von Danemarck', the Damask 'Mme Hardy' and recurring groups of *R. centifolia* 'Fantin Latour'. The ends of these beds on both sides are closed with short runs of box hedge 914 mm, 3 ft, wide, leading the eye on to the next transverse yew hedge, which is clipped at 2.1 m, 7 ft, to conceal the 1.8 m, 6 ft, high fruit cage in the *potager* immediately below. The area of cultivated ground for vegetables is just under 334 m², about 400 sq. yds, including the fruit cage, but excluding the space taken up by four pyramid apple and pear trees, 3 m, 10 ft, apart on either side. In this case these trees stand in soil which is useful for catch crops of lettuces.

In the middle of the *potager* is a round pool, 3.7 m, 12 ft, across with brick sides raised 610 mm, 2 ft, standing in a wide central gravel pathway. The 914 mm, 3 ft, wide beds on either side of the path are for flowers for cutting—coreopsis, gladioluses, delphiniums, dahlias, peonies, pyrethrums, and scabious. Wires along the transverse path can be used for cordon bush fruit, runner beans and sweet peas.

The length of the plot allows the house to be, as it were, built well up into it and still leave a good length of garden in view from the terrace but allowing also for a greenhouse to be made in the north-east corner, out of view from the main windows and the terrace, and close to the house in the interests of obtaining a short run of electric cable. This position is to an extent at the expense of some light, depending chiefly on the height at which the hedges are kept. In the case of these somewhat highly wrought little gardens this alternative is considered preferable to putting the greenhouse in full view. The greenhouse with its frames and some spare ground are separated by a wall, 2.4 m, 8 ft, high, from the side terrace on the left of the house and by a hedge from the drive. In front of the house a wide band of grass runs towards the road boundary and returns in front of the Portuguese laurel hedge. These grass areas are raised 152 mm, 6 in, above the drive level by pre-cast concrete edging in order that cars reversing gently enough should, as it were, "feel" these little retaining walls with their back wheels and avoid driving on to the grass.

Figure 12 shows a garden for a detached house in a row of similar houses.

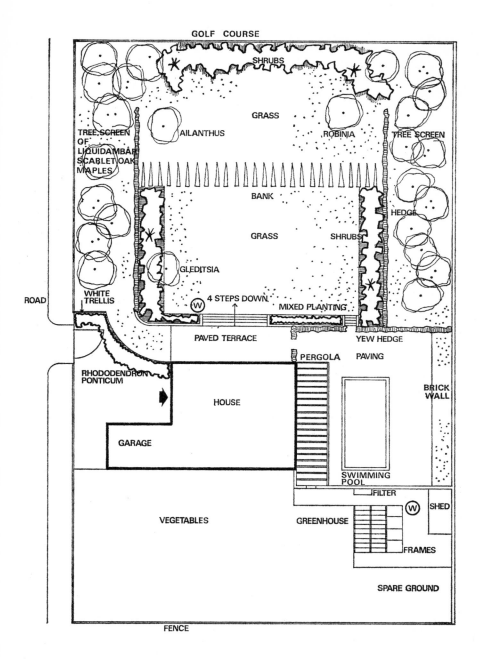

GOLF COURSE

SHRUBS

GRASS

AILANTHUS

ROBINIA

TREE SCREEN
OF
LIQUIDAMBAR
SCARLET OAK
MAPLES

TREE SCREEN

BANK

HEDGE

GRASS

SHRUBS

GLEDITSIA

WHITE
TRELLIS

W 4 STEPS DOWN

MIXED PLANTING

ROAD

PAVED TERRACE

YEW HEDGE

PERGOLA   PAVING

RHODODENDRON
PONTICUM

BRICK
WALL

HOUSE

GARAGE

SWIMMING
POOL

FILTER

W SHED

VEGETABLES

GREENHOUSE

FRAMES

SPARE GROUND

FENCE

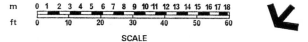

m   0 1 2 3 4 5 6 7 8 9 10 11 12 13 14 15 16 17 18
ft   0   10   20   30   40   50   60

SCALE

Figure 12

The frontage is 36.6 m, 120 ft, by 54.9 m, 180 ft, depth. The garden faces south-east; the soil is acid.

The entrance is from a road to the left (north-east). Advantage has been taken of this to leave enough space at the bottom boundary for a kitchen garden, approximately 375 m², 450 sq. yds, excluding the greenhouse, frames and some spare ground. The greenhouse is within 7.5 m, 25 ft, of the house, thus providing a fairly short run of cable for heating. For the same reason the swimming-pool is about the same distance away from the corner of the house, the filtration plant being housed between the greenhouse and a 1.8 m, 6 ft, wall that screens the lower end of the pool from the whole kitchen garden area. The swimming-pool measures 9.1 m by 4.6 m, 30 ft by 15 ft, and is set in an area of paving, 15.2 m by 9.7 m, 50 ft by 32 ft, excluding that part of the paving under the pergola. The width of the paving to the right of the pool is 3.7 m, 12 ft, to give good width for sunbathing and garden chairs. At the further edge is a band of grass, 2.4 m, 8 ft, wide to soften the angle of the paving with the 1.8 m, 6 ft, high boundary wall. On the opposite side of the pool, a pergola 3 m, 10 ft, wide is built out from the end of the house, clothed with vines planted in 'pockets' taken out of the paving. At the upper end (to the south-east), the pool area is bounded by a yew hedge with a 914 mm, 3 ft, opening leading down to the lawn by a flight of steps. To the right of the lawn is a 2.4 m, 8 ft, wide bed of plants.

From the house terrace, which is 3.6 m, 12 ft, wide, four steps, 6.1 m, 20 ft, wide, lead down to the lawn, across which is a downward slope of 609 mm, 2 ft, 1 in 20, to a grass bank 2.7 m, 9 ft, wide, on a rake of 1 in 3, which is easily mowable with any kind of machine. From the bottom of this bank another lawn runs on for 9.1 m, 30 ft, sloping 152 mm, 6 in, a gradient of 1 in 60, and ending in a bed of shrubs, in this case largely rhododendrons, *Enkianthus* and *Pieris*. In the upper lawn is a single *Gleditsia triacanthos* and in the lower lawn an *Ailanthus* and a *Robinia pseudacacia*. On either side are 6.1 m, 20 ft, wide screens of trees, *Acer negundo*, *A. platanoides*, liquidambar and scarlet oaks.

A curving line of *Rhododendron ponticum* screens a small forecourt from the garden, the curve being returned at right angles to the left boundary by white trellis, 3 m, 10 ft, high, through which the rhododendrons can be seen from the garden.

Figure 13 shows a country garden of about 4600 m², rather more than 1 acre, overlooking the village churchyard; the boundaries on three sides are holly hedges, that to the south-west against the churchyard is a brick wall, 1.2 m, 4 ft, high. With an acre at disposal there is for the first time room for a tennis court, one moreover that can be placed out of the main view of the windows of the house. For the first time too there is room for a drive, although of only 36.6 m, 120 ft, between the road and the forecourt of the house.

The kitchen garden to the left of the drive measures 18.3 m by 30.5 m, 60 ft by 100 ft, over 551 m², 666 sq. yds, excluding the greenhouse, frames, shed and spare ground. The hard court 33.5 m by 17 m, 110 ft by 56 ft, is tucked in against the south-eastern boundary; this may result in inconvenience in retrieving the few balls that are sent over the top of the 2.7 m, 9 ft, high enclosure, but this disadvantage is considered to be outweighed by the advantage of keeping the tennis court out of view from the house. To the left of the forecourt, through beds planted first with tulips and then geraniums, a path leads on to the paved side terrace from which, through two more beds of mixed planting, access is obtained to the swimming-pool, 6.1 m by 11.2 m, 20 ft by 37 ft, in a paved surround from which is the way in to the tennis court. The

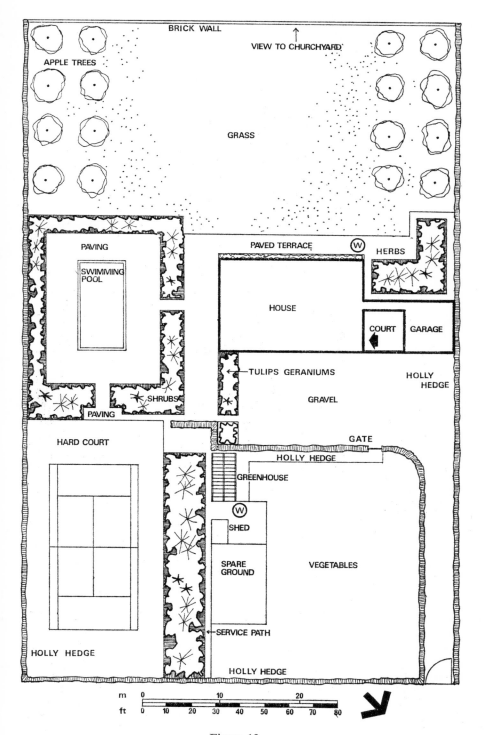

BRICK WALL

VIEW TO CHURCHYARD

APPLE TREES

GRASS

PAVING

SWIMMING
POOL

PAVED TERRACE　Ⓦ　HERBS

HOUSE

COURT　GARAGE

TULIPS GERANIUMS

HOLLY
HEDGE

SHRUBS

GRAVEL

PAVING

HARD COURT

GATE

HOLLY HEDGE

GREENHOUSE

Ⓦ

SHED

SPARE
GROUND

VEGETABLES

SERVICE PATH

HOLLY HEDGE

HOLLY HEDGE

m　0　　　　　10　　　　　20
ft　0　10　20　30　40　50　60　70　80

Figure 13

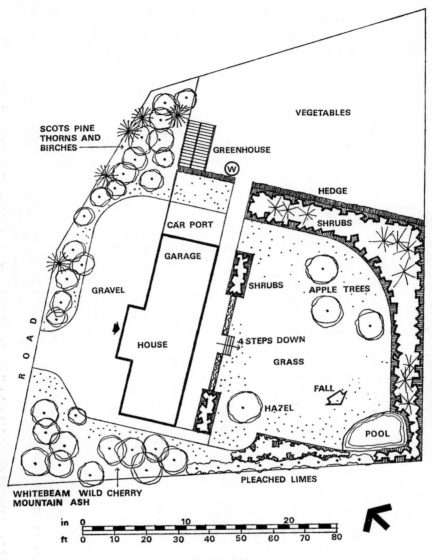

SCOTS PINE
THORNS AND
BIRCHES

VEGETABLES

GREENHOUSE

HEDGE

W

CAR PORT

SHRUBS

GARAGE

GRAVEL

SHRUBS

APPLE TREES

R O A D

HOUSE

4 STEPS DOWN

GRASS

FALL

HAZEL

POOL

WHITEBEAM WILD CHERRY
MOUNTAIN ASH

PLEACHED LIMES

in 0   10   20
ft 0   10   20   30   40   50   60   70   80

Figure 14

house terrace is 3 m, 10 ft, wide, there being a narrow bed against the house for scented plants. To the right is an area for herbs. To either side of the lawn, standard apple trees are planted, 6.1 m, 20 ft, apart, as much for their blossom as for the fruit.

Figure 14 shows a garden of about 1470 m², between a quarter and half an acre. The frontage to the road is about 44 m, 145 ft, and the average depth 33.5 m, 110 ft. Small plantations of trees on either side of the entrance gates screen the house from the road. To the north-east are a vegetable garden and greenhouse, divided from the rest of the garden by a yew hedge. This house was built between

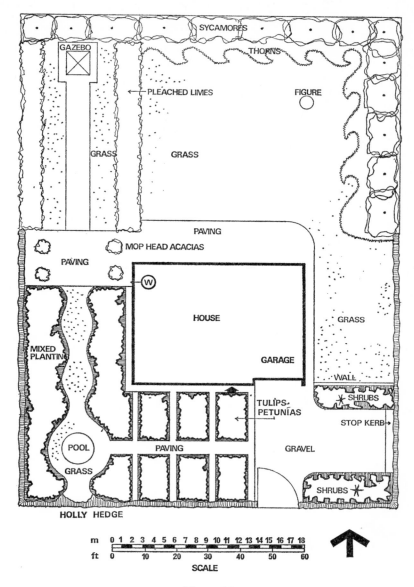

Figure 15

the wars on a part of an orchard, and some of the old trees remain. The hazel in the lawn below the terrace is unusual but the present owners did not have the heart to cut it down, although it takes light from the windows on that side of the house. Winter aconites have been naturalized underneath and in February, at the time of Candlemas, they twinkle in their green toby ruffs at the catkins swinging above them. The pool, at the lowest part of the garden, is bordered on two sides by gigantic gunneras and rheums. The pleached limes screen the house next door. On the south-east boundary there is a beech hedge and on the

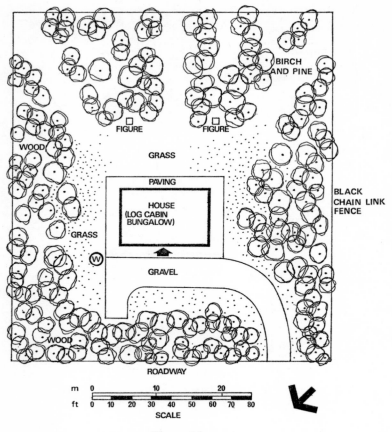

Figure 16

inside of this a mixed screen has been planted, yews, laurustinus, Rugosa roses and, at intervals, the 'Lanarth' *Viburnum* horizontally branching over the edge of the lawn. This garden is fortunate in having a very effective piece of 'borrowed' landscape, the spire of the village church beyond the southern corner.

Figure 15 shows a level garden of rather less than half an acre, facing north. The frontage is 36.6 m, 120 ft, and the depth 48.8 m, 160 ft, giving an area of 1782 m², 2133 sq. yds. The house was so sited to leave most of the garden to the north. The garage is intended for one car only. No attempt has been made to screen the small formal front garden from the forecourt, the six beds being planted with tulips followed by petunias. This opens into a long garden running from south to north which has on either side of a grass path wide beds of mixed planting with sinuous curves to their edges and contains also a pool. North of this is a small paved courtyard with four mop-head acacias (*Robinia pseudacacia* 'Inermis'). From this a paved path leads between grass panels bordered by pleached limes to a gazebo from which there is a view directly southwards into the pool garden. There is a small paved area on the north side of the house and beyond this a lawn of about 167.2 m², 200 sq. yds. To the east of this lawn is a shelter belt of sycamores planted 4.6 m, 15 ft, apart and returning all the way

50

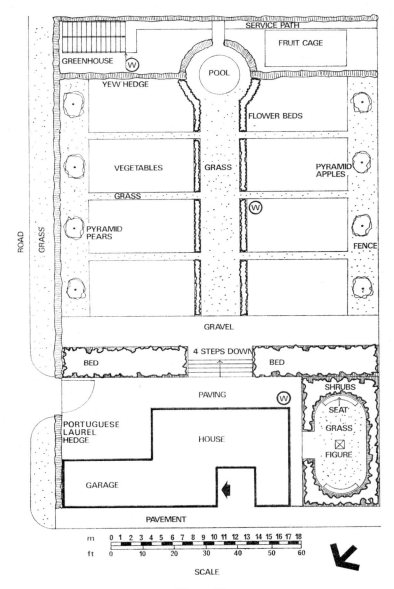

Figure 17

along the north boundary behind the gazebo. In front of the screen of sycamores, thorns are brought out in a toothed pattern. There is a white figure of Poppaea in the lawn.

Figure 16 shows a level garden of a little less than three-quarters of an acre. The frontage is 48.8 m, 160 ft, and the depth 54.9 m, 180 ft, giving an area of 2676 m², 3200 sq. yds.

The house is a log cabin bungalow. The garden is entirely a mixed wood of birch and pine. An area of paving 1.8 m, 6 ft, wide has been laid all round the

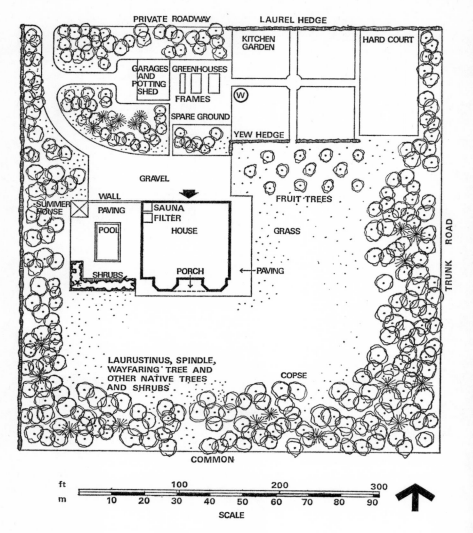

Figure 18

house, but beyond this is grass, which is rough and mown only occasionally, leading to the wood through which three *allées* have been cut in *patte d'oie* arrangement to give direct views to open country beyond and to prevent a feeling of claustrophobia. There is no garage. The wood is kept clear of brambles, suckers and scrub growth and there is no hedge between the grass and the wood, so that stems of the trees can be seen intact, and the view of the two sculptured figures is unimpeded. The garden is fenced on all sides with 1.8 m, 6 ft, high black chain link netting and the owner, who is a recluse, is trying to make a small nature reserve.

Figure 17 shows a garden of about a third of an acre on a corner site sloping down from the house and facing south-east. The frontages are 48.8 m, 160 ft, and 30.5 m, 100 ft, giving an area of 1488.4 m², 1777 sq. yds.

52

The whole garden here is a decorative *potager*. Four wide steps down from the terrace lead across a gravel path directly into the garden arranged symmetrically on either side of a 3.7 m, 12 ft, wide grass path bordered by 610 mm, 2 ft, wide flower beds and terminated by a circular pool. The fruit cage and the greenhouse in this case are at the far end. The latter can be seen above the 1.8 m, 6 ft, high yew hedge from the terrace and there is a 39.6 m, 130 ft, run for the electric cable for heating the greenhouse, but this has to be accepted to give as large a garden as possible and keep the house close to its roadside boundary. There are four pyramid apple and pear trees on either side standing in grass. The area of cultivable kitchen garden excluding the paths is about 418 m², 500 sq. yds. To the right of the house and leading from the surrounding paving is a small secret garden, mixed planting surrounding an oval panel of grass with semi-circular seats at either end and a white figure of La Calisto.

Figure 18 shows a garden of over four acres around a medium-sized family house. The frontages are 134.1 m, 440 ft, to the main road, and 128 m, 420 ft, to the private road, giving an area of 17,168 m², 20,533 sq. yds.

The entrance is from the private road, which leads on to other similar houses. The drive curves past a screen of pines to the forecourt. There is immediate access to the garages by a subsidiary drive to the left. The boundary to the private road and to the property beyond to the west is a Portuguese laurel hedge. The southern boundary is a loose screen of native trees including *Acer campestre*, *Viburnum lantana*, *Euonymus europaeus* (spindle tree) and wild rose. The boundary to the main road at the east is a mini-copse of *Sorbus aria*, *Sorbus aucuparia*, birches, thorns and wild cherry, the mini-copse averaging 18.3 m, 60 ft, wide. There is a small orchard of twelve standard fruit trees about 9 m, 30 ft, apart which screen the hard court at the bottom end of the kitchen garden, which measures approximately 36.6 m by 39.6 m, 120 ft by 130 ft, about 1446 m², 1730 sq. yds, including some flower beds along the main paths. To the west of the kitchen garden are the two greenhouses and frames, potting shed and store, with spare ground to the south. The kitchen garden complex is separated from the orchard by a yew hedge with an opening in the middle.

At the west side of the house is a large swimming pool, 12.2 m by 7.5 m, 40ft by 25 ft, with paved surround, beds for mixed planting to the south and west, a summer house in one corner and a sauna bath built in to the corner of the house itself. The heating and filtration plant is housed in another compound inside the house. No other flower beds are provided, most of the area to the south and east being grass, which is used for croquet and occasionally as grass tennis courts.

The garden shown in Figure 19 is designed for a small cottage in a village by the sea. This garden has an appreciable slope towards the south-west; a kitchen garden at the back falls to the levelled platform of the cottage and the front garden continues the slope towards the road. The plot to the north-east of the road has a frontage of 14.6 metres, 48 ft, and an average depth of 26.5 m, 85 ft. The entrance is by four steps up from the road through a white handgate in the middle of a white palisade fence standing on top of a wall of local stone. The 1.2 m, 4 ft, path of whitish shingle leads straight to the storm porch and the front door. There are wide beds of flowers and shrubs on either side of the path; the flowers include in the front gazanias and thrift, backed up by lavender, rosemary, echinops and eryngium with a stiffening of shrubs—*Olearia haastii*, *Berberis darwinii*, *Hebe* (*Veronica*) 'Bowles' Hybrid', Warminster broom (*Cytisus praecox*), Spanish gorse (*Genista hispanica*) and *Genista Lydia*, and

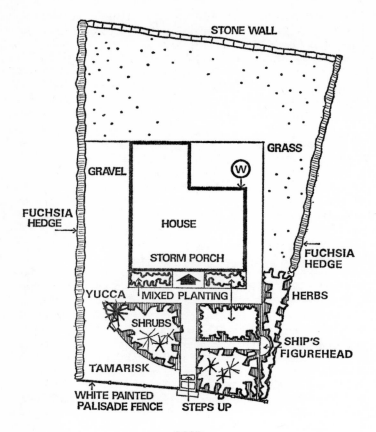

STONE WALL

GRASS

GRAVEL

W

FUCHSIA
HEDGE

HOUSE

STORM PORCH

FUCHSIA
HEDGE

YUCCA   MIXED PLANTING

HERBS

SHRUBS

SHIP'S
FIGUREHEAD

TAMARISK

WHITE PAINTED
PALISADE FENCE   STEPS UP

ROAD

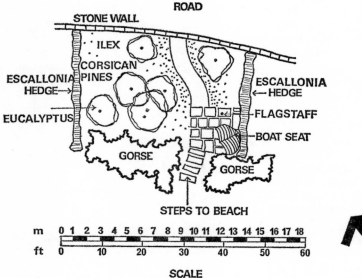

STONE WALL

ILEX

CORSICAN
PINES

ESCALLONIA
HEDGE

ESCALLONIA
← HEDGE

EUCALYPTUS

FLAGSTAFF

BOAT SEAT

GORSE

GORSE

STEPS TO BEACH

| m | 0 1 2 3 4 5 6 7 8 9 10 11 12 13 14 15 16 17 18 |
| ft | 0   10   20   30   40   50   60 |

SCALE

Figure 19

hybrids of *Rosa spinosissima*, 'Frühlingsgold', 'Frühlingsmorgen' and 'Stanwell Perpetual'. In the top corner of the left-hand bed is a large specimen of *Yucca gloriosa*; at the bottom of this bed a token screen of tamarisk, *Tamarix pentandra*, disguises the path branching to the left of the front gate and leading up the side of the house to a small yard at the back for dustbins and a coal store. There are fuchsia hedges on both side boundaries and, at the back, a rough drystone wall built in Jack-and-Jill fashion. Behind the flower bed to the right of the front gate is a small garden for herbs with an old ship's figurehead in the middle.

Across the road is a small garden on the sloping cliff leading down to within 6.1 m, 20 ft, above the beach. This consists mainly of rough grass which is mown only two or three times a year, through which a pathway winds down the slope to a flat area, about 3.7 m, 12 ft, square, paved out with local stone on which the sawn-off half of a pulling boat is up-ended and fitted with a seat looking directly out to sea and making an observation point. Here also is a flagstaff that in these surroundings looks perfectly in place, but is generally an unsatisfactory component of gardens inland. In the sloping rough grass are planted a number of ilexes and Corsican pines and, for good measure, a *Eucalyptus gunnii*. At the lower end of this little garden is a bank of common gorse, *Ulex europaeus*, never out of flower, and on both sides, hedges of *Escallonia* 'Crimson Spire'. A winding and slightly precarious flight of steps leads down from the observation platform to the sea beach below.

Figure 20 shows a garden of twelve and a quarter acres by an estuary in the south-west of England. It has a frontage of 182.8 m, 200 yds, and a depth of 274.2 m, 300 yds, making an area of 50,167 m², 60,000 sq. yds.

The approach drive is through gates from a lane down a slope at a gradient of about 1 in 8 to a gate in a walled courtyard. To the right are stables and a garage, to the left a walled garden. To the right of the house is a conservatory built between the house and a wall 2.4 m, 8 ft, high retaining the terrace of the house from the rising ground to the west. The first 30 m, 100 ft, or so of this is taken up in a grass slope and beyond this, still on rising ground, is a windscreen of *Rhododendron ponticum* in two or three irregular lines, and beyond this again are three lines of sycamores. This screen continues on down to within 15.2 m, 50 ft, of the estuary and is an efficient protection against south-westerly gales. The house terrace is 6.1 m, 20 ft, wide and gives on to an area of sloping grass falling 914 mm, 3 ft, over a distance of 45.7 m, 150 ft. From the edge of this irregularly shaped lawn a winding path leads down through woodland to the quay, beyond which is a tidal inlet of the sea. The woodland has been largely cleared of lichenous scrub oak and has now been planted with a number of exotic plants, *Magnolia sargentiana robusta*, *M. mollicomata*, *M. salicifolia*, *Camellia* × *williamsii* 'Donation', *C.* 'Cornish Snow', *C. granthamiana*, *C. sasanqua*. There is a large rampant *Camellia reticulata* 'Captain Rawes' over the gateway in the top courtyard, but the owner decided not to have any *Camellia japonica* varieties. Other trees are *Pinus radiata*, the Monterey pine, and *Cupressus macrocarpa*—the latter in this case planted more or less in isolation in order that it should develop its true outline, like that of a cedar—*Arbutus menziesii*, *Drimys winterii*, a grove of *Myrtus apiculata* (*M. luma*) and, at the lower end in full view from boats approaching, a number of Umbrella pines, *Pinus pinea*.

The old conservatory, still heated by antiquated 102 mm, 4 in, pipes, houses a number of tender plants, *Hoya carnosa*, *Plumbago capensis*, *Jasminum polyan-*

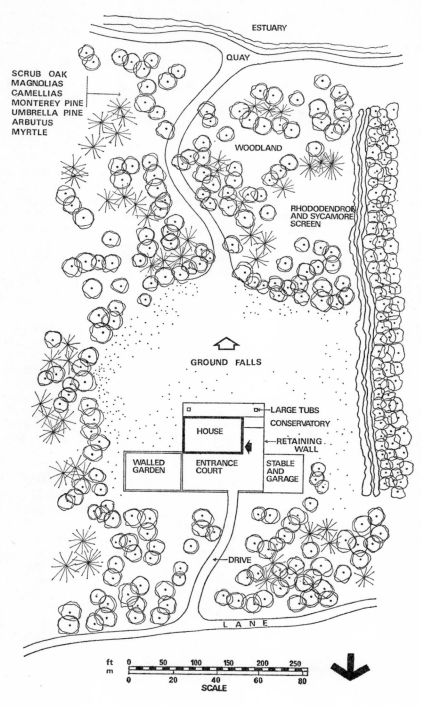

ESTUARY

QUAY

SCRUB OAK
MAGNOLIAS
CAMELLIAS
MONTEREY PINE
UMBRELLA PINE
ARBUTUS
MYRTLE

WOODLAND

RHODODENDRON
AND SYCAMORE
SCREEN

GROUND FALLS

LARGE TUBS

CONSERVATORY

HOUSE

RETAINING
WALL

WALLED
GARDEN

ENTRANCE
COURT

STABLE
AND
GARAGE

DRIVE

L A N E

ft
m

0   50   100   150   200   250
0   20   40   60   80
SCALE

Figure 20

thum, Stephanotis and, in tubs, *Luculia gratissima, Rhododendron* 'Lady Alice Fitzwilliam', *Rhododendron cilcealyx.* Two large tubs, 914 mm, 3 ft, square on the terrace are planted with the old blue African lily (*Agapanthus umbellatus* of gardens), which in this climate can stand out of doors all through the winter.

Figure 21 shows an estate of over 100 acres where the house has been built below the crest of a wooded hill, roughly horseshoe shaped. The drive from the road passes the lodge and then crosses a bridge over the stream and a cattle grid and goes on uphill through a mixed wood of lichened oaks, lime, hornbeam, field maple, ash and alder, the latter predominating on the lower slopes. One or two squints have been cut through on either side to show up glades where bluebells are flourishing, having colonized empty spaces in woods as soon as trees have fallen or have been taken out, allowing light to get in. The woods are predominantly of pedunculate oak trees, which characteristically have an attractive wild flora beside the bluebells: primroses, wood anemones, enchanter's nightshade, woodruff and many others including foxgloves, the wild *Digitalis purpurea*, with flowers along one side of the stem only. Between the edges of the drive and the wood on both sides there are verges of rough grass allowed to grow fairly long and mown only two or three times a year when the cow parsley has died down. There are no groups of daffodils in these grass verges.

The entrance courtyard gives ample space for cars to be driven up to the front door and turned round in the drive, without reversing. Opposite the front door of the house, the grass in front of the wood is wider and more closely mown. There are no shrubs or decorative plants at the edges of the wood, so that the stems of the trees can be seen rising from ground level, but away to the left three large drifts of daffodils have been planted of about a hundred in each, white 'Beersheba', yellow 'Carlton', and the buttered-eggs colours of 'Polindra'. These lie back, as it were, against the wood and are well separated by good spaces of grass between each group. There are no *allées* cut in this wood to let in the cold north-east wind, but on either side of the house where there is also some woodland, *allées* have been cut to give vistas to the farther country.

The house itself is a large, comfortable Victorian stucco building, with the almost evergreen rose 'Félicité et Perpétue' covering much of one part of the front. *Pyracantha* 'Lalandei' now covers the other side, having been trained out horizontally. In beds on either side of the front door are evergreen shrubs which have taken the place of the original Victorian laurels and aucubas. The planting now is mainly composed of the evergreen *Viburnum davidii* with, for their winter and spring smells, *Sarcococca humilis* and *Skimmia japonica* 'Fragrans'. There are also two large tubs filled with an acid compost, and containing camellias, now 1.8 m, 6 ft, high. These tubs are made like Versailles *caisses* with detachable sides, but instead of being exact cubes they are slightly taller, measuring 1.1 m high by 914 mm square, 3 ft 6 in by 3 ft square. The pink camellias, 'Elegans', are beautiful in flower in the early spring, and their evergreen foliage through the year is distinguished. They are put here because a north aspect is the best for camellias. Between the front of the house and the drive there is a stretch of turf 3 m, 10 ft, wide, retained at the drive edge by steel edging of the kind seen in quadrangles of Oxford colleges. Without this steel edging repeated trimming back with an edging-iron would cause the turf to recede, leaving beyond the gravel a strip of soil into which weeds would quickly gain an unwelcome foothold. Generally there is little in front of the house, partly because it faces north,

57

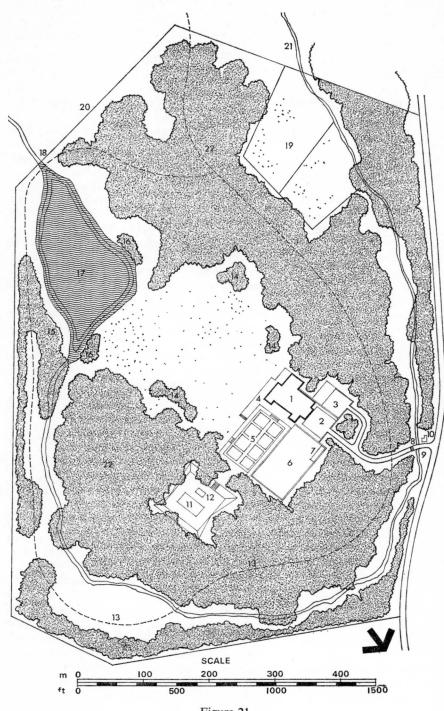

SCALE

| m | 0 | 100 | 200 | 300 | 400 |
| ft | 0 | 500 | 1000 | 1500 |

Figure 21

KEY

1. House
2. Forecourt
3. Garage yard
4. Main terrace
5. Flower garden
6. Walled kitchen garden
7. Greenhouse
8. Cattle grid
9. Bridge
10. Lodge
11. Tennis court
12. Swimming pool
13. Bridle way
14. Tree groups in grass
15. Poplars
16. Willow
17. Lake
18. Weir
19. Paddock
20. Perimeter fence
21. Stream
22. Mixed woodland

but also because a degree of formal severity is appropriate here where visitors arrive for the first time.

If, instead of going inside ourselves, we turn to the right and then round the end of the house, we see again mown grass leading up to woodland and in the grass a large old *Arbutus unedo*. It must have been planted soon after the house was built, and since then has been lovingly pruned over the years to a clear main stem of about 1.5 m, 5 ft, and above this branching into a romantic twisted framework. This evergreen tree, a native as it happens of Britain and fairly common in Ireland, is a member of the Ericaceae Family, which includes the rhododendrons, and whose members usually demand an acid, lime-free soil— but this arbutus is perfectly content on calcareous soil. It is known as the straw-berry tree because its fruits a little resemble strawberries; they persist from one year to the next until the flowers appear in the autumn, when both fruit and flowers are seen together. At the base of this tree are several *Cyclamen nea-politanum* 'Album'; the white flowers in autumn are outstandingly beautiful, and because they cling to the ground so closely and have no significant height, their presence does not compromise the bole of the Arbutus rising from the ground. It is, unfortunately, a very expensive little corm to buy, but a dozen put in in the first place will increase over the years and spread outwards, the more so if before flowering time they are well dusted with leaf soil to catch the resulting seeds.

The wood beyond has been thinned considerably to allow the planting of some exotic trees, and some Scots pines have been put in to provide, together with the predominating oaks, a degree of top cover against frost in early spring. The forest floor is old and rich, with a pH just on the acid side of neutral, but not really acid enough for such as *Magnolia salicifolia*, *Liquidambar styraciflua*, enkianthus, *Pieris* and, of course, rhododendrons, but a fine specimen of *Davidia involucrata* flourishes, and there is great beauty in the large double-flowered white cherries standing in front of the wood.

On the south side of the house the terrace is 7.3 m, 24 ft, wide, a dimension which happens to correspond with Le Nôtre's recommendation, that the width of the terrace should be equal to the height of the house from ground to cornice; [1] and the length of the terrace is 15.2 m, 50 ft. This is the size that was originally made to form a platform for the house, but it is too large an area to be paved over entirely. In practice, this family, with four undergraduate children and their friends from time to time, find that a width of 5.5 m, 18 ft, and a length of 9.1 m, 30 ft, is amply large for garden chairs and tables, and paving has been laid over this area. The rest of the platform is taken up as follows. There is a 610 mm, 2 ft, bed running in front of the house under the windows; this is planted entirely for scent; a few permanent evergreens or ever-greys, lavender and rosemary, with good space between for wallflowers in the spring and tobacco plants, heliotropes and stocks in the summer. There are also two plants of the lemon verbena on either side of the garden door into the house. At the far end of the terrace and beneath the 914 mm, 3 ft, high parapet wall, is a 1.2 m, 4 ft, wide bed filled with flowering plants which, with one exception, shall not grow taller than the parapet wall, but be contained by it (any of them that throw a spray above the desired level are appropriately pruned). These plants include *Potentilla arbuscula*, *Phlomis fruticosa*, *Salvia lavandulifolia* (*S. hispanica*), rosemary, lavender, *Alchemilla mollis*, *Campanula poscharskyana* and catmint—all muted colours,

[1] Cited by Russell Page in *The Education of A Gardener*.

in order not to draw attention away from the landscape beyond. There is a very real danger of letting fly with colour and making the foreground and middle distance so emphatic as to distract the attention from contoured hills, trees and grazing sheep in the distance. The length of the terrace has, as it were, been brought in on either side by making grass panels 3 m, 10 ft, long by 5.5 m, 18 ft, wide (from the back to the front). The terrace was made some years ago of natural York stone, when this material was less expensive than it is now. Its large size has been relieved by bands of slate 229 mm, 9 in, wide, two running transversely and two from front to back, giving a panelled effect. The use of slate for this purpose is exceedingly subtle, because in certain lights and from certain angles it does not make an emphatic contrast with the stone.

The park slopes on gently past a neck of woodland to the lake. On the terrace and standing close to the house are four large tubs like those in the front of the house, with mop-headed bay trees which have to be trundled away to the cold greenhouse in October to protect them from the frost. On the terrace also are some large Florentine terracotta pots planted in summer with tumbling scented-leaved geraniums, *Pelargonium tomentosum* and *P.* 'Clorinda'. These pots are not used for spring flowers, such as tulips and wallflowers, which would look stuck-up. The steps down to the park are 5.5 m, 18 ft, wide, with 356 mm, 14 in, wide block treads and 114 mm, 4½ in, stone risers. On the outer side of the wall some native volunteers have established themselves, the red and white valerian, the blue-flowered alkanet, and ivy-leaved toadflax.

To the east the house terrace returns and gives on to more steps leading down to the flower garden, with the walled kitchen garden behind it. The flower garden is divided up by gravel paths edged with wooden boards, with 229 mm, 9 in, box planted just inside the boarding. Here are beds of peonies, irises, lilies, anemones, campanulas, delphiniums (Belladonna varieties), *Achillea filipendulina* 'Gold Plate', verbascum, clove pinks, crinums, and some roses. Against the kitchen garden wall and facing south, the Banksian rose and *Rosa × anemonoides* (*R. sinica anemone*) and wintersweet, together with a number of cistus such as *C. laurifolius* and *ladaniferus*, which in the hot sun gives off a smell of cigars—not cigar smoke, but of Havanas taken from their cabinet and rolled before being lighted. On the opposite side of the garden looking towards the north is a collection of hellebores, *H. niger, orientalis, corsicus, foetidus* and *viridis*.

Inside the kitchen garden there are greenhouses, peach cases against the south-facing wall, a good frame yard, and generous space for the storage of loam, peat and leaf soil; four compost bins, a large incinerator, and a fruit cage, leaving good space for propagation and cultivating vegetables. Then, leading on from the flower garden, a special place has been made for a hard court and swimming-pool. The ground has been excavated in the shape of a square to a depth of 1.8 m, 6 ft, retained by vertical brick walls, and the soil thrown up all round to make rounded banks, which have been turfed over. On the new excavated low level, which is about 2.7 m, 9, ft below the top of the new grass banks, the hard court and swimming-pool have been put in, and the surrounding area partly turfed but largely paved. The reason for this expensive operation was to keep these intractable elements out of sight from any part of the garden, except from the top of the steps leading down.

The stream runs on round the property and widens out into a lake, which has been made by damming and making a weir at the lower end. The water running over this weir drives a ram, which supplies auxiliary water to storage tanks behind the kitchen garden. When the lake was first made it was intended that it should hold trout and it was excavated to an average depth of 2.4 m, 8 ft, at which depth it still remains owing to conscientious cleaning and dredging so that the water is cool enough for trout, but in one or two places it is sufficiently shallow for small colonies of the larger waterlilies. In the grass round the lake, fritillaries have been planted, and on the farther bank bright-stemmed plants, in particular *Cornus alba* 'Sibirica', the Westonbirt dogwood, and the scarlet willow, *Salix chrysostella*.

Chapter 3

Foundation Planting

Foundation planting means, first, the provision of shelter to create an equable climate inside the garden, the planting of hedges to define the boundaries and then of those trees and plants that in years of maturity will set the pattern and dictate the character of the garden.

SHELTER IN SMALL GARDENS

In small gardens, although there is seldom enough room to plant sheltering trees in much depth, useful protection can be afforded by one or two rows of medium-sized trees planted close together to windward. In choosing trees for this, their ultimate height must be considered in relation to the size of the garden. For example, a row of massively framed trees, Norway maples, willows or poplars, or the evergreen Leyland cypress, could dwarf a small garden, and make it lop-sided and claustrophobic both for the owner and for his plants. It is much better to decide upon trees that, when mature, will settle down at about 6.1 m, 20 ft, as for example mountain ash, which can be planted for windscreen purposes as close as 1.2 m, 4 ft, apart and can usually be bought as high as 3 m, 10 ft, thus providing a degree of shelter fairly quickly. The trees should attain a height of 5.5–6.1 m, 18–20 ft, in ten years and ultimately reach 6.1–7.6 m, 20–25 ft. Many thorns or May trees, white, pink or red and both double and single-flowered, when planted close together also give good winter shelter. Thorns are planted the same distance apart as mountain ash, but are slower growing. Like other deciduous trees, when they approach maturity their lower branches become thin at their bases; when this happens it is advisable to plant hedges in front of them to stop the wind under their skirts. Any of the deciduous or evergreen hedging plants referred to later can be used for this, in particular holly, hawthorn, beech and yew—the last of these, however, not on a boundary because yew is poisonous to cattle. Privet is not a good plant for this purpose because it makes such high demands on soil moisture and nutrients and even at a distance of 1.8 m, 6 ft, it would add to the root competition that is bound to build up among the screening trees when planted as close as 1.2–1.8 m, 4–6 ft, apart.

DECIDUOUS SHELTER BELTS FOR LARGER GARDENS

For larger gardens where there is room to plant in depth there is a wide choice of trees capable of reaching to almost any height without dwarfing the garden. Most of them can be bought at a height of 1–3 m, 3–10 ft. The trees are again planted 1.2–1.8 m, 4–6 ft, apart in alternating (staggered) rows; for example, in a strip 1.8 m, 6 ft, wide there would be three rows and in a strip 9.1 m, 30 ft, wide, six rows.

The most wind-hardy deciduous tree is the sycamore, *Acer pseudoplatanus*, the one to defy real gales as on the sea coasts in the west country. Le Sueur, in *Hedges, Shelter Belts and Screens* (in *Country Life* in 1951), suggests that when they are planted in depth 1.5 m, 5 ft, apart in staggered rows it is desirable to widen the intervals on the exposed edge. In maturity the effectiveness of sycamore is all the better for a low screen of *Rhododendron ponticum*, pruned to prevent it getting leggy if the soil is acid. On neutral or alkaline soils holly or *Thuja plicata* would do instead and may reach 6.1 m, 20 ft, in ten years.

Other good deciduous screening trees include Norway maple, *Acer platanoides*, which is rather faster growing than sycamore, probably reaching 7.6 m, 25 ft, in ten years. It is capable of attaining a height of 18.3 m, 60 ft, or more under favourable conditions but may not always do this when on duty in very exposed situations. These are well-branched, wind-hardy trees whose leaves have good red-brown autumn colour, though in common with all the other deciduous trees they are far better put in as 'feathered' trees—that is, branching from the ground upwards and not trimmed to clear stems. The native field maple, *Acer campestre*, is also useful for shelter, though is not quite so fast growing, taking about fifteen years to reach 3 m, 10 ft, and is more spreading, but it is a good plant to choose on alkaline soils. Willows are among the fastest growing British trees and the white willow, *Salix alba*, is often used as a wind-break, in this case planted about 3.7 m, 12 ft, apart and pollarded 2.1 m, 7 ft, high; this process will cause it to throw up numerous vertical branches at 12.2 m, 40 ft. Both this willow and its near relative the blue willow, *Salix alba* 'Coerulea', make beautiful screens in wet places. For this purpose they may be planted in gardens between 9.1 and 12.2 m, 30 and 40 ft, apart, bearing in mind their ultimate spread. Both of them are used as wind-breaks in the fruit areas of the Long Ashton Research Station of the University of Bristol, where alders are also used, *A. incana*, the grey alder, and *A. cordata*, the Italian alder.

Poplars are also very fast growing. The most interesting ones to choose would be some of the balsam poplars, among them *P. trichocarpa*, which is a 27.3 m, 90 ft, tree when fully grown; these should be planted 3 m, 10 ft, apart in several rows. Their unfurling leaf buds in spring release the heady fragrance of Chanel No. 5. When there is not much depth in which to plant a screen, Lombardy poplars, *Populus nigra italica*, are very useful because their branching extends almost from the ground upwards and they also can attain considerable height, 27.3 m, 90 ft. In a single row they can go in 1.8–2.4 m, 6–8 ft, apart, or in a double row 3 m, 10 ft, apart in both directions, but unless there is a good width of garden to leeward they could be unacceptably overwhelming and their tight, remorselessly fastigiate habit could look a little curious striding across some landscapes. Most of the poplars have wide-spreading, very thirsty root systems which extract so much water that they can cause clay soils to contract and lead to subsidence under buildings—therefore poplars are not for planting within 15.2 m, 50 ft, of buildings or important roads.

EVERGREEN SHELTER BELTS

One of the most useful coniferous trees for planting to give shelter is *Thuja plicata*, which has an ultimate height of up to 30.5 m, 100 ft. It is a narrow tree and for planting by itself as a screen can be put in as close as 610 mm, 2 ft, apart. Plants can be bought at 1.5 m, 5 ft, high or more, but smaller plants at 610 mm, 2 ft, settle in better and would probably overtake larger ones in a few years. It is a rapid grower and flourishes best on good loam. Leyland cypress, *Cupressocyparis leylandii*, is said to be the fastest-growing conifer in Britain. This too is probably capable of reaching 30.5 m, 100 ft, and trees can be put in 914 mm–1.2 m, 3–4 ft, apart. It is not particular about soil and is generally adaptable. Hillier's *Manual of Trees and Shrubs* reports that plants from cuttings have reached a height of 15 m, 49 ft 2 in, in sixteen years, even on a relatively poor site. *Chamaecyparis lawsoniana*, Lawson's cypress, is another tree capable of attaining about the same height as the first two. The foliage is rather more tightly compact than that of *Thuja* and the tree is, if anything, even narrower. It is fairly fast growing, getting to 3 m, 10 ft, in ten years. For screening it can be planted 610–914 mm, 2–3 ft, apart. These two cypresses can be bought and planted at 1.5 m, 5 ft, or more. *Cupressus macrocarpa*, the Monterey cypress, although at one time hideously abused as a hedging plant inland, is a fine screening plant when allowed to grow taller in the south-west near the sea. This flourishes in ordinary good soil and can be planted 914 mm–1.2 m, 3–4 ft, apart.

Pines can be transplanted only at small sizes, usually under 610 mm, 2 ft, and some may even be supplied in pots. *Pinus sylvestris* is probably the best, certainly for inland; it can be planted 1.5 m, 5 ft, apart in both directions to make in time a many-stemmed resinous quietness with branches just touching overhead. To make good shelter belts in maturity they must be planted in considerable depth so that invading wind is baffled by the alternated bare trunks. The Corsican pine, *P. nigra maritima* (*P. laricio*), can be used in the same way but is the better tree to choose for positions near the sea. Plantations of the common spruce, or Christmas tree, *Picea abies*, make effective if quite alien-looking screens when planted in depth and 1.8m, 6 ft, apart, to be thinned later. Spruce prefers rather moist heavy soil and is good on heavy loams and clays; it resents a smoky atmosphere. This too is capable of reaching 30.5 m, 100 ft, but under forestry conditions is felled long before it gets to this height. For really damp or peaty land the Sitka spruce, *Picea sitchensis*, would be the better tree to choose, also planted at 1.8 m, 6 ft, apart.

MIXED DECIDUOUS AND EVERGREEN SCREENS
A mixed screen may give the most effective protection without being the most beautiful. *Thuja plicata*, as has been seen, is reasonably fast growing, wind-hardy and shade-tolerant and will not be suppressed by fast-growing deciduous trees. Lawson's cypress and the Leyland cypress can also be used alternated with deciduous trees; so too can pines, although these have to be planted very small and are slow growing. Le Sueur (op. cit.) cites a successful high elevation screen, 381 m, 1250 ft, up in North Wales, of two rows of sycamore 1.8 m, 6 ft, apart and four rows of Scots pine 1.4 m, 4 ft 6 in, apart planted in loam over slaty rock.

Before entirely leaving the subject of protective planting it is worth recording some shrubs that in the south-west are useful in conjunction with taller trees: *Olearia macrodonta*, growing to 4.6 m, 15 ft, or more, and the more familiar and smaller *Olearia haastii*, about 1.5–2.4 m, 5–8 ft, and hardier; also some of the escallonias, such as 'Donard Seedling' or 'Crimson Spire', both of which will get up to about 1.8 m, 6 ft, tall. In Cornwall bamboos are also employed for wind screening at lower levels.

HEDGES
Boundary hedges, as distinct from wind screens, are usually kept clipped to 1.8m, 6 ft, or less. They do of course provide useful wind screening low down but their chief use is to define the boundaries of a property and to deter trespassers,

1. Lyegrove, Gloucestershire: a vista through the gateway built in 1927 by G. H. Kitchin, the Bristol architect. At the far end is the old stone summer house. The wrought-iron gates in the foreground are of satisfyingly robust construction.

2. Lily pool in the summer garden at Lyegrove. The massive stone piers with ball finials and shell-headed arches frame the view to the west, of tall beeches from which rooks in their nests call in querulous content at evening in the spring.

3, and 4. Hornbeam hedges meticulously maintained, and pleached hornbeams showing the perfect finish to the process described on page 134, at the Hunting Lodge, Odiham.

5. Prospect from the terrace at Buckhurst Park, Ascot. This shows good detail close to the house leading on through splendid vistas to open country beyond.

6. York-stone steps on a firm radiused curve, grass panel between beds of lavender, and generous terrace steps.

7. Small formal garden with box-edged beds on an interestingly varied grid pattern.

8. Topiary in an enclosed garden close to the house. A refreshing 'breakfast parlour' on warm mornings.

9. Quadrangle at Trinity College, Oxford. The use of round stones, cobbles and bricks gives interesting relief to the more usual coursed stone paving.

10. A small courty—
at Eton. The photogra—
illustrates how a gr—
amount of detail a
interest can be int—
duced and harmoniou—
reconciled in a very sm—
space.

11. Weeping willow.
the waterside is the b—
place for these tr—
which grow rapidly t
great size and can s—
overwhelm a sm—
garden.

12. Terrace in high summer. It belongs to the house described on pages 48 and 49.

13. Bridge with larch trellis over the stream at Ninfa.

14. Loggia at Iford Manor.

15. Summer house with square trellis sides and classical columns and, originally and usefully, a clock in the pediment. The balls at either end of the swimming-pool give it an architectural value. Burghfield Old Rectory.

whether on four feet or two, for properly looked after they are longer lasting and more attractive than wooden fences. The composition of a boundary hedge depends generally upon the exterior surroundings; the best ones in the real country are hawthorn and holly, the two together making an ornamental 'tapestry' hedge.

Hawthorns, or 'Quicks' as they are known when used for hedging, are planted 305 mm, 1 ft, apart in a single row. When first planted the apprentice hedge will look thin and spindly, as if it would never come to anything, but after two years what it has been about is evident, namely making the beginnings of a first-class boundary hedge, protective and daunting with thorns, twiggy and closely inter-textured. Even under regular clippings a hawthorn hedge usually manages to produce a few May blossoms on the side. It is the external hedge par excellence for country gardens and yet its built-in yeoman aristocracy makes it no intruder in cosiest suburbia.

Hollies are put in 610 mm, 2 ft, apart in a single row and, being evergreen and therefore always to some extent transpiring through their leaves, are best planted in late April or in May so that in a warming soil temperature their roots can quickly establish working contact with the soil and push up supplies of moisture. They are slow growing, taking about ten years to make a hedge 1.8 m, 6 ft, high, very tough when established but needing to be nursed through their first spring and summer and to be well watered and mulched in spring and again in early autumn while the soil is warm. Temporarily rigged screens of hurdles or hessian or even old sacks tacked to stakes will protect them from the north and east winds if these scourges persist after planting and will do much to assure survival during the first critical summer. The common holly is *Ilex aquifolium*, with prickles at the edges of its leaves; when established a hedge would stop a bull and a double row give pause to an elephant, particularly the variety 'Ferox', the male hedgehog holly that has spikes not only at the edges of its leaves but also on the surface. For ordinary garden purposes the hybrid hollies *Ilex* × *altaclarensis* 'Camelliifolia' and 'Hodginsii', have smooth-edged leaves and are, psychologically at least, more comfortable to live with near the house.

Where boundaries do not give on to fields or commons, certain plants can be used for hedging which would tend to look sophisticated out in the wild. Among these is the Portuguese laurel, *Prunus lusitanica*, quite different from the common laurel, having much darker more pointed leaves, resembling bay leaves. It makes a distinguished hedge, its large shiny leaves rippling in the sunshine. It is also acceptably quick growing. In my own garden it was being pruned at 2.4 m, 8 ft, seven years after planting. Plants are put in 610 mm, 2 ft, apart in a single row preferably at the end of March or in April and must be well cared for in the first spring and summer.

The common laurel, cherry laurel, *Prunus laurocerasus*, has the merit of being a good shade-tolerant plant. It is fairly rapid growing, useful but rather plain with its large, coarse leaves, and not quite so hardy as the Portuguese laurel. Plants are put in 610 mm, 2 ft, apart again if possible in the spring.

The common privet, *Ligustrum ovalifolium*, is a maligned and misunderstood hedging plant. Its detractors condemn it as greedy, but a more compassionate word to use would be hungry. It needs, and takes, a lion's share of water and nutrients to sustain its rapid growth and should be allowed 1.8 m, 6 ft, distance from other plants. Whatever may be thought of it, it is to me at any rate a more acceptable hedging plant than the prissy cypresses that have been pressed into almost universal service chiefly because so many of them are quick growing; their lighter green feathery foliage, compressed into geometric shapes by clipping to which they are not truly amenable, and their tendency to remain for some years as unhappy pyramids make them, by comparison with yew, fakes and impostors.

Lawson's cypress, *Chamaecyparis lawsoniana*, has already been referred to as a screening plant. There is a selected strain of it known as 'Green Hedger', which is much used for evergreen hedges planted 610 mm, 2 ft, apart. This plant flourishes on deep moist neutral loam.

Leyland cypress, also previously mentioned as a screening plant, is probably the most popular of all hedging plants at the present time because its rate of growth is exceedingly fast, 914 mm, 3 ft, or more in a year when established, and it can be planted as far apart as 914 mm, 3 ft, thereby reducing the number of plants required. As for most hedging plants there comes a time when its ultimate height has to be determined, but until then its growing point should not be cut out. To me this plant has a quality of dreariness, difficult to account for but probably due to an antipathy to its flat, fan-shaped foliage and relentlessly boring medium green colour, quite unlike the inky black, needle-like foliage of yew.

Thuja plicata, also mentioned as a screening plant, is commonly used as a clipped hedge planted 610 mm, 2 ft, apart, for which purpose it is satisfactory although not elegant, but it is useful under conditions of shade, which it will endure better than many other hedging plants.

In the country where a garden overlooks a common and there is enough space it is attractive to make a loose screen instead of a hedge. The plants for this could include the laurustinus, *Viburnum tinus*, which although slow growing at first soon expands into a dark, evergreen billowing screen with tight pink pin-points of buds in the winter, opening to white clustered flowers in the spring. It is not a native plant, but the rest of the screen could consist of some of the many plants found growing in ancient hedgerows; beech, hawthorn, wild rose, the wayfaring tree (*Viburnum lantana*), the spindle tree (*Euonymus europaeus*), field maple, hazel, ash, elm, bird cherry, blackthorn, plum, crab-apple, dogwood, elder, guelder rose, holly, honeysuckle, hornbeam, oak, poplar, privet, rowan, silver birch, Spanish chestnut, sycamore, wild cherry, willow. These are taken from a list of forty-eight trees and shrubs which may be found in *Fieldwork in Local History* by W. G. Hoskins. They all amalgamate well and such a screen provides good nesting sites for birds. Unless it is wished to let some of them grow up as hedgerow trees the whole plantation will have to be trimmed at least every other year.

TREES FOR SMALLER GARDENS

It will be found when looking back in old or middle age that the true elements of a garden are trees, grass, water and the sky. Trees lift up your eyes from your boots, from your knee-high roses and your awkward middle-distance rhododendrons to the serene heaven of sky and clouds which they inhabit. A tree is by nature tall and the taller it is the better, having due regard to considerations of scale—a tulip tree 24.4 m, 80 ft, or more in a garden the size of a lawn tennis court might be an uncomfortable companion; something much more homely, no taller than an old apple tree about 5 m, less than 17 ft, high, is what is needed here. The important thing seems to be that the tree should lift up your eyes without being so close to you as to make you crane your neck. In the smallest gardens trees 6.1–9.1 m, 20–30 ft, will be in scale. Two universal trees for such gardens are whitebeam and mountain ash. The former, *Sorbus aria*, although officially capable of getting to 12 m, nearly 40 ft, will take very many years to do it, and can be thought of for practical purposes as a 6.1 m, 20 ft, tree. When grown in the open it has a fine symmetrical outline, branches widespreading at the base, reducing in length towards the top to make a tapering head. The chief joys of this tree are the grey undersides of the leaves, flashing when ruffled by the wind, the white flowers in May and the red berries in the late summer. It is a good single tree in grass, interesting also in a quincuncial planting or on the outskirts of a large garden at the edge of woodland mixed with yews, with the dark foliage of which its grey leaves make a striking contrast. It is most at home on the chalk, but adaptable enough for most gardens where the soil is not strongly acid, or thin sand.

The rowan also flourishes in all ordinary garden soils, with a slight preference for peaty, rather acid soils. This is the mountain ash, *Sorbus aucuparia*, familiar by the side of burns in Scotland; it makes a higher head or crown than the white-beam and is a more delicate tree. This native rowan will grow to 7.6 m, 25 ft. It has pinnate leaves, white flowers and conspicuous bright red berries towards the end of the summer, and the thin foliage casts only moderate shade. A smaller version is *Sorbus vilmorinii*, only 5.5 m, 18 ft, and very delicate with its fern-like foliage and drooping clusters of pink berries.

Other trees for small gardens are the thorns, of which Bean, in *Trees and Shrubs Hardy in The British Isles* (1914, 1933), wrote 'None make lovelier lawn trees'. To take one of these only, 'Paul's Scarlet' has an ultimate height of about 6.1 m, 20 ft, and an equal spread. In my garden its branches droop a little under the weight of flowers and foliage, causing them to be curved almost to the ground with long-lasting crimson (not really scarlet) flowers at the end of May. It is slower growing than either the whitebeam or the rowan, but well worth planting by those with a little patience, and deserving also of careful shaping and pruning if found in a newly acquired, previously planted garden.

Some small deciduous exotics can be very effective in small gardens or in enclosed parts of much larger gardens. The Judas tree, *Cercis siliquastrum*, 6.1 m, 20 ft, will sometimes, when pruned to a single stem, develop an intriguing contorted outline, but its chief glory is in its mauve-crimson pea-shaped flowers borne in abandoned profusion on the old black wood before the leaves appear. A little smaller at 4.6 m, 15 ft, and 3.7 m, 12 ft, are some of the Japanese cherries; of these *Prunus yedoensis*, the Yoshino cherry, is among the earliest to come into flower; the bare branches are crowded with pale pink to white almond-scented single flowers in March. The tree has a good, rather pendulous outline, useful in small enclosed courtyards and also in the front gardens of houses close together or semi-detached. *P. serrulata* 'Longipes', also known as 'Shimidsu Sakura', comes into flower much later, after the middle of April. The blossoms are double, pink in bud, opening to white, and give very great density of colour. This tree has a wider spreading top than *P. yedoensis*, making it less attractive in outline when the flowers are over and in the winter. Some may tend to regard these as over sugary, pretty, suburban trees, but when seen in full flower the most spiteful cynic must find them hard to resist. This sort of criticism is more justly levelled at some of the flowering crab-apple trees. *Malus* 'Eleyi' is one of these, theoretically capable of 6.1 m, 20 ft, but usually lower, pendulous in shape with light crimson flowers in May and purple foliage. Another is *Malus flori-bunda*, similar but with clearer pink flowers. To me these are really cosmetic trees, suited to occasional 'doll's-house' surroundings and with little good bone behind their musical comedy sweetness. To return to the cherries, there is one special one, 'Ukon', *P. serrulata* 'Grandiflora' or 'Luteo-Virens', to 6.1 m,

20 ft, and of equal spread, which in April has remarkable yellow-green flowers, palely luminous in the noonday light but taking on a strange pallor when dusk draws on. I doubt if this is a tree for the gardens of small houses close together. It does not go with brickwork or small-scale enclosures. It needs green foliage and tall grey walls a long way off, as at Lyegrove.

The Venetian sumach, known also as the 'Wig Tree' and the 'Smoke Tree', *Cotinus coggyria* (formerly *Rhus cotinus*), is most often a bush up to 3.7 m, 12 ft, but can be very satisfactorily pruned into a small tree—mine is still only 2.1 m, 7 ft, high after twenty years, and has an interesting, slightly contorted, clear stem; a graceful little tree of considerable character, to be planted by itself and not mixed up with other shrubs, in July and for most of the rest of the summer covered with the pinkish cloud of its plume-like inflorescences. Another related tree, *Rhus typhina*, the stag's-horn sumach, is different in character. Taller, about 6.1 m, 20 ft, with very large pinnate leaves 305–610 mm, 1–2 ft, long, turning rich red in autumn, and large erect panicles covered with small yellow flowers; several of these panicles seen together look a little like a stag's horns. The whole plant is covered with brown hairs, almost fur. It has low forking branches and, by comparison with the Venetian sumach, is a coarse tree, but this very coarseness gives it a certain attraction, particularly to some landscape architects with a developed *penchant* for foliage. It is used with success in context with modern white-walled buildings, but is not a good mixer with other shrubs.

Many of the trees that give outstanding autumn colour become large specimens, but one which will not grow to more than 4.6 m, 15 ft, and could well be used in small gardens on acid soils, is *Photinia villosa*. A native of Japan, Korea and China, it is a member of the Rosaceae, having white flowers in May and bright red berries, not unlike our native hawthorn, but in autumn the scarlet and gold foliage is perhaps the most brilliant of all the autumn foliage trees. It needs an acid soil to bring out its best colours and a warm summer to ripen its wood; it can be very well planted with other trees, including evergreens, to give contrasting foliage colour.

There are other trees larger than those so far referred to which, although generally more at home in medium-sized or large gardens, can sometimes be found a place in the smaller ones. The common almond, now to be known as *Prunus dulcis*, is for me one of the most beautiful trees of the spring. Its cold pink blossoms on bare boughs, seen against stone walls in a college quadrangle, are unforgettable, and yet it is also, I think, perfectly acceptable and at home in quite small suburban front gardens, even when seen against brickwork. It has a reputed height of 6.1 m, 20 ft, and a spread of a little less.

Magnolias as trees (as opposed to bushes) fairly quickly become both wide and tall and can soon overwhelm a very small garden, but both *M. denudata* (the Yulan) and its offspring, *M. × soulangiana*, are beautiful and dramatic trees best planted singly towards corners or against a contrasting background of taller trees, hedges or walls. They are really more suited to much larger gardens, where they can grow to their full size and still be contained by a background, and be far enough away to be seen as a whole. Either the Yulan or *M. × soulangiana* could be planted 9.1 m, 30 ft, apart in parallel lines in wide lawns, to bring in the lateral dimension and prevent the garden appearing to fall away inconclusively sideways, a function which is also performed by pleached trees, as at Chatsworth.

Good small evergreen trees are hard to come by. The best, but alas slow growing and obtainable in the first place only as a small plant, is *Arbutus unedo*, the

Killarney strawberry tree, theoretically capable of getting to 12.2 m, 40 ft, but seldom seen much above 6.1 m, 20 ft. It certainly grows wild in Ireland but is not admitted as a native by Clapham, Tutin and Warburg in their *Excursion Flora of the British Isles*. It is unusual in being tolerant of lime in the soil, belonging as it does to the Ericaceae, a family that includes many calcifuges, such as rhododendrons. It has oval shiny leaves, the white flowers in drooping clusters making their appearance late in the year from October to December, at which time the fruits from the previous year's flowers still hang on the tree. The fruit resembles a strawberry in appearance, but although harmless to eat, has a disagreeable taste. If left alone *Arbutus unedo* will often grow as a tall shrub with several stems, but it can be pruned to a single stem to give it a picturesque contorted branch structure and a spreading crown. It is hardy in the south of England, and according to Bean has withstood temperatures down to —1.1° C., 30° F., at Kew.

Its cousin *Arbutus menziesii* is most generally seen in milder districts and sheltered aspects in the south and west but is often hardy in the Home Counties when protected from north-east gales. It is taller, up to 12.2 m, 40 ft, a real exotic from California. This is the beautiful 'Madrona', with flowers, also white, in May, in upright terminal panicles, followed by yellow pea-sized fruits, and most notable for its beautiful warm cinnamon-coloured bark. Yet another west-country aristocrat is *Myrtus apiculata* (*M. luma*), a myrtle, about 6.1 m, 20 ft, from Chile, but naturalized in some southern Irish gardens. W. Arnold-Forster (*Country Life*, 1948) wrote of this: 'The most beautiful use of it I know is a little grove in the woodland garden of Lanarth, where the orange trunks stand on either side of the path, with a snow of flowers overhead among the dark leaves.' But this is a tree for what Compton Mackenzie[1] described as 'the life-giving west from which love and music shall come until the day of the seven whirlwinds and the crack of doom'. Those of us who garden in prosaic parts will have to make do with cotoneasters, for small evergreen trees. Not much liked by me, but for men of stout heart here are three that are semi-evergreen: *Cotoneaster salicifolius*, 3 m, 10 ft, much berried; *C.* 'Cornubia', 4.6 m, 15 ft, much berried; and *C.* 'Exburyensis', arching, and loaded with yellow fruits.

After the small-scale trees and before considering what I think of as warrantable trees—trees of forest dimensions, oaks, beeches and ashes, trees which oneself when young could climb into—there are many trees of intermediate size and character which can be planted in almost any surroundings, including medium-sized gardens and enclosed parts of much larger gardens. Some of these have special attributes.

To begin with some of the smaller of these for general purposes; the great white cherry, *Prunus* 'Tai Haku', 11 m, 36 ft, is a much more robust tree than the smaller Japanese cherries referred to earlier and quite capable of standing on its own in fairly spacious surroundings, although it can be at its most effective in a group of three, 11 m, 36 ft, apart, their spreading branches just not touching in maturity. I have also seen it in the context of a fairly wide, smooth but fast-gliding trout stream, where its densely white, heavy head of flowers was exceedingly beautiful. This is not to suggest that it is a tree that needs to get its roots into water; in this case the river bank was fairly steep and the tree several yards away. Another large cherry is the winter cherry, *P. subhirtella autumnalis*, 6.1 m, 20 ft, which ought to be near enough to the house to be seen from the windows,

[1] *The West Wind of Love*, 1940.

for the sake of the white flowers thinly spaced on bare branches in winter, its wide-spreading framework and rather denser show of white flowers again in May.

Our native wild cherry, *P. avium*, 15.2–18.3 m, 50–60 ft, is quite a different plant. It is the wild gean or mazzard, familiar in the chalk country on the outskirts of beech woods still dark from winter, or as Housman noted, standing 'about the woodland ride'. Its lovely single flowers are fugitive and too often sent scattering down the indifferent winds of May. For this reason, and because the whiteness of the flowers is denser, the double-flowered version, *P. avium* 'Flore Pleno', is probably better for gardens. It has been known for two centuries and presumably arose as a sport from the common gean. Whichever may be chosen, single or double-flowered, these trees need some space, at least in front of them, to be properly appreciated. Bean (op. cit.) described the wild cherry as one of the most beautiful of all flowering trees, and for me this is certainly true. There are trees with more spectacular flowers; anyone who has seen the Asiatic magnolias in flower in Cornwall will never forget them, but all the time they maintain an outlandish air of improbability partaking of the quality of a dream; but the wild cherry is a credible daylight miracle.

To come down a little in size, and in order not entirely to overlook the genus *Malus*, there are two well out of the doll's-house scale. One is *M. hupehensis*, 7.6 m, about 25 ft, upright growing, covered with white flowers in May and June, followed by yellow fruits tinged with red. The other is *M. tschonoskii*, taller, having a strongly ascending habit of growth. Both of these could find useful places in small gardens, as well as in the enclosures of larger ones, kept for preference to the sides, even in lines of two or three.

Orchard apple trees are in the genus *Malus*, and are in many ways the perfect lawn trees for medium-sized gardens. When fully grown to 6.1–9.1 m, 20–30 ft, and covered with pink and white blossom in May, these single orchard trees are as beautiful as anything that can be found, and are delightful to sit under at midsummer. In my own garden I inherited an old 'Cockles Pippin', not particularly good for its fruit, but having a splendid firm outline all the winter and glorious blossom in the spring. To plant a new one in these days one would probably choose a dual-purpose tree like 'Blenheim Orange' in standard form. The fruit of this can be picked, stored and eaten as dessert from November to January, or cooked and put into pies. Some others with especial beauty of blossom are the dessert apple 'James Grieve', which is a recognized pollinator for 'Cox's Orange Pippin', and the cooking apples 'Annie Elizabeth' and 'Arthur Turner'.

Pears too are beautiful garden trees. Their white blossom comes earlier than that of apples and small branches of it cut in December and kept in water indoors or, better, in a cool greenhouse, will burgeon from bare twigs. Pears, *Pyrus communis*, to 9.1 m, 30 ft, have an upright habit of growth and look at their best standing against a building, near an old farmhouse for example.

Before entirely giving up our borrowings from the orchard, we could consider what I like to think of as a Merrie England trio, quince, medlar and mulberry. Quinces, *Cydonia oblonga*, to 5.5 m, 18 ft, and of about equal spread, grown to rounded bushes or trees on short trunks, are often twisted in outline and full of character. The dark green leaves are felted a little on the undersides, and in May the plant is covered with a cloud of flowers which are white or whitish-pink; the large fruits are like pear-shaped apples and decorative in their golden-yellow colour. (They are cooked with apples to give sharpness to a pie, and also make a very good jelly.) Quinces flourish well near moving water, a little stream for instance, but I have one, an attractive lawn tree, which is nowhere near water, and seems very content.

Medlars deserve to be cultivated for the unusual beauty of their large five-petalled flowers, white or pale pink, with in some lights a tinge of yellow on account of the yellow stamens in the centre. The tree is *Mespilus germanica*, and can grow to about 6.1 m, 20 ft. Professor Saintsbury is said to have considered medlars to be the ideal fruit to marry to port, but as they are not considered fit for eating until they are more than a little rotten it needs a braver man than I am to take them on in a dish of dessert at the end of a dinner party.

The mulberry of gardens is the black mulberry, *Morus nigra*, up to 6.1 m, 20 ft. It is an excellent lawn tree, particularly in gardens with a sense of enclosure. It is late coming into leaf. The deep crimson fruits ripen in great numbers in August; some are taken avidly by wild birds hungry after the moult, but many fall to the ground and lie in profligate abandon. Although sweet, they are also sub-acid, and pleasant, if a little insipid to eat when well ripened at the end of a hot summer. The leaves are large and closely packed, so that in full leaf the tree makes a dense mass against the sky, and in winter it has a rugged, picturesque outline.

A tree just below full size in weight and character is the false acacia, *Robinia pseudacacia*, which looks well in any company and for almost any garden, except the smallest. It has a potential height of 21.3 m, 70 ft, and in maturity a noble and wide spreading head and a deeply furrowed trunk. It has so much of the quality of elegance that it demands positions where it can be a cynosure, not taking its place in woodland. It can be planted in lines or avenues, for preference in the context of tall buildings or roads, or as a specimen tree in smooth lawns, but needs to be viewed from a distance not less than 30.5 m, 100 ft. Beautiful in its spare branching and foliage, and its white scented flowers in the summer, it is a fast-growing tree and when planting it regard must be had to its ultimate size, something which was once embarrassingly borne in on me after I had been responsible for putting one of them into an Oxford quadrangle. It grew fast and spread so widely that it became the source of polite remonstration from a for-bearing don, whose windows were darkened at noonday in the summer. The golden-leafed version, *Robinia pseudacacia* 'Frisia', has a stature of only 10.6 m, 35 ft, when fully grown, and is easier to place in smaller gardens. Three together, 10.6 m, 35 ft, apart so that the heads will just not touch in maturity, on a shallow mound, would be an enchanting eye-catcher towards a corner of an enclosed garden or against the background of other trees. The honey locust, *Gleditsia triacanthos*, with a greatest height of about 15.2 m, 50 ft, is a smaller, more delicate version of the false acacia. Its branches are thin and this, with its lacy sparse foliage, is responsible for its light shade. It is a narrow tree, the width being about 9.1 m, 30 ft, and slower growing than the false acacia. The honey locust grows well in ordinary good garden soil, preferably neutral or slightly acid, and endures smoke and dust in town gardens.

The variegated box elder, *Acer negundo* 'Elegans', at 7.6 m, 25 ft, high provides good foliage contrast through the bright yellow marginal variegation of the leaves, sparkling in the sunshine. The red chestnut, *Aesculus* × *carnea* 'Briottii', 9.1 m, 30 ft, a much smaller tree than the more familiar horse chestnut, could also come into this company. It has upright panicles of crimson-pink flowers, although the colour has a bricky-deadness, a certain flatness; but this is a robust tree for a medium-sized garden, where it does not produce conkers and is not subject to depredation from small boys throwing up sticks and damaging its branches.

Cornus kousa, from Japan and Korea, 6.1 m, 20 ft, is a beautiful tree for a warm sheltered district in moist, slightly acid soil. It has proved to be quite hardy at Kew, for instance, but would be doubtful much farther north. Its charm lies in the butterfly bracts of creamy-white flowers in June in company with other shrubs but rising above them (see Figure 10). *Cornus florida*, the flowering dogwood from America, up to 4.6 m, 15 ft, tall, is more spectacular, having larger bracts also in May, looking as though a cloud of butterflies had come to rest on the tree. In Britain it is safe only in the south where it will not suffer from spring frosts, and planted high enough to make sure that it is never caught in a frost pocket. It also needs a hot summer to ripen its wood. By contrast with these two, *Cornus mas*, 4.5 m, 15 ft, and with a spread of up to 7.5 m, 25 ft, the 'Cornelian Cherry', is a European plant, usually much branched and tending to become twiggy, benefiting from studied pruning after flowering to preserve a spare outline to show off the flowers on the bare twigs in February; these are pale lemon-yellow in colour. It has to an extent been superseded by the Chinese Witch-Hazel, which I think is unfortunate, because it is the more adaptable of the two, growing quite contentedly in alkaline soils. It looks its best at the edge of thin woodland where its flowers lighten the darkness of a lingering winter. None the less the Chinese witch hazel, *Hamamelis mollis*, is a very beautiful small tree with fragrant golden-yellow flowers like narrow strips of ribbon borne on naked twigs at midwinter. Not perhaps for the usual small garden because the winter flowers are soon over, and also because it is not a tree to put into close company with other plants. It needs a good free space of, say, 6.1 m, 20 ft, all round it, for instance an enclave in rather open woodland, and it prospers best in slightly acid, moist, but not waterlogged soil, and can look very well at a key point of a garden, with water not far away, as in the Savill Gardens in Windsor Great Park.

Pyrus salicifolia pendula, the willow-leaved pear, has small creamy-white flowers in April and pendulous growth. It can get to 6.1 m, 20 ft, and has narrow, willow-shaped leaves, silvery above and below early in the season, the upper surfaces turning to shining green as the year progresses. It can be planted in association with many other shrubs and gives good foliage contrast against summer green and early autumn colour.

Many trees, besides their ordinary shapes in which we know them, have, as they say in horticultural terms, 'thrown sports' or mutations, both weeping and fastigiate with shapes approaching that of the Lombardy poplar. One of the largest of our native trees, the common beech, has both forms. The weeping one generally supplied as *Fagus sylvatica* 'Pendula' is variable, but usually the branches tend to grow from the head outwards at first horizontally and then descending sharply and vertically towards the ground, making a rather ungainly green cage. The weeping ash, *Fraxinus excelsior* 'Pendula', is also a bulky tree when fully grown; the descending branches are long-jointed, resulting in lengths of bare stems 457 mm, 18 in, or so between the leaves. The best of the large weeping trees is the weeping wych elm, *Ulmus glabra* 'Pendula', which has large leaves closely draped and overlapping along the far more graceful downward curves of the branches, making an umbrageous tent in summer. Weeping trees are notoriously difficult to place in a landscape, partly because of their domed and generally low outline but more because their branches in turning downwards away from the sky are doing the opposite to what we look for in trees, like a disastrous wrong note at a concert. They are chiefly for curiosity, best put perhaps where their circular shape can be matched—in the middle of a geometric formal garden of beds and paths, or as a focal point at the end of a wide grass *allée* with a tall solid hedge or a screen of trees behind it. I knew of one planted near front gates where high-spirited girls used to hide and make very unladylike noises when visitors came in.

Weeping trees sometimes fit in well on riverside lawns, ash and elm better than beech, whose natural home is on the upland chalk far away from marsh and stream. But the most traditional weeping tree for the riverside is the weeping willow, *Salix babylonica*, a native of China and according to Bean (op. cit.) brought here in 1730 by a Mr Vernon, a Turkey merchant from Aleppo. He got it from the river Euphrates and planted it in his garden at Twickenham Park. This is the weeping willow which Napoleon loved, and under which he was buried on St Helena. Many slips of this tree have been brought to Europe, including this country, and presumably are still to be found. It can grow to 15.2 m, 50 ft, and to at least as great a width. In a small garden it can, like an awful cuckoo in a nest, very soon dominate and suppress all other plants owing to its very rapid growth and spread, but overhanging a river and with ample lawns behind it at midsummer when it seems that nothing can go wrong with the world, its green, enclosing tent is a fine and private place for dalliance in a punt. When the autumn comes it lives up to its French name of *Saule pleureur*, whispering of nothing but *tristesse*.

A first-class tree for riverside lawns is the Indian bean, *Catalpa bignonioides*, 12.2 m, 40 ft, and when fully grown, of an even greater width. The very wide-spreading head and frequent branching, together with the large overlapping leaves, combine to give a very dense shade. The tree has the great merit of producing flowers late in the summer, in July and August, long after most other trees have ceased to blossom. These flowers are borne in large panicles, 229 mm, 9 in, long, having, when seen from a distance, the colour of lilac, but on closer view composed of both purple and yellow spots on a white background. The rate of growth is slow, and when first planted at 1.8–3 m, 6–10 ft, it is a gawky specimen and needs a certain amount of faith and patience to preserve a belief in its ultimate excellence.

Gardeners in the south-west of England and on the west coasts of Scotland and Ireland are fortunate in being able to plant certain very beautiful exotic trees which are not hardy outside these regions. They are all seen at their best in woodland, that is, growing in deep forest-floor material, well watered but also well drained, and most of them also in the partial shade of old woodland, providing not only shade but a top cover against unseasonal frost. *Rhododendron arboreum*, 9.1 m, 30 ft, heaves its huge trusses of blood-red flowers towards the sky from February to April. It requires an acid soil, of a pH not above 5.6. There are several Asiatic magnolias which rapidly grow into large trees, most of them deciduous and also precocious in that the flowers are borne on naked branches, before the leaves come out. *Magnolia campbellii* has enormous flowers as big as a man's head, varying in colour from rose-pink to deep pink in February and March. The flowers are not produced until the tree is about twenty years old and by then it will probably have developed a clear stem of 12.2 m, 40 ft, or so, so that it is best appreciated when looked down upon from above, which means planting it half way up a hillside with winding walks by means of which it is possible to get above the tree. *Magnolia mollicomata* is similar, but will produce its equally sensational flowers at an earlier age, from seven to ten years. The most spectacular of all is *Magnolia sargentiana robusta*, whose even larger crimson-pink flowers are borne early in the spring; it becomes a large, spreading tree, up to 9.1 m, 30 ft, high. Frost is seldom experienced in the far west, but on the rare days when it does occur it can cause damage to the flowers of these trees, unless they are well protected within a wood with the top cover already referred to of pines and oaks. Another magnolia is the delicious *M. salicifolia*, a smaller tree, about 6.1 m, 20 ft, thriving as a part of the woodland, that is, not having large clearings specially made for it. Its six-petalled white flowers are 102 mm, 4 in, across and open flat; the bark of this tree is strongly lemon scented.

Other plants for these south-western paradises are camellias, notably the *C.* × *williamsii* hybrids which, together with some of the many *C. japonica* types, will be referred to later with other shrubs in Chapter 7. But there is one, *Camellia reticulata*, which can reach tree size, 9.1 m, 30 ft, particularly when planted against a high wall like wistarias and the evergreen *Magnolia grandiflora*. It is an extravagant, romantic plant, with very large 152 mm, 6 in, flowers, essentially single with prominent yellow anthers (but there are some new semi-double varieties); its large, handsome, evergreen reticulated leaves are beautiful all the year, even when the flowers have gone.

FULL-SCALE TREES

These I have referred to as warrantable trees, growing to 15.2 m, 50 ft, or over, massive and unmistakable as trees, rather than vigorous bushes which have been pruned to make small trees out of them; all are for larger gardens, where they can be seen from a distance. A rough and ready rule might be that to look to the top of a tree without craning one's neck one should stand no closer than one and a half times the height of the tree, which represents an angle of about 35° from your feet on the ground to the top of a tree. Thus, to contemplate in comfort a tree 30.5 m, 100 ft, high, one should stand 45.7 m, 150 ft, away, a distance considerably greater than the length of a full-size tennis court.

There are some trees which, by virtue of qualities of slenderness, comparative infrequency of branching and thinner leaf cover, seem most fitting, as it were, in captivity; that is, as the architect would say, 'reading' with buildings, as, for instance, in college lawns and large gardens in which they are seen together with buildings. Such a one is the silver maple, *Acer saccharinum* (*A. dasycarpum*), 24.4 m, 80 ft, with a spread of 18.3 m, 60 ft, a tall, elegant tree with considerable delicacy of poise and outline. The silver undersides of the leaves, on long flexible twigs, flicker and dance in the wind; they have a good red and gold autumn colour; a tree to plant as a single specimen or in groups of three to five, rather close together, perhaps 6.1 m, 20 ft, apart, to make, in time, a composite head. It is light-demanding, not a tree for mixed woods, and flourishes on ordinary good soil, neutral or with a tendency to acidity. The 'Tree of Heaven', *Ailanthus altissima* (*A. glandulosa*), from China, can attain 24.4 m, 80 ft, although it does not very often do so in this country. It is a wide-spreading tree, to 21.3 m, 70 ft, but notwithstanding this still has about it an aspiring feeling. Its large, pinnate, ash-like leaves, 457 mm, 18 in, long, are comparatively sparsely disposed, so that it does not cast a heavy shade. The greenish flowers in late June and July are in terminal panicles, the male and female flowers usually confined to separate trees. The male flowers have a goat-like smell, repellent to sensitive natures, who are advised when buying a tree to insist on the feminine gender. The 'Tree of Heaven' endures the smoky atmosphere of towns with equanimity, and is a good tree to choose for large gardens or for parks on the outskirts of industrial towns, needing deep, rich soil, a little on the acid side. The tulip tree, *Liriodendron tulipifera*, from America where it reaches a great height, will grow in this country to 27.3 m, 90 ft. It is densely foliaged, but its sweeping branches maintain a fairly open structure, and it is generally taller than its width—about 18.3 m, 60 ft—giving it a beautiful soaring outline. It can be immediately identified by its leaves, 152 mm, 6 in, long, which look as if they have been cut off at the end. The flowers in June and July, shaped like tulips, pale yellowish-green, have to be looked for high up among the foliage but, when recognized, have a cool, mysterious charm. In autumn the leaves turn to golden-yellow and when fallen lie in wind-ruffled drifts on the ground below. Tulip trees need ordinary, good deep soil, neutral or slightly acid. They are fairly rapid growing.

Next in this list of graceful trees might be the silver birch, *Betula pendula* (the weeping silver birch is *B. pendula* 'Youngii'). This grows to 24.4 m, 80 ft, in thin, peaty, rather dry acid soils, has a spare branching habit and sparse leafage, casting only a thin shade. The width at 9.1 m, 30 ft, is small, so that it projects a rather narrow outline of branches drooping downwards at their outer edges. It is frequently adumbrated in architects' drawings in a context of buildings, with which its delicate framework makes a telling contrast. For me it is familiar with pines, and it is also a tree of mixed woodland.

The birch of moist, acid soils is *B. pubescens*, the white birch, whose bark peels in papery layers off its rugged trunk. This, too, goes well with Scots pines or in groups of three to five planted closely together.

Just as there are two universal trees for small gardens, whitebeams and the mountain ash, so there are two large trees, lime and plane, which can be planted in any position and in any company, provided that there is enough space around them. The best lime is *Tilia euchlora*, the green-twigged lime. At 15.2 m, 50 ft, with a spread of 6.1 m, 20 ft, it is a full-sized long-lived tree, whose brilliant, glossy green leaves do not drop honeydew as the leaves of so many other limes do. It has strongly scented yellowish-white flowers in July, is fairly fast growing, and needs a deep rich soil, preferably above a limestone formation. The large leaves are closely inter-textured and therefore cast a deep shade. A lime alley in torrid summer weather is one of the coolest places that can be found, and a group of eight or ten planted to form a rotunda would make a good termination to a vista. It is also *par excellence* the tree for pleaching (see Appendix D). This green-twigged lime is smaller than the common lime, *Tilia vulgaris*, 30.5 m, 100 ft, but it does not develop burrs as the common lime does. There is another lime tree which is one of the most beautiful of all lawn trees, *Tilia petiolaris*, the weeping or pendent silver lime, whose habit is quite different from that of the round-headed weeping trees which have already been referred to. Its branches become pendent as the growing point continues upwards, making, instead of a round-headed gnome's house, draped curtains of green leaves and scented flowers. The result is that the tree, of unexcelled beauty of outline and scale, can reach to 24.4 m, 80 ft, or higher. The flowers, in August, are very strongly scented, the fragrance being perceptible from many yards away. Bean (op. cit.) wrote that 'Bees find something narcotic in the flowers, as they may be seen in the evenings lying in scores beneath the tree, and many do not recover'. There is much dispute over whether or not any flowers are poisonous to bees, but fair evidence that some honeys, in particular rhododendron honey, are poisonous to man.

The other general-purpose tree for all seasons is the plane. The London plane is *Platanus* × *hispanica* (*P. acerifolia*), a large tree, 27.3 m, 90 ft, with a spread of only a little less. It will grow well in any reasonable soil that is not strongly acid or strongly alkaline, and although frost- and wind-hardy it is not generally used for wind-screening. It succeeds well in smoky atmospheres, a quality which presumably has given it its name, it is fairly fast growing and the piebald bark is always gay. It is effective as a shade tree but does not cast such a dense shade as limes and beeches. In France and Italy it is planted by the thousand alongside the roads. I have paced out the distance between them when planted in avenues, and found it to be between 10 and 11 m, 33 and 36 ft. Often in France it is cut back ruthlessly each year. It may be thought of as a town tree but is also a good tree for a large garden. There is a fine specimen at Magdalen College, Oxford, one of the plants raised from seed discovered by Jacob Bobart, the Keeper of the Botanic Garden, in 1665 amongst a parcel of seeds sent from Montpellier. It is thought to be a hybrid between the occidental plane and the oriental plane, *Platanus orientalis*. This latter, unfortunately, is not as widely planted in Britain as it might be, probably because it is slower growing, but it lives to an immense age and is sometimes as large as the London plane. It has a shorter, more rugged trunk, and the branching structure begins lower down.

Another large tree too much neglected is the walnut, which again can be used in any company and in almost any position. The tree generally planted for nuts is *Juglans regia*, the common walnut, 24.4 m, 80 ft, and an approximately equal spread. Selected varieties—'Broadview', 'Buccaneer' and others—are available from specialist nurseries such as Hillier's at Winchester, and if the tree is to be planted for nuts it is important to make sure of getting one of these special kinds which have been grafted, because seedlings are generally valueless for nuts. Rooks and squirrels are likely to take the nuts as they become ripe, and if it is impossible to protect them, those which can be reached may as well be picked before the shells harden, usually in July, and pickled. But if all fails, a man who has planted walnuts can sit back and project his thoughts into the future of his grandchildren, for whom the trees will be worth great sums as timber when mature. *Juglans nigra*, the black walnut, is a more ornamental tree and capable of great height, some specimens reaching 27.3 m, 90 ft; in my experience this is a rapid-growing tree. Typically it has a fairly short trunk and branches from low down. It has a massive framework of branches and large pinnate leaves which, being made up of a number of leaflets, do not cast a very dense shade, needs deep but rather light soil, preferably above a limestone formation, is rather less hardy than the other and not always successful in the north. It is an outstanding deciduous tree with noble, aristocratic bone, with no trace of effeminacy, more suited to being brought near a house than such rugged characters as oaks and Spanish chestnuts. Walnuts make good avenues and are effective also in lines alongside a drive, planted 9.1 m, 30 ft, apart. The leaves of both walnuts are fragrant and refreshing when bruised or rubbed, which may account for their general freedom from aphids and other insects.

To consider next what may be thought of as the wilder trees; the common alder, *Alnus glutinosa*, has a potential height of 18.3 m, 60 ft, and a spread of 7.6 m, 25 ft. It is a fair-sized tree most often seen by streams and pools, with its branches sweeping low over the water: it is a very good tree for such a position. Its shiny bright, attractive heart-shaped leaves, tapering towards the stalk, are unexpectedly large. The grey alder, *A. incana*, has grey leaves, does not require wet waterside conditions, and is a useful tree to plant for its foliage on any normal soil and in woodland. The Italian alder, *A. cordata*, taller at 24.4 m, 80 ft, is another tree of value in its own right for specimen planting or in a mixed wood. It has large heart-shaped leaves, tapering away from the stalk, larger than either of the other two referred to above, and erect, egg-shaped fruits. It is proving to be a good tree for windscreens.

The English elm, *Ulmus procera*, 27.3 m, 90 ft, is a native tree, tall, towering, in beauty absolute in the English pastoral landscape, but fallible, as all beauty must be, for its unstable roots, and its tendency to drop branches. Now, also tragically threatened by a league between a despicable beetle and a malevolent fungus known as Dutch Elm Disease. Soon, with luck, immune or at least resistant strains will have been developed, and in the meantime injection with a systemic fungicide is showing promise. A tree of these proportions is not really a garden tree; it belongs in the fields and hedgerows where it may soon be planted again for future generations to see its beautiful pale-gold foliage against an autumn sky.

The weeping wych elm, *Ulmus glabra* 'Pendula', has been referred to as the best of weeping trees. In its ordinary form it is also a fine four-square tree of full 30.5 m, 100 ft, size, with much larger shiny leaves than the English elm. It is also, unfortunately, at present prone to Dutch Elm Disease, but one day will be planted again as a distinguished specimen or in mixed woodland. The Cornish elm, *Ulmus stricta*, is a narrow tree, usually a maximum of 12.2 m, 40 ft, wide but still tall at 24.4 m, 80 ft, when fully grown. It is a good-sized tree along a drive or to make avenues; good also as an isolated specimen when its pointed silhouette makes good contrast with rounder-headed trees. It grows in any normal soil, provided there is an adequate supply of water and good drainage.

Aesculus hippocastanum, the common white horse chestnut, at a potential of 27.3–30.5 m, 90–100ft, and of an almost equal spread, is a full-sized tree in all aspects, thick trunk, wide branching, dense cover, casting a heavy shade from the large leaves, which are some of the first to turn in autumn to crimson and gold; but the chief glory is in the candles of white flowers in May, seen everywhere in Paris at that time of the year. A fine tree for avenues, planted 15.2 m, 50 ft, apart, a double avenue is a most impressive spectacle. It is a splendid shade tree in pasture for cattle, but the shade is so thick that little grass will grow under it. A good lawn tree also, where it can be given enough clear space to be seen from a distance, but when looked at from higher ground the rounded top gives it a slightly 'dumpy' appearance. Chestnuts thrive in deep rich soils, well drained but not moist, and can be used also in mixed woodland. The red chestnut, *Aesculus* × *carnea* 'Briotti', has already been referred to among smaller trees for domestic scenes. *Castanea sativa*, the Spanish or sweet chestnut, is a rugged tree with a massive trunk often spirally furrowed as the tree branches in maturity. The large, handsome leaves overlap and cast dense shade. In July the catkin flowers, consisting of yellow-green feathery plumes, are a fine sight at high summer. While a little robust for all but the largest gardens, they are good trees in large lawns or in parks, for example the magnificent avenue of Spanish chestnuts at Croft Castle, five miles from Leominster in Herefordshire, a National Trust property. If a tree is to be planted for the sake of its nuts, 'Marron de Lyon' is the variety to look for. Spanish chestnuts succeed in normal, good garden soil with adequate water and drainage. The tree is hardy, but betrays its origins from districts near Vallombrosa in being happier in warm southern situations.

The common ash, *Fraxinus excelsior*, is another tree attaining 27.3 m, 90 ft, with a spread only a little less at 21.3 m, 70 ft, in Britain where it is a native, but it will grow into a larger tree in warmer latitudes of Europe. It sometimes has a considerable length of clear stem under an open crown and a comparatively slender framework of branches for its height. It prospers on moist, alkaline soils, and is often seen near water, with which it seems to have an affinity. A good tree for river banks, but not so low down as to have its roots permanently submerged. Its characteristic smooth black leaf buds open to large pinnate leaves, 254 mm, 10 in, long, and the purplish flowers are borne in dense panicles in April, turning to the familiar keys in late summer. Ash trees were one time seen as hedgerow trees in the lines of ancient thorn hedges, and grown for timber for the framework of axles and farm carts and the handles of tools. For planting in the landscape, ash is beautiful in a context of lakes or large pools. In Scandinavian mythology it was Yggdrasil, the Tree of the Universe and of the world.

Fagus sylvatica, the common beech, is another 27.3 m, 90 ft, giant with a spread at least as great, a thick trunk branching from low down if growing in the open, but if close planted in a wood making long clear stems, ashen-grey and smooth. It is a light-demanding tree so that in mixed woods it soon dominates other trees and plants, towering resolutely and suppressing almost everything within its shade. Its natural habitat is the upland chalk, alkaline and well drained, upon which it throws its shade and a deep carpet of leaf soil. It is one of the trees most used by eighteenth-century improvers as, for instance, at Stourhead where, alas, its life has been demonstrated to be between a hundred and two hundred years, much less than that of limes, for example. It was planted in large numbers just below the tops of swelling grass hills in Wiltshire and Berkshire to make those beautiful 'hangers'—hanging woods.

The spread of a full-grown beech tree grown in the open, about 30.5 m, 100 ft, is a space that no one would allow for in the first planting of a beech wood. They would be put in 2.1 m, 7 ft, apart to draw them up, and for the same reason are sometimes inter-planted with conifers such as the Norway spruce, or the western hemlock, *Tsuga heterophylla*, which in its early stages flourishes in light shade. The first thinning of beeches is done when the trees are 6.1–9.1 m, 20–30 ft, high and thereafter about every ten years until the trees stand at their final spacing of 9.1 m, 30 ft, apart like the columns in the nave of a cathedral. The beech is a real heavyweight specimen tree in grass and can also be planted in groups of perhaps five trees as close together as 5.2 m, 17 ft, or to make impressive avenues at 15.2 m, 50 ft, apart.

Hornbeam, *Carpinus betulus*, in some ways resembles a scaled-down beech; about 18.3 m, 60 ft, high and of almost equal spread. It would be the better tree to choose on lower-lying, moister soils. There is a fastigiate hornbeam, *C. betulus* 'Fastigiata', which in maturity develops an attractive candle-flame outline. Hornbeam and beech are two of the best plants for hedges, planted in a double row, 457 mm, 18 in, apart. Both retain their russet foliage (hornbeam a little greyer than beech) through the winter, undergoing only a brief period of about three weeks of bareness while the new green leaves unfold.

The last of our deciduous giants is *Quercus robur*, the pedunculate or English oak, our most familiar forest tree, with an ultimate maximum height of something in the region of 18.3 m, 60 ft, and a spread of well over 21.3 m, 70 ft, making it one of the most massive native trees, with exceedingly stout trunk and sturdy, four-square branching. The English oak is immensely long-lived, slow and resolute in its growth. A splendid tree to find and take over in a large garden and worthy of expert examination and, if necessary, tree surgery. Such a savage, untamed tree is a little uncouth to bring close to a house and much better seen at some distance away in a context of fields and sky. A fine tree also for avenues, as in the famous double avenue at Bucklebury in Berkshire. Because of the open framework and wide branching an oak wood gives a comparatively light and mainly dappled shade, resulting in a rich and varied flora of wood anemones, wild violets, primroses, woodruff and bluebells in the clearings.[1]

The flora under durmast oaks, *Q. petraea*, is less varied, but usually includes honeysuckle, holly, hawkweed and foxgloves. Oak timbers were used for ship-building; two thousand trees were needed to build one 74-gun ship in the eighteenth century. For these purposes it was the English oak, *Q. robur*, that was planted because of its angular branching, providing ready-made grown knees and crucks. It is less useful for this now, and as a timber tree it is the durmast oak that is grown for its straighter timbers. Oaks grow best on strong land, that is, in deep, rich, neutral loam. To make an oak forest in these days acorns or seedling plants are put in 2.1 m, 7 ft, apart to draw them up and, after the removal of conifers if planted, the seedlings are thinned to 6.1–7.6 m, 20–25 ft, and thereafter thinned each ten or twelve years until the trees stand at their final spacing of 12.2 m, 40 ft, apart.

There are many other oaks. The Turkey oak, *Q. cerris*, is a taller tree than either of the above two, and narrower in outline. The timber is of little value, but the tree is quicker growing, and used for avenues; for example the Fairmile at Henley-on-Thames was planted with Turkey oaks when the ancient elms were felled. The Scarlet oak, *Q. coccinea*, is a smaller tree, probably not much taller than 18.3 m, 60 ft, with a spread of rather less. It came from Canada and the United States, and is planted here for its golden-crimson foliage in autumn, giving good contrast in a mixed wood and striking also as a specimen tree in grass. It is better suited by drier soils than are the other oaks so far referred to, in well-drained, upland situations. The evergreen oak, *Q. ilex*, will be considered later with other large evergreen trees.

Before considering the latter, there are three larger exotic trees which are planted almost entirely for their autumn colour. On alkaline soils few trees can match the colours of the wild cherry, our native beech and the guelder rose, but the following three all need an acid soil to give the special conditions necessary for the production of anthocyanin, which causes the bright orange, scarlet and crimson colours in the leaves of deciduous trees before they fall.

Nyssa sylvatica, the tupelo, can grow up to 30.5 m, 100 ft, with an attractive columnar outline, has large leaves 127 mm, 5 in, long, turning to brilliant crimson and gold in the autumn. In its native North America it is seen near swamps, but here it is better suited by rich acid soil in full exposure to sunlight. It is effective at the outside edges of mixed plantings, where its bright colour can shine out.

The sweet gum, *Liquidambar styraciflua*, has reached a height of 22.9 m, 75 ft, in Britain, but in its native United States is a giant at 45.7 m, 150 ft. It tends to make a narrow pyramidal head while young, which suggests that an imaginative gardener with space to spare could make an elegant little grove of these trees, planted about 6.1 m, 20 ft, apart at the end of a grass walk leading to a gate in the wall.

Parrotia persica is a smaller tree at 6.1 m, 20 ft, very wide spreading. The large leaves turn crimson in the autumn, and its flowers in March are attractive with their bright red stamens.

Between the deciduous and evergreen is that curious deciduous conifer the swamp cypress, *Taxodium distichum*, tall, tapering to 27.3 m, 90 ft, having a width of only 9.1 m, 30 ft, with a generally cypress silhouette. After it has shed its

---

[1] *The Oxford Book of Wild Flowers.*

leaves in the autumn it is left with a delicate 'fishbone' structure all the winter. In spring the unfolding of its soft green foliage is one of the tenderest and most beautiful sights of that season. A tree for acid soil and the waterside—so much so that if its base becomes inundated, as happened to a specimen at Kew for example, it continues to thrive but develops processes known as 'knees' at the bottom of its trunk. Supreme for the sides of lakes in large gardens, with generous space around for its height and outline to be appreciated.

TALL EVERGREEN TREES

Tall evergreen trees are valuable for the dense, solid mass which they pose against the sky, something quite different from, but complementary to, the exploring, changing outline of deciduous trees and making a good contrast with them. The most impressive must be the Lebanon cedar, *Cedrus libani*, with a tiered height of 30.5 m, 100 ft, and at least an equal spread. In gardens large enough to accept its majestic proportions it is the supreme lawn tree, with immensely cool shade on summer afternoons—shade so dark as to seem as though vitality has been drained away from it. Cedars grow well on most soils; some good examples can be seen at Hambleden in lawns by the side of the Thames, but they flourish also on lighter soil. The branches can be damaged and broken by heavy snow, and if a new owner taking over a garden finds large specimens, he would be advised to have them surveyed by a tree surgeon and, if necessary, strengthened with cables. Like other evergreens, it cannot be transplanted at a height much above 914 mm, 3 ft, and will probably be supplied in pots. Thereafter its rate of growth is, unfortunately, slow—12.2 m, 40 ft, in forty-three years, according to Miss Colvin.[1] A tree, perhaps, for one's grandchildren, but none the less one which we should recognize as our duty to plant.

Two other cedars are the deodar (*C. deodara*) and the Atlas cedar (*C. atlantica*) (the former with drooping branches, the latter with ascending branches); both, by comparison with the cedar of Lebanon, are parvenus. The blue cedar, *C. atlantica* 'Glauca', together with the blue spruce, are much given to being ceremonially planted on the occasions of visits by Superior Persons.

Thuja plicata (Arbor-vitae or western red cedar), which has already been referred to for windscreens and hedges, is not, of course, a cedar at all. It is very much more like one of the *Chamaecyparis*, having fan-shaped flat leaves which, unlike those of the *Chamaecyparis*, have a refreshing resinous smell when crushed. When planted alone it is a full-sized tree up to 30.5 m, 100 ft, with a spread of 9.1 m, 30 ft, giving it a cypress-like outline. Not an attractive specimen tree and not amalgamating well in mixed deciduous woodland, always appearing a rather spiky intruder, but it is very useful as a windscreening plant, mixed in with hard woods, and is shade-tolerant. This *Thuja* is often planted to make hedges and can be put in as large as 1.5 m, 6 ft, high or more, provided it is well cared for in the first spring and summer after planting. Once established it is fast growing.

The Corsican pine, *Pinus nigra maritima* (*P. laricio*), up to 30.5 m, 100 ft, with a spread of 24.4 m, 80 ft, has been referred to as a windscreen tree, particularly in maritime districts. It can also be planted in little groups from two to five together on one side of a main vista. This pine grows well in fine, well-drained, even poor soils. It can only be safely transplanted when very small and is slow to make a start, but once settled in will begin to put on height fairly rapidly. The

---

[1] *Trees for Town and Country*, Brenda Colvin *et al.*, 1949.

native Scots pine, *Pinus sylvestris*, is a nobler tree inland, capable of 24.4 m, 80 ft, and usually with a narrower spread of the order of only 15.2 m, 50 ft. In youth it is something of a fastigiate tree, the branches growing from ground level, and unattractive when grown close together in Forestry Commission plantations. But as it approaches maturity it sheds its lower branches and assumes its characteristic outline of tall reddish trunk, sparse branching and a noble crown. Scots pines are majestic when seen in groups of from three to five or more on high ground; the combination of their spreading, flat-topped heads and blue sky on a still day is one of beauty and tranquillity. This tree is useful also in mixed woods, where it makes good top cover with oaks and other trees to protect rare exotics like magnolias and rhododendrons. It has a preference for light sandy acid soils, but will flourish in most ordinary soils provided that they are well drained. Like all the pines this one must be planted young.

Pinus pinea, the umbrella pine or stone pine, is not usually seen in this country much above 7.6 m, 25 ft. The tree is unmistakable for its very broad umbrella-shaped crown, familiar in the Italian landscape. It is tender and will not flourish out of the south and west, where it can be very beautifully placed when the sea can be seen under its spreading branches. This, too, has to be planted young and is slow growing. It prospers in light sandy soils. One other which is not reliably hardy outside the south and west is *Pinus radiata* (*P. insignis*), the Monterey pine, but in mild gardens by the sea it is a wonderful tree, growing to 30.5 m, 100 ft, and having when mature a trunk 1.8 m, 6 ft, thick, rugged and dark brown. Although, like the others, it has to be put in when small, once established it grows really quickly at the rate of 914 mm, 3 ft, per year. The leaves are rich green in colour, not so dark as those of the others.

Chamaecyparis lawsoniana has already been referred to as a screening and hedging plant. As a specimen tree it can get to 30.5 m, 100 ft, at which height it may have a spread of only 6.1 m, 20 ft—even slimmer than the *Thuja* but usually denser. This can be transplanted in sizes up to 1.8 m, 6 ft, if it is solicitously looked after in its first spring and summer by watering the roots, spraying the foliage, putting on a mulch when soil conditions are wet and warm, and screening from wind if possible. The plant needs a good, deep neutral soil, is fairly hardy against wind and frost, but rather less suited to maritime districts than some of its close relations. There are very many different varieties of *C. lawsoniana*; I counted eighty-six in Hillier's *Manual of Trees and Shrubs*. A prospective enthusiast will find many of them in nurseries and botanic gardens. For our purposes here perhaps four would serve as examples: *C. lawsoniana* 'Allumii', blue-green foliage; *C. l.* 'Erecta Viridis', bright green; *C. l.* 'Fletcheri', grey-green, almost bluish foliage; *C. l.* 'Kilmacurragh' is a narrow columnar tree with dark green foliage, with a suggestion of Glendalough.

The Italian cypress, *Cupressus sempervirens*, grows to about 15.2 m, 50 ft; very tightly fastigiate, almost pencil-like in outline. It is generally tender outside the south and west although it seems to become hardier as it gets older, with the result that it will often survive to old age in districts around Oxford, for example, if it can be protected in its infant years. With the umbrella pine it is familiar in Umbria and Tuscany, where they both seem natural and at home along the narrow, dusty roads which St Francis trod. The umbrella pine is good by the sea, but this Italian cypress is difficult to place; in our cold northern climate it seems more a kind of trick than a serious part of a garden, and even when dragged into Italianate attempts it fails to make these convincing.

Cupressus macrocarpa, the Monterey cypress, has already been considered as a windscreening tree in coastal districts. It is also a magnificent isolated specimen for the south and west, where it will grow to 24.4 m, 80 ft, with at least an equal spread when mature, and when it has cast off its youthful pyramidal outline it branches out horizontally like a cedar of Lebanon, and is exceedingly beautiful in Cornwall and south Devon when given generous space around it near the sea. The foliage is bright green. It requires a good soil, neutral or slightly acid, and is quick growing.

The evergreen oak, *Quercus ilex*, at 27.3 m, 90 ft, and a spread of 36.6 m, 120 ft, is a truly massive evergreen tree when fully grown. Unlike all those ever-greens so far considered, it is not a conifer with needle-like foliage, but has much larger leaves, 51 mm by 25 mm, 2 in. by 1 in. The ilex makes one of the very darkest outlines against the sky and is a fine contrast with deciduous trees. It is a good lawn tree, perhaps looking its best when planted in pairs but not popular with professional gardeners on account of the shedding of some of its evergreen leaves in May, causing a good deal of unseasonal sweeping up. I have seen the tree looking particularly well growing above a tall boundary wall on a roadside. This evergreen oak is only reliably hardy in the south of Britain, but is a good sea-coast plant and can be used as a wind-break. It is said to make a good clipped hedge for this purpose; I have not seen it treated in this way here, but I noticed a hedge of it in the Vatican Gardens in Rome. It is slow growing and must be planted at a small size, 305–610 mm, 1–2 ft, high.

Taxus baccata, the native English yew, is probably best known for making hedges, but it is by nature a tree 13.7 m, 45 ft, high with a potential spread of 18.3 m, 60 ft. It is one of the longest-lived native trees, slow growing at first but no sluggard at making a clipped hedge once established. It is exceedingly hardy and wind-firm, and thrives best in soil over chalk, although it will grow per-fectly well in all gardens except those with extremely acid soils. Yews can be transplanted at sizes up to 1.8 m, 6 ft, high but at this size plants are expensive and run some risk of failure from drought and cold winds in the first spring and summer. Planting ought to be done either in October or in April when the soil is warm and the roots can quickly re-establish contact with soil moisture. A safe size at which to transplant yews for hedging is 457–914 mm, 1½–3 ft, 508 mm, 20 in, apart. Yews will in time become effective tall specimen trees in large gardens, or they can be planted as a part of a mixed visual screen such as I have, the other plants being beech, laurustinus, *Rosa rugosa* and the 'Lanarth' *Viburnum* at the edges. The inclusion of the last caused some eyebrow raising by the experts, but it quickly worked out very well, the viburnum spreading out forwards at intervals towards the light. Yew is a good shade bearer and is seen to good effect in mixed woodland along with holly, box and privet.

The Irish yew is *Taxus baccata* 'Fastigiata', which grows to about 6.1 m, 20 ft, with a spread of 3 m, 10 ft, making a tall, closely packed pyramid, and a very much better tree than Lawson's cypress where a green obelisk effect is needed: in solemn rows on either side of a bowling alley, for example, in a large garden, or to make a square. This plant needs average rich, well-drained soil, on the alkaline side of neutral. From mature age onwards the fastigiate branches tend to fall outwards and usually need to be held in with wires.

CLIMBERS

Foundation planting will include some of those larger climbing plants and wall shrubs which take many years to come into their own. Among these is the evergreen *Magnolia grandiflora*, a large tree in its native southern United States and often seen as a free-standing tree in south Europe, but generally trained up sunny walls of houses in our warmer counties. One of the named clones grown from cuttings is desirable because plants raised from seed may take twenty years or more to bear flowers. The flowers are large, creamy-white with a strong refreshing lemon scent, between July and September. As in the planting of all climbers, the planting 'pocket' should be thoroughly prepared, if necessary enough paving or other surface material being temporarily removed to enable a hole 914 mm, 3 ft, square and deep to be excavated, the bottom broken up, a little coarse filling material put in followed by a layer of animal manure, and the rest of the hole refilled with fresh topsoil before the paving is replaced. Plants growing against walls receive less water than those growing in the open because rain usually falls at a slant, and at times will entirely miss the foot of a wall; also, the heat from the sun stored in a wall makes growing conditions warmer than out in the open, with a resulting increase in evaporation.

Wistaria sinensis is a deciduous wall plant. Once established, and if well planted as indicated above, it will grow rapidly on wires and from an early age produce its mauve or deep lilac-coloured scented flowers in long racemes in May.

Vines are best suited to pergolas, but can be grown against a house wall with support. Some of the outdoor grape vines after a few years make massive stems and will envelop large areas of a wall. Those from which wine can be made after hot summers are 'Golden Chasselas', also known as 'Royal Muscadine', and 'Madeleine Royale', both white, and 'Pirovano 14', black. The grapes on my 'Golden Chasselas' are a beautiful sight in autumn, full of mellow fruitfulness, but attempts to harvest them for wine-making are foiled by wasps and mildew. The most impressive decorative vine is *Vitis coignetiae*, which is fairly quick growing and has enormous leaves, 305 mm, 1 ft, which turn a magnificent coppery crimson in the autumn. One which, unlike the others, is self-clinging, is *Parthenocissus henryana*. The leaves of this one are quite small, of a velvety dark green with silvery-mauve variegation.

Some climbing roses can be considered to be part of foundation planting. 'Mermaid' has single, large golden yellow flowers, not scented, and shining dark green foliage; a fairly fast grower when established, having a height potential of something like 6.1 m, 20 ft, it is well worth putting in at an early stage. It is best on a south-western wall, but is one of the few which will also grow well and flower on a north or east wall. It will flower from June to October. At St Mawes, in Cornwall, I have seen flowers on New Year's Day. Two other roses which can give tall wide cover are 'Madame Alfred Carrière', double white, and the old 'Gloire de Dijon', with buff-coloured flowers flecked with touches of rose.

A shrub usually grown against a wall which takes some years to produce flowers regularly is the wintersweet, *Chimonanthus praecox*; it needs a warm south wall or a warm angle facing south-west. At midwinter its bare branches are covered with small goblin-yellow flowers, very strongly scented. The old 'japonicas' are useful against north and east walls, in which position they will not put on height very rapidly and therefore should be planted at an early stage of making the garden. They are now known as *Chaenomeles*, and good ones to choose are 'Atrococcinea', deep crimson; 'Nivalis', white; or, 'Knap Hill Scarlet'.

The climbing hydrangea, *H. petiolaris*, is another very good plant for a north wall or a shady position, or both of these together. It is self-clinging, making itself fast to its wall with aerial roots, and capable of getting up to 4.6 m, 15 ft, if given the opportunity. In summer it has large whitish hydrangea-like flowers, and large oval leaves, pointed and toothed. It is deciduous, but its brown-red stems in winter are attractive and its pointed buds at midwinter full of promise of things to come in the summer.

Climbing plants such as clematis and less vigorous climbing roses can be put in at a later stage of making the garden, and are included in the chapter on secondary planting.

BULBS

Bulbous plants which are to be naturalized can be put in at an early stage to give them time to increase and multiply. The most important are the smallest, those which will make pools of gentle colour under trees without compromising their integrity. Snowdrops can be planted as dry bulbs in the autumn, in which case they should be put in 25–76 mm, 1–3 in, apart in large random drifts. They are better transplanted as green plants when in full growth, preferably just after flowering. The native wild snowdrop is *Galanthus nivalis*, which flourishes best in partial shade. A large-flowered one, *G. elwesii*, with conspicuous dark green marking at the base of the flowers, flourishes equally in full sunshine. The rate of planting for snowdrops can be calculated at about eighty per square metre, a little over 1 square yard. Winter aconites, like snowdrops, are inexpensive and can be planted in large numbers in the same sort of situation at the same density. Snowflakes, *Leucojum vernum*, are the *perce-neiges* of the Alpine spring, flowering a little later than snowdrops. They are put in at about the same rate. Grape hyacinths make sheets of blue in April, beautiful under trees, particularly magnolias before the leaves come out; they are planted at between thirty and eighty per square metre.

The wild bluebell is *Endymion non-scriptus*; the small corms are planted in August–September at 305 mm, 12 in, apart in large drifts in open glades in woods. The wood anemone, *Anemone nemorosa*, can be bought as little stick-like roots and planted at the same rate.

All the above are put in at about 102–152 mm, 4–6 in, deep.

Cyclamens are planted 51–76 mm, 2–3 in, below the surface and about 305 mm, 1 ft, apart. This works out at only nine to the square metre, the reason being that cyclamen are naturally spreading, increasing from seed. This seed can be trapped as it ripens by sprinkling leaf soil over the plants and on the surrounding ground when the seed is being produced in July. *C. coum* can be had in separate colours; crimson—a rather hectic magenta crimson—pink, and white. *C.* 'Atkinsii', a close relative, is available in similar separate colours and has attractively marbled leaves. Both of these begin to flower in December and continue until the end of March. Two autumn-flowering cyclamen are *C. europaeum* with lightly silvered leaves, and crimson flowers; and *C. neapolitanum*, which flowers from July to October or November, rosy pink, often with tones of magenta, and finely-marked variegated leaves. The most beautiful of all is the white *C. neapolitanum* 'Album' which, unfortunately, is very expensive.

In long grass in water meadows, the native snake's-head fritillary can be planted at much wider spacings, about 1.8 m, 6 ft, apart, and not in drifts or groups like the smaller bulbs. *Fritillaria meleagris* is a slender plant about 305 mm, 1 ft, high, the flowers like lanterns hanging downwards, mysteriously dim, chequered dark purple and white with green veining, coming out on the first day of May.

The best daffodils for naturalizing are the native wild daffodils, *Narcissus pseudonarcissus*, often seen in fields by streams; they are a true native plant only about 203 mm, 8 in, high, primitive, bicolor trumpet daffodils, with pale creamy-yellow perianths and deeper yellow trumpets.

Chapter 4

Terraces, Steps and Paths

After the foundation planting, the next part of the garden to be made could be that closest to the house. It is visually of importance because it makes a platform for the house to stand on and is the meeting point of architecture and landscape, leading the house out into the garden and accomplishing the transition from hard, inanimate artifact to the organic world of trees and plants and turf. It is also the place for chairs and tables for such out-of-doors existence as the climate allows. For scale, the width of the whole terrace platform can be equal to the height of the house, from ground level to cornice. In larger houses this may result in a terrace width of 7.6 m, 25 ft, which, while satisfying as far as overall dimensions go, may have a stony, hard appearance if it is all paved. As described in the notes to Figure 21, this can be relieved by making beds for low plants against a parapet wall, or by a low clipped hedge at the outer edge of the paving and a narrow bed for scented plants against the walls of the house. This narrows the breadth of stone, and its length can be reduced by laying panels of turf at either end, reducing the paved area to 3–4.6 m, 10–15 ft, by 6.1–7.6 m, 20–25 ft. If, as is usual, the terrace faces towards the south, it will be an advantage to provide shelter at the eastern end. A solid wing wall of the same material as the house may look very well, provided it ends in a resolute looking pier, and it will look all the better if it has a solid door. If this wing wall is fairly high, about 3 m, 10 ft, it will give protection from wind for a distance of about 9.1 m, 30 ft, along the terrace, which should be room enough to draw chairs into on bright days in March when the wind is keen. By contrast with solid walls, hedges filter the wind and considerably reduce its speed to a distance of about six times their height. This sort of shelter is excellent for plants in a garden, but probably too draughty on a terrace.

The preparation for laying a stone surface must start with locating the damp-proof course on the house—a line of slate or bituminous felt between courses of bricks a little above ground level. The finished surface of the paving should be at least 51 mm, 2 in, below this. The foundation of 102 mm, 4 in, of hard filling material, clinker, gravel or brick hardcore, must be laid to slope away from the house at a gradient of not less than 1 in 100 if the paving is not pointed, but if the paving is pointed a rather sharper fall, about 1 in 80, would be more prudent. If there is a bed or a hedge at the outer edge of the terrace, the soil in this will usually take the water that runs across, but if the paving ends abruptly against a parapet wall, a line of small weep holes, about 51 mm, 2 in, in diameter, should be put in at intervals of 1.8 m, 6 ft.

A thin layer, 38 mm, $1\frac{1}{2}$ in, of fine ashes is the best bed on which to lay the paving stones. The paving stones are spot bedded, that is, given five dabs of mortar on the undersides, turned over, laid in position, and gently tapped to a level. Random rectangular or any paving with uneven edges should be pointed after laying, but sawn natural stone or artificial paving material is better left unpointed, the slabs being butted up tightly and sand brushed into the joints. This gives a better appearance and takes some of the rainwater down between the joints.

Real natural York stone, so frequently used in the past, is nature's non-slip material, and is still in many places the best stone that can be obtained, but it has now become so expensive as to be prohibitive. Fortunately, perfectly satisfactory artificial stones are now made, and when once 'weathered' by rain and dust (the process, if necessary, being accelerated by a sloshing over with a mixture of cow dung and milk) are as nice looking as any that one could want. These garden slabs are made in different sizes; a few of them are supplied as large slabs 900 mm by 600 mm, a fraction of an inch less than 3 ft by 2 ft, but these are exceedingly heavy and really need professional masons or 'slabbers' to put down; 600 mm by 600 mm, about 2 ft by 2 ft, slabs are about the largest that can be managed by an amateur, while 450 mm by 450 mm, about 17¾ in by 17¼ in, are even more convenient. Below this size slabs tend to look fussy, and the many different paving patterns recommended by the suppliers have the same effect and should be avoided. Through-jointed square slabs are the most becoming in nearly all places except the very largest terraces, which may call for the 900 mm by 600 mm size laid coursed.

To prevent large expanses of paving looking staring, relief can be effected in different ways, for example by slate bands, 229–305 mm, 9–12 m, wide, in long horizontal lines, crossed towards each end by transverse lines, to suggest panelling. The same sort of effect can be got from 229 mm, 9 in, band of bricks on edge used in the same way. Odd corners can be laid with granite sets or sea-shore cobbles, and these can also be worked into a design over the main part of the terrace, both of these materials being visually very good because their multiple small units break up the flatness and give a contrasting texture; but they are uncomfortable to walk over, particularly to women with their narrower shoes and heels, and are best kept away from main routes, the way to steps for instance. Pebble mosaic was used on the floors of Arab patios, in Spain, and in the squares of many cities abroad, when they are sometimes laid in radiating patterns like overlapping fish scales.

Bricks are also used for paving. In some contexts, perhaps with large Tudor houses, they preserve the ancient atmosphere, but they have their disadvantages; they give no relief to the colour and texture of a brick-built house and they do not throw up the light, either on the terrace itself or into the windows of the house, in the way that the lighter colours of stone do. Also, brick paving can become slippery in dark places where it is not regularly walked over, and can be very dangerous for steps. Too many different materials—stone, slate, bricks, cobbles, sets—on one terrace are a mistake. Two or, at the most, three different surfaces give sufficient contrast without appearing to be busy and confusing.

Gravel is one of the least expensive surface materials, but has certain disadvantages on a terrace in that it becomes soft after rain, and gets picked up on shoes and brought into the house in wet weather, but apart from these it provides a safe, non-slip foothold in all conditions of weather. It is, as it were, 'flexible' and can be laid over undulating or sharply sloping levels, where stone would not only look awkward but would be dangerous in frosty weather. Besides all this, its colour is sober and unobtrusive. Gravel is a mixture of stone, sand, silt and clay, its composition varying from district to district, so it is advisable to rely on trustworthy local experience, and to take material that is known to give a firmly bound surface. It binds together partly under compression, causing interlocking of the particles, which are then temporarily cemented together by the silt and clay, and in some cases because the soft stone compound breaks down to powder to form a cementing medium when wet.

It is the very best material for paths, which are among the first things to be put in. It is not too unpleasant in summer to make one's way along grass paths between flower beds even on wet days, but it is entirely unacceptable to slither and possibly fall on muddy tracks in winter in the course of necessary journeys, perhaps in darkness, to the toolshed, the woodpile or the greenhouse. Therefore good firm paths, wide enough for two to walk abreast, at least 1.2 m, 4 ft, and preferably 1.5 m, 5 ft, wide, cambered to the edges, leading to the working parts of the garden should be laid down at an early stage. It will in the course of time prove to be more efficient and more economical to lay edging to the paths, 31.8 mm, 1¼ in, thick cedar boarding in the politer parts, and concrete edging in the kitchen garden; this concrete edging can be entirely concealed if a box hedge is planted on its inside.

The first essential for a flight of steps is that they should be safe and reassuring, and seen to be so. There is an old rule of thumb formula for the ratio of tread to riser—twice the rise plus the 'going' (the breadth of tread) equals 22–25 inches, i.e. between these limits. This is now expressed in rounded off millimetres as $2 \times$ rise (R) $+$ going (G) $= 575$ mm to 630 mm. Two examples will illustrate this.

First beginning with the riser, pre-determined at, say, 152 mm, about 6 in: 2×152 mm $= 304$ mm. If 304 is deducted from the lower limit of 575 the remainder is 271 mm—about 10⅝ in. If it is deducted from the upper limit of 630 the remainder is 326 mm—about 12⅞ in. The tread width should therefore be between 271 mm and 326 mm. The latter would be much more comfortable in a garden, where one expects to be able to put one's whole shoe on the tread without the overlapping that has to occur on most stairs indoors, where there is simply not room to allow more than 254 mm, 10 in, or so for the treads.

For the second example, the breadth of tread is predetermined at say 350 mm, just under 14 in. Deducting this from 575 mm, the lower limit, gives a remainder of 225 mm, for twice the riser; half of this is 112.5 mm, between 4¼ and 4½ in. Deducting 350 mm from the upper limit of 630 leaves 280 mm, 140 mm for one riser, or about 5½ in. Block steps, in which the tread and riser are in one with no overhanging nosing, are the most attractive. Steps, whether wide, or narrow and turning, are one of the architectural elements that can give charm and drama to gardens, whether descending in a straight flight or, in order to get to a lower level without too much projection, going down a few steps, first to a landing, and then turning left and right to go down narrower flights at right angles. Where there are steps leading down from the terrace, a parapet wall or low hedge at the far edge of the terrace gives at least a psychological sense of security.

Chapter 5

Lawns

Stretches of grass are indispensable to give areas of horizontal space to make a contrast with the vertical principle of trees. In formal surroundings many lawns may appear to be level, although in practice they will probably have an imperceptible fall of about 1 in 100 for the sake of drainage. In large gardens of considerable slope, lawns have to be terraced, but again finished to shallow rakes. Less formal gardens are all the better for recognizably sloping grass.

A lawn is a community of plants living at uncomfortably close quarters, to which they are to some extent naturally adapted, but they are also subject to systematic defoliation, to which they are not adapted, a practice that causes restricted root growth. Therefore, in common with other things that grow, lawns need appropriate consideration and sympathy in their treatment. Like all plants they need water, drainage, light and a fertile soil—fertile in the true sense of the biological implications of structure, nutrients and a flourishing population of micro-flora.

Because of this, good drainage is a first consideration at the planning and construction stage. The best and easiest way is, as has been seen elsewhere in this book, the provision of a slope with means of disposal of the surface water, by running it into flower beds, pools, lakes, or the next man's garden. If the proposed lawn cannot be given a fall, and if it is at the foot of higher ground, a French drain may succeed in trapping the water before it gets on to the lawn. In severe cases it may be necessary to carry out artificial drainage by one of the methods outlined in Chapter 1, and to make sure that the subsoil above the drains is reasonably porous by, if necessary, digging in peat, compost, lime and some of the seaweed conditioning materials. If the topsoil which has been previously removed is of satisfactory quality, this is replaced to a depth of 102–152 mm, 4–6 in, spread, regulated to level and, unless the area is enormous and such a process is not practical, methodically trodden or 'heeled' all over to consolidate the soil. This process does not, as might be expected, produce a state of compaction in the finished lawn. After the treading, the ground is raked again to produce the final tilth—a fine friable surface on to which the seed is sown, preferably in two operations in opposite directions. If the tilth is perfect, a light rolling after the sowing is useful, but if the surface is at all sticky it is better to omit this. In any case, the seed should not be covered deeply. Some seeds, including those of 'Browntop', are so small that they can be smothered and killed.

If seed is to be sown, temporary retaining laths should be fixed wherever the lawn abuts on a hard surface like paving. These should stand 51 mm, 2 in, above the path or paving, so that when the seed has germinated, the surface consolidated down, and the laths have been removed, the finished grass will be 25 mm,

1 in, higher than the paving, enabling cylinder types of mowers to be used right out to the edges. If preparatory work is properly carried out, better lawns are produced from seed than from turf. This means properly cleaning the ground of weeds and coarse grasses in the two months mid-June to mid-August, by hoeing. If a suitable seed mixture is then employed a good lawn will result, consisting in the early stages at any rate of the chosen grasses; but in fact the botanical composition of lawns nearly always changes, depending on which grasses best survive under the method of management practised, on local conditions of soil and moisture, and what grass population may exist near by upwind to supply the seeds of volunteers, which will gain a footing in rolled-down wormcasts or bare places. That ubiquitous vagrant *Poa annua*, for example, is almost certain to start an immigrant population. *Poa annua* is also a useful grass in shade, but is not, I believe, commercially available although I have occasionally obtained small supplies from 'cleanings' from seed testing stations or large seed merchants.

Before sowing the seed at the end of August, a base fertilizer is raked in. The choice of seed depends on the height of cut which is to be maintained on the established lawn. Generally lawns are cut much closer than is good for them. If they were kept at 19 mm, $\frac{3}{4}$ in, many troubles such as fungus infection, invasion by weeds and volunteer grasses, and susceptibility to drought would be avoided. Convention dictates that bowling greens and putting greens should be mown to as short as 5 mm, $\frac{3}{16}$ in, or even a little less, and there are only two reasonably fine grasses that will withstand such close mowing, 'Browntop' (*Agrostis tenuis*) and 'Chewing's Fescue' (*Festuca rubra fallax*), but not, unfortunately, the true 'Creeping Red Fescue', and many other good grasses.

For a fine garden lawn to be mown no closer than 19 mm, $\frac{3}{4}$ in, a good seed mixture would be:

'Creeping Red Fescue'	
(Pedigree S59)	35 per cent
'Browntop'	30 per cent
'Chewing's Fescue'	35 per cent

For less fine, but durable, garden lawns over large areas also mown to 19 mm, $\frac{3}{4}$ in:

'Creeping Red Fescue'	
(not Pedigree)	30 per cent
'Chewing's Fescue'	30 per cent
'Crested Dogstail'	30 per cent
'Browntop'	10 per cent

On dry soils 'Chewing's Fescue' could be replaced by *Poa pratensis*, smooth-stalked meadow grass, the blue grass of America, but when this is included the grass should not be mown shorter than 25 mm, 1 in, and should be given good supplies of nitrogen through the growing season. On moist soils 'Chewing's Fescue' could be replaced by *Poa trivialis*, rough-stalked meadow grass, which will withstand mowing to 19 mm, $\frac{3}{4}$ in, but it is a much coarser grass. All the above would be sown at 42.5 g per m², 1$\frac{1}{2}$ oz. per sq. yd. I have omitted rye grass because of its untidy and unattractive appearance and the difficulty of producing a good mown finish from a lawn containing a high proportion of it.

There are no grasses that really thrive in shade under mowing conditions. *Poa nemoralis* was once included in the seed mixtures for shade, and it is true that it is found wild in shady woodland, but it will not withstand mowing at all. The best that can be done is to use a mixture of grasses which are a little less resentful of shade than others and, above all, not to mow the resulting lawn closer than 25 mm, 1 in. Such a mixture might be:

'Chewing's Fescue'	50 per cent
Rough-stalked meadow grass	30 per cent
'Browntop'	20 per cent

If rye grass can be accepted, 35 per cent or so of it could be put in at the expense of some of the 'Chewing's Fescue' and rough-stalked meadow grass.

After the lawn is sown the seed will take from three to six weeks to germinate. It is in the next two or three months that the very important process of establishment takes place, during which the owner must not become neurotic about stones and weeds. There is certain to be a large crop of weeds when a lawn is sown in spring, because it will not have been possible to fallow the ground to take out weeds germinating from seeds in the soil; owing to low soil temperatures in the months before sowing—probably February and March—weed seeds will not germinate for hoeing out, as can be done before August sowing. Many of them, however, will be annual weeds and will 'mow out' in the course of the first cuts with the mower, but coarse grasses must be taken out by hand. It may also be necessary to take out in this way some of the larger weeds such as docks, which might otherwise smother the young grasses. The first cut is made when the grasses are about 51 mm, 2 in, high. The area should first be rolled with a roller sufficiently heavy to push in the stones; this will temporarily flatten the grasses, but as soon as they have sprung up again a rotary mower should be used. The next cut will also probably be with a rotary in about two weeks' time. After this it will be possible to begin to use a cylinder machine with the blades set really high at 51 mm, 2 in, and gradually lowering them through the season to 19 mm, $\frac{3}{4}$ in, or 25 mm, 1 in, if *Poa pratensis* has been used, which will be short enough for the first season. At midsummer a dressing of a complete fertilizer will help during the establishment period. In dry weather the sprinkler will have to be kept going more often than will be necessary in later years. In the autumn a dressing of a fertilizer containing little or no nitrogen should be put on and also, if it can be afforded, a bulk dressing of peat, or peat and grit sand mixed together, at from 907 g–1.8 kg per m², 2–4 lb. per sq. yd, to true up the surface.

Making a lawn with turf has both advantages and disadvantages. The process is, as it were, instant, and it often happens that a new garden only comes to life when the turf is put down; turfing can be done at almost any time between October and March, and even in other months if the turf can be got from cutting grounds then, and if a water supply can be guaranteed to stop turfs curling up in really dry weather; and finally turfing avoids the anxiety which besets a gardener confronted with a great population of weeds germinating with the grass seed, though this is seldom as serious as at first appears.

Chapter 6

Water

Even the smallest gardens can have a fountain of water rising scintillating in the sunshine and falling back into a pool. Information given in Appendix A should enable anyone to calculate and decide on the type of pump to work a fountain and on its installation.

Pools as distinct from ponds will usually be, if not on a terrace, at least in formal surroundings, and on this account are better in regular shapes—square, rectangular or round. Small prefabricated pool bodies made in fibreglass can be bought in sizes up to about 1.5 m, 5 ft, across and 457 mm, 18 in, deep (there are other weird and far from wonderful shapes, wiggles and wobbles that should be eschewed), but in many cases a larger pool would be needed to be in scale with its surroundings; even a moderate-sized terrace needs a pool of from 3 to 3.7 m, 10–12 ft, in diameter and probably 610 mm, 2 ft, deep. These are best constructed in reinforced concrete which, if properly made, is unlikely to crack and leak. It is worth taking the trouble and going to the expense of employing skilled labour to do this work to avoid the frustration of a leaking pool—leaks are notoriously difficult to find and repair in later years. Pools on a terrace are immensely improved by having raised moulded copings around them, for without these they can appear to be simply holes in the paving. They are even more effective if they stand raised 610 mm, 2 ft, above the level of the terrace, or at a junction of paths further out into the garden. When this is done they are surrounded by brick or stone walls with stone copings that will form a seat from which to lean over and observe at close quarters the slow perambulations of aldermanic goldfish, waterboatmen and the occasional marauding descent of the terrifying Great Diving Beetle. A water depth of 610 mm, 2 ft, is usually enough to prevent fish from being frozen solid in the winter and for the cultivation of some water lilies.

Pools intended only as fountain basins, that is without fish or water lilies, can be comparatively shallow, only 305 mm, 1 ft, or so deep, and the water can be kept clear of algae, and even toned a little blue, by the addition of copper sulphate; such pools may be even further refined with a lining of mosaic tiles. If water lilies, other aquatic plants and fish are to be introduced a balanced economy will have to be established. At the initial stages, as with the sowing of grass seed, neurosis can too easily set in. When first stocked the water in the pool will be turbid, but if the stocking process is properly carried out it should begin to clear in about six weeks. The flat waterlily pads will shade a good proportion of the water surface, oxygenating plants will be regularly carrying out their necessary functions, fish will be contentedly feeding on any possible mosquito larvae, and by then the water will become transparent, although pale porter-coloured. Once a state of equilibrium has been attained, the pool or pond should not be emptied and refilled, otherwise the whole waiting-period will have to be gone through again.

For a water depth of 914 mm, 3 ft, or more the white *Nymphaea* 'Gladstoniana' would be the most suitable. For rather shallower pools a choice could be made from *N.* 'Marliacea Albida', white, *N.* 'Marliacea Carnea', pink, and *N.* 'Escarboucle', red. *N.* 'Marliacea Chromatella', yellow, will flourish in slightly shallower water, while *N. odorata turicensis*, soft rose, and *N.* 'Laydekeri Purpurata' need only 302–610 mm, 1–2 ft, of water. In really small pools *N. pygmaea alba*, white, and *N. pygmaea helvola*, yellow, can manage in a depth of only 102–254 mm, 4 –10 in, but it would not be possible to keep fish at such a shallow depth.

Oxygenating plants will also be necessary. Suitable ones are *Callitriche autumnalis*, a submerged plant useful because it persists in the winter and is eaten by fish, *Fontinalis antipyretica*, another submerged oxygenator, and *Myriophyllum spicatum*. A number of Ramshorn snails should also be put in as scavengers. For small to medium-sized pools the best fish are ordinary goldfish; in larger pools where they have length in which to display their athletic activities Golden Orfe can be included; these are slender fish swimming near the surface in shoals, in summer rising to flies, and it would seem a pity to introduce them into small pools where their natural activity cannot be exercised. Generally these pools are best with a clean bottom, which will look more attractive if a thin layer of shingle is laid over it. For this reason water lilies and any other aquatics are best planted in specially designed perforated polythene pots or small plastic crates which can be obtained from the supplier of the plants. These keep the soil in round the roots and to an extent prevent its spreading and becoming silt on the bottom. Planting in these containers results in less vigorous growth of the water lilies, which may be an advantage in small pools, and also makes it possible to lift and divide the plants if this should be required. In these pools, as opposed to ponds, marginal plants are not advisable, for they destroy the principle of flatness which makes such a good contrast with a fountain jet and their irregular 'fuzz' is out of place in formal surroundings.

By contrast, ponds are more in the nature of small lakes, usually larger than pools nearly always of irregular shape and with a natural clay or muddy bottom, but they can be made artificially by excavating to the required depth and then lining the excavated area with a membrane such as butyl rubber, as referred to in Chapter 1 for making storage reservoirs. These ponds, with their tadpoles, frogs and newts, ancient carp and tench, waterboatmen and dragonflies, are the paradise of small boys. Here too snails will be needed as scavengers, and with a muddy bottom one of the fresh-water mussels can also be put in; the Zebra mussel, *Dreissena polymorpha*, is said to be most suitable because its larvae do not attach themselves to young fish. Larger water lilies can probably be used, such as *Nymphaea* 'Gladstoniana', which has large white flowers and requires up to 2.4 m², 20 sq. ft, and a depth of at least 914 mm, 3 ft. There are many other aquatic plants, notably the water hawthorn, *Aponogeton distachyum*, with flowers projecting a little above the water surface and long leaves lying flat. Ponds are also *par excellence* the place for marginal plants, in particular the yellow flag, *Iris pseudacorus*, with its bright yellow flowers in summer. Others are irises such as *I. chrysographes* 'Rubella', 457 mm, 18 in, with plum-coloured flowers, and *I. kaempferi* hybrids in a number of shades including white, pink, violet and yellow, 762 mm, 2 ft 6 in. *Aruncus sylvester* is tall, impressive with heavy plumes of creamy white flowers, 1.5 m, 5 ft. *Hemerocallis* will grow in most soil conditions including damp ones near water, reaches 610–914 mm, 2–3 ft, high and comes in a great variety of colours, largely yellow, orange and bronze, but also pink. Among the primulas are *P. beesiana*, which has rosy carmine flowers and is about 610 mm, 2 ft, high; *P. bulleyana*, which has orange-apricot flowers and stands 610 mm, 2 ft; *P. denticulata*, with lilac-coloured flowers, 305 mm, 1 ft; *P. florindae*, like a giant cowslip, 914 mm, 3 ft; *P. helodoxa*, yellow, 914 mm, 3 ft; *P. japonica* in white, pink or crimson colours, 610 mm, 2 ft; and *P. pulverulenta*, crimson, 610 mm, 2 ft.

By my own small pond I have two giants; the 'boss' giant is *Gunnera manicata*, occupying the commanding position in the angle where it has the benefit of a downpipe from a neighbour's gutter and the overflow of my own pond. Its enormous leaves, nearly 1.8 m, 6 ft, across like elephant's ears, reach a height of 2.4 m, 8 ft, by midsummer. The plant has the largest leaves of any in this country, outside a tropical greenhouse. In the south of England it is, for practical purposes, hardy, provided its crown is protected in winter, the best protection being its own leaves cut down when they begin to fade in the autumn. It needs a deep moist loam and is most at home by the edges of pools or slow streams. I wish I knew its familiar name in Brazil, where it came from, for had it been known in England when country names like 'Lords and Ladies' and 'Priest's Pintle' were invented, its thick, upright, brownish-purple inflorescences would not have failed our ribald vernacular.

Challenging the *Gunnera* in authority is *Rheum palmatum*, a giant rhubarb, with leaves almost as large, a little thinner in texture and developing earlier. My group of three plants reaches a height of 2.4 m, 8 ft, in June, when the cream-coloured flowers appear on ascending stems well above the foliage. This does not demand a position so near to water as the *Gunnera*, though it needs deep rich loam and adequate moisture to sustain its massive superstructure of foliage.

Between these two at the far end of the pond I have three or four plants of what I knew as *Senecio clivorum*, but which must now be called *Ligularia dentata*. These, too, are waterside plants, reaching to 1.2 m, 4 ft, with large heart-shaped leaves; the flowers in July and August are borne in flat-topped clusters or corymbs and the colour is hot orange, which is acceptable at the time of the year when spring is already far away.

Under these in summer *Hosta sieboldiana* is able to hold its own in the shade, and in the spring, and before the giants unfold their leaves, we have late white daffodils 'Cushendall' and 'Foggy Dew'. In dry summers, notwithstanding the natural moisture, we provide fairly massive watering through a hose, without which the *Rheum* in particular begins to flag.

Chapter 7

Secondary Planting

A bed of shrubs, when the plants approach maturity and create underneath them sufficient shade to suppress weeds, will need very much less maintenance than either a mixed border or a herbaceous border. Since such a bed will be on view not only when it is in flower and leaf, but all through the winter also, it is advisable to include a proportion of evergreens to give it some body then.

Here to consider first is a general list of plants that will flourish on neutral or alkaline soils, in which rhododendrons, camellias and others will not grow; the evergreens should be of a more refined, as it were domestic, character than those that would be planted on a boundary; for example *Viburnum rhytidophyllum* is too coarse a plant for this purpose. Evergreens suitable for positions about the middle or back are: × *Elaeagnus ebbingei*, 2.7 m, 9 ft, with large leaves, grey-green above and silvery on the undersides; *Garrya elliptica*, the same height, with matt-surfaced grey-green oval leaves and, its chief attraction, long jade-green catkins in winter; *Mahonia japonica* (once known as *M. bealii*), 1.5 m, 5 ft, with large green leaves and long drooping racemes of very fragrant pale yellow flowers in winter; *Viburnum* × *burkwoodii*, 2.4 m, 8 ft, which has large heads of sweetly scented flowers in April and good dark evergreen foliage; *Choisya ternata*, 1.8 m, 6 ft, the Mexican orange blossom, whose large white flowers in May are also scented (its foliage too is aromatic when crushed but, although perfectly evergreen, goes a rather washy light green in winter); *Osmanthus delavayi*, 1.8 m, 6 ft, has very small evergreen leaves, but its white flowers are produced in great numbers in April, and once again are deliciously scented.

The heights of all the plants given in this chapter are approximately their maximum at or near maturity, and many of them will take a number of years to reach these heights. As pointed out in Appendix D, some sort of compromise must be worked out between the size of the plants when supplied, and their ultimate dimensions in both spread and height. These evergreens are usually supplied as fairly small plants (British Standard 3936, *Nursery Stock* Part I, *Trees and Shrubs*, indicates that 457–762 mm, 18 in–2 ft 6 in, is a normal size at which to expect to buy × *Elaeagnus ebbingei*, for example) and, further, they are often slower growing than deciduous shrubs which may be put in with them. This is a real difficulty but there are two ways of tackling it: one is to plant the deciduous shrubs at a respectful distance from the small evergreen ones, being content to wait for a year or two for the latter to fill out; the other is to buy the tallest sized evergreens that can be found as good bushy robust specimens, not drawn up or spindly, preferably container-grown, and at the same time to buy smaller-sized deciduous shrubs to give the evergreens a start and to avoid their being overlaid and turned into gawky specimens.

It is a mistake to plant rigidly in rows, tallest at the back, middle sized in the middle, shortest at the front; a more interesting effect is obtained by some imaginative contouring, bringing some of the taller (but seldom the tallest) towards the front. Tall deciduous shrubs to consider are: *Amelanchier laevis*, 6.1 m, 20 ft, covered with white flowers in April, and with good autumn colour in the foliage; lilacs, *Syringa vulgaris*, 3.7–4.6 m, 12–15 ft, 'Katherine Havemeyer', double purplish-lavender, 'Maud Notcutt', single white, and 'Buffon', single pink, fading to indescribable hyacinthine paleness. These all give colour and smell delicious in May. Later, in July, but also strongly scented, are the *Philadelphus*; 'Beauclerk', at 1.8 m, 6 ft, is not so tall as some others, which can so easily look ungainly.

Some of the taller shrub roses will give good colour on and off most of the summer, for example, the hybrid musks: 'Moonlight', semi-double, almost white; 'Vanity', bright pink, single; 'Will Scarlet', semi-double, crimson-scarlet; these will all make about 1.8 m, 6 ft. There is also the rose 'Nevada', creamy-white, 2.1 m, 7 ft. In the same height bracket are *Hydrangea paniculata* 'Grandiflora', creamy-white flowers, about 1.8 m, 6 ft; for late summer and autumn, *Hibiscus*, about 2.4 m, 8 ft: 'Blue Bird', single clear blue, 'Hamabo', single pink with crimson centre, 'Woodbridge', ruby, and 'William R. Smith', single white. *Buddleia alternifolia* has lilac-blue flowers crowding its arching, exploring branches in June.

Shorter, medium-sized deciduous plants are *Viburnum carlesii*, which is for me one of the most charming small shrubs in my garden, for it seems to have a knack of developing an attractive spreading and a little contorted growth, and bears its white flowers (pink in the bud) in attractive corymbs early in the spring, refreshingly scented; *Deutzia × rosea* 'Carminea' is covered with pretty pink flowers in May and June; *Hypericum* 'Hidcote', 1.5 m, 5 ft, produces large yellow saucer-shaped flowers in August, and is very effective when seen with some of the grey-foliaged plants, in particular *Senecio laxifolius*, 914 mm, 3 ft. This has its own yellow flowers in June and July, but the reason for planting it is for the grey of its foliage, to my mind the perfect grey-foliaged plant, not white and staring but none the less giving a very good contrast with green leaves. It has an excellent habit of growth, apparently an inborn sense of how to display itself with perfect manners; a plant to put not only towards the middle, but also in the front. Another grey-foliaged shrub of about the same height is *Phlomis fruticosa*, whose foliage is darker than that of the *Senecio*, more of an elephant grey. Its flowers are hooded, yellow, the yellow of lacquered bronze. There is another deciduous plant that I regard as indispensable, *Lavatera olbia* 'Rosea', 1.5–1.8 m, 5–6 ft, with bluish-pink cup-shaped flowers from July to October, well mated with grey foliage and having a lax, extrovert habit of growth.

Somewhere about the middle is the place for other roses, some of the Rugosa varieties. 'Rosaraïe de l'Haÿ', 1.5 m, 5 ft, has wine-red flowers, deepening to purple as they age, and *R. rugosa alba*, at the same height, has pure white flowers and is probably the most strongly scented of all the Rugosas, which, apart from their flowers, are interesting for their characteristic rough, wrinkled foliage. There are many old roses—Cabbage roses, Gallicas, Damasks—which can be mixed in with shrubs in a bed of this sort, and towards one end of a bed in a position where it can be easily picked and smelt, I would include a Moss rose, the common pink moss, *R. centifolia muscosa*, and make room somewhere for another favourite, the Centifolia rose, 'Fantin-Latour', about 1.5 m, 5 ft, with blush-pink full-petalled flowers.

For the front edge, apart from an occasional grey-foliaged shrub, evergreens are *Skimmia japonica* 'Fragrans', rather under 914 mm, 3 ft, having strongly scented white flowers as early as February; and *Salvia lavandulifolia*, grey-green aromatic foliage and bright blue flowers in June (this plant has a tendency to spread forwards from the edge of a bed onto paving). The rock roses are also good for a forward edge: *Helianthemum* 'Supreme', about 152 mm, 6 in, with crimson flowers, and *H.* 'Wisley Primrose', at the same height, with soft yellow flowers; both of these have grey foliage and a procumbent habit of growth. In positions fully exposed to the sun, both lavender and rosemary are very good ever-grey plants. The Dutch lavender, about 610 mm, 2 ft, has markedly grey foliage and soft lavender-blue flowers in July and August. The 'Hidcote' lavender is a smaller plant, about 457 mm, 18 in, with less grey foliage but much darker purplish flowers. Rosemary can grow into quite a large bush but still looks very well at the edge, particularly on a corner. *Rosmarinus officinalis* at 914 mm–1.2 m, 3–4 ft, has lavender-blue flowers in April and May, and makes in time a sprawling bush. Shorter ones, 610 mm, 1–2 ft, are 'Severn Seas' and 'Tuscan Blue'; both have more brilliant blue flowers than the common rosemary. *Viburnum davidii* is stated to have a height of 610 mm, 2 ft, but in my own garden it is getting on for double that, so that after many years it may become a little large for the front, but none the less it is an excellent shrub, with dark evergreen leaves with deeply etched veins. Its white flowers in May are relatively inconspicuous, and so are its blue berries, which never seem to be borne in great numbers. There is a small × *Cistus corbariensis*, about 610 mm, 2 ft, high, grey-foliaged with white flowers between June and August, which like other cistuses needs full exposure to the sun.

Comparatively low deciduous shrubs to plant with the evergreens just referred to are *Philadelphus* 'Manteau d'Hermine', usually not more than about 1·1 m, 3 ft 6 in, unusual in a mock orange, and useful for its white fragrant flowers at high summer. *Potentilla* 'Elizabeth' is another absolutely indispensable shrub to be used whenever possible. In winter its bare twiggy outline is not particularly attractive, but its great virtue is that it produces its pretty canary-yellow flowers in great numbers all through the summer from May till October. It is, in fact, quite as "perpetual" as any rose.

On acid soils there are many calcifuges which can be grown—the following are deciduous. The best of all the deciduous azaleas is the wild (but not native) *A. pontica* (*Rhododendron luteum*), 2.1 m, 7 ft, with very strongly scented yellow flowers in May, and bright autumn foliage. It is a spreading bush and best at a corner of a bed, preferably in light woodland where it will get shade for a part of the day. The Exbury and Knap Hill hybrid azaleas will in time get up to 1.8 m, 6 ft, but take some years to do it. They come in many colours; the nicest are shades of fawn, biscuit and cream, but there are also bright oranges and bright crimson-scarlets.

Japanese maples give very good foliage contrast; *Acer palmatum* 'Dissectum Atropurpureum' is said to be able to reach to 1.8 m, 6 ft, but is exceedingly slow growing; it has finely cut coppery-purple leaves in summer turning scarlet in autumn. Another is *A. palmatum* itself, capable of getting to 4.3 m, 14 ft, after a long time and having some of the brightest autumn colour—nothing glowed more brilliantly at Westonbirt when I was there on the second of November in one year; *Corylopsis spicata*, 1.8 m, 6 ft, but often less, has delicate primrose-yellow scented flowers in March. *Enkianthus campanulatus* 2.1 m, 7 ft, has biscuit-yellow bell-shaped flowers in clusters in May and is of graceful erect growth, elegant when seen above a lower shrub in the foreground; *Fothergilla monticola*,

2.1 m, 7 ft, with white flowers like bottle brushes in April and with fine autumn colour, is perhaps not entirely hardy outside the milder counties; *Hydrangea macrophylla* 'Blue Wave', 1.5 m, 5 ft, and 'Lanarth White', 762 mm, 2 ft 6 in, both flower July to August.

Leading the evergreen calcifuges is a horde of rhododendrons. Some of the cast-iron hardy hybrids are not really so bad as one considers them to be when in jaundiced mood—in fact 'Pink Pearl', when well grown, is a beautiful flower; an old plant 3 m, 10 ft, high on a short leg in a big tub is a real spectacle in May. 'White Pearl' and 'Mother of Pearl' are paler versions and good plants; 'Britannia' and 'Doncaster' are red and 'Letty Edwards' is yellow. In the RHS *Rhododendron Handbook* and in Hillier's *Manual of Trees and Shrubs*, rhododendrons are graded as to hardiness, as follows:

H4 Hardy anywhere in the British Isles.
H3 Hardy in the south and west and along the
        seaboard, and in sheltered gardens inland.
H2 Requiring protection in the most sheltered garden.
H1 Usually only safe in a greenhouse.

All the hardy hybrids so far mentioned are rated H4, but there are one or two others also rated H4 which have more charm: 'Cilpinense', 914 mm, 3 ft, has loose trusses of flowers, white flushed with pink, in March; 'Bow Bells', 762 mm, 2 ft 6 in, pale pink bell-shaped flowers, light green coin-shaped leaves; 'Harvest Moon', 1.8 m, 6 ft, creamy-white; and 'Naomi Stella Maris', buff, shaded lilac-pink, and fragrant. Amongst those rated H3 are 'Bric-à-Brac', 762 mm, 2 ft 6 in, white flowers with chocolate-coloured anthers in March; 'Fusilier', scarlet bell-shaped flowers; 'Loderi King George', up to 6.1 m, 20 ft. This is one of the most beautiful rhododendrons in woodland, excellent in a corner where rides cross, the large flowers pink, soon turning to white. Rhododendrons in some circumstances are good screening plants, and for this purpose are planted 1.2–1.8 m, 4–6 ft, apart, undiluted, but where they are needed to contribute to a general effect in a bed of shrubs they should be well mixed in with deciduous plants and evergreens of less oppressive density.

Some other good calcifuge evergreens are *Kalmia latifolia*, an elegant plant, 1.8 m, 6 ft, wide and spreading, with bright pink flowers in large clusters; *Eucryphia glutinosa*, 3.7 m, 12 ft, has white flowers in July and August, and the larger *E.* 'Nymansay', up to 9.1 m, 30 ft, has scented white cup-shaped flowers in August; *Pieris forrestii* 'Wakehurst', 2.1 m, 7 ft, with cream-coloured flowers, rather like those of lily of the valley, in April, is chiefly planted for its brilliant red young foliage. I doubt if the very studied formal flowers of *Camellia japonica* mix in well in a bed of this kind, but there are camellias of looser habit and with looser flowers also, particularly the *C.* × *williamsii* hybrids such as 'Bow Bells', rose-pink and semi-double, and the justly famous 'Donation', bright pink and semi-double. The very pretty 'Cornish Snow' is a hybrid between *C. cuspidata* and *C. saluenensis*, and has a crowd of white flowers along the branches.

There are some shrubs more suited to what might be called an assembly rather than a thorough-going bed, shrubs which either do not amalgamate well or have so much individuality in their outline that they need space all round them. A position in front of an old wall might be a good one to choose for these. Some deciduous shrubs of this sort are *Viburnum fragrans*, 2.7 m, 9 ft, which has white, pink-tinged flowers, very strongly scented, almost all through the winter from November until well into February; *Magnolia sieboldii*, formerly known as *M. parviflora*, up to 4.6 m, 15 ft, has white open flowers with a central boss of purple stamens; *M.* × *soulangiana*, 6.1 m, 20 ft, and very wide spreading, has large upright chalice-shaped flowers, mainly white but stained with purple at the bases, but this plant does not really come into its own until it reaches some height because the flowers are so large as to be out of scale on a small young plant. *Clerodendron trichotomum*, 3 m, 10 ft, has white very fragrant flowers in September; this seemed to be planted all over the West Country when I made a September tour with the Garden History Society one year. Finally, there are *Hamamelis mollis*, the Chinese witch hazel, 3.7 m, 12 ft, with scented yellow flowers like strips of ribbon from December to February; *Rosa primula*, 2.4 m, 8 ft, primrose yellow to white flowers in May and foliage scented like incense and free on the air, i.e. it is not necessary to crush the leaves to release the scent; and *Viburnum plicatum tomentosum* 'Lanarth', 2.7 m, 9 ft, high and spreading to at least 3 m, 10 ft, which bears white flowers on horizontal tiered branches in May, and is an exceedingly beautiful plant.

Evergreen calcifuges for this so-called assembly could include many varieties of *Camellia japonica*, which grow well against a wall facing north or north-west, and in time can get to 3 m, 10 ft; they flower in March and April: *C. j.* 'Elegans' is a deep peach-pink, anemone form; 'Adolphe Audusson' is deep red showing yellow stamens, semi-double; 'Latifolia' is another semi-double, rose-red; 'Mathotiana Alba', white, large formal double. For a position where it could display its rather drooping, spreading habit of growth, there is 'Lady Clare', semi-double, peach-pink. The size of camellia flowers is getting larger and larger; two that I have noticed, for those who care for such things, are *C. j.* 'Drama Girl' and a *C. reticulata* hybrid, 'Buddha', both having enormous deep pink flowers. *C. reticulata* has been mentioned in Chapter 4. Some of the best known are immensely attractive, tall growing and very good against a wall, varieties such as 'Captain Rawes' and what is now known as the Wild Form being treasures for milder counties.

The mixed border is popular because it needs less skilled and painstaking maintenance than a purely herbaceous border. The intention is to provide as much colour as possible with a high enough proportion of shrubs to restrict the maintenance commitment. It will include a number of herbaceous plants, chiefly to give blue colour and the general density of colour which is difficult to achieve with shrubs alone, and also roses and lilies. The shrub content can include any of those so far referred to with an emphasis on the grey-foliaged *Senecio* and *Phlomis*, the yellow *Hypericum* 'Hidcote' and the yellow *Potentilla* 'Elisabeth'; in a warm climate under a wall, *Myrtus communis*, and, when applicable, such calcifuges as *Kalmia*, *Eucryphia*, and some of the smaller, daintier rhododendrons, but azaleas may be too brassy for this bed. Some midsummer roses will provide bright colours of red, pink, yellow and white. More white, and an entirely different structure, will come from lilies—*Lilium candidum* on alkaline soils and *L. regale* on more acid soils. Blue can come from some of the irises, salvias, delphiniums and campanulas referred to later in this chapter, and early colours, red, pink and white, before the roses come into their own, from peonies. Grey foliage and edging can be drawn from those proposed for herbaceous borders.

In the days when herbaceous borders could be devotedly cared for by the lady of the manor, assisted by an under gardener expressly engaged for this alone, effects of shimmering beauty could be achieved in waves of gentle contoured colours. Now, with the scarcity and high cost of labour, it is difficult to make a success of an all-herbaceous border, but those with a mind to try could start with a restricted vocabulary based on colours, as follows.

YELLOW:

Doronicum caucasicum 'Miss Mason'	305–457 mm, 12–18 in	March/April
Paeonia mlokosewitschii	610 mm, 2 ft	April
Euphorbia polychroma	305–610 mm, 1–2 ft	April/May
Iris 'Buttermere'	914 mm, 3 ft	June
Iris 'Ola Kala'	914 mm, 3 ft	June
Helianthemum 'Wisley Primrose'	152 mm, 6 in	May/June
Oenothera missouriensis	229 mm, 9 in	June/August
Coreopsis grandiflora 'Badengold'	914 mm, 3 ft	July/September
Achillea 'Gold Plate'	1.2–1.5 m, 4–5 ft	July/August
Achillea 'Moonshine'	610 mm, 2 ft	July/August
Verbascum bombyciferum (*V.* 'Broussa')	1.5 m, 5 ft	July/August
(this is a punctuation, spike, plant)		
Rudbeckia 'Herbstsonne'	1.8 m, 6 ft	July/September

WHITE:

Iris 'White City'	1.1 m, 3 ft 6 in	June
Iris 'Cliffs of Dover'	914 mm, 3 ft	June
Paeonia 'Festiva Maxima'	610–762 mm, 2 ft–2 ft 6 in	June
Scabiosa caucasica 'Miss Wilmott'	610 mm, 2 ft	June/October
Campanula persicifolia 'Snowdrift'	914 mm, 3 ft	June/August
Crambe cordifolia	1.8 m, 6 ft	June
Phlox 'White Admiral'	914 mm, 3 ft	July/September
Romneya coulteri	1.5 m, 5 ft	July/October
Anemone × *hybrida* 'Honorine Jobert'	762 mm, 2 ft 6 in	September/October

PINK:

Paeonia lactiflora 'Lady Alexandra Duff'	610–762 mm, 2ft–2 ft 6 in	June
Dianthus 'Cherry Clove'	381–457 mm, 15–18 in	June/July
Monarda didyma 'Croftway Pink'	610–914 mm, 2–3 ft	June/September
Lavatera olbia 'Rosea'	1.5–1.8 m, 5–6 ft	July/October
Phlox 'Dodo Hanbury Forbes'	914 mm, 3 ft	July/September
Sedum spectabile	381 mm, 15 in	August/September
Anemone hupehensis 'September Charm'	762 mm, 2 ft 6 in	August/October
Aster amellus 'Brilliant'	610 mm, 2 ft	August/October

RED:

Helianthemum 'Supreme'	152 mm, 6 in	May/June
Aquilegia 'Crimson Star'	610 mm, 2 ft	May/June
Papaver orientale 'Goliath'	914 mm, 3 ft	May/June
Paeonia lactiflora 'Felix Crousse'	610–762 mm, 2 ft–2 ft 6 in	June
Monarda didyma 'Cambridge Scarlet'	762 mm, 2 ft 6 in	June/September
Lychnis chalcedonica (scarlet)	914 mm, 3 ft	July/August
Lythrum virgatum 'Rose Queen'	914 mm, 3 ft	July/August
Pentstemon 'Garnet'	457 mm, 18 in	July/September

BLUE:

Geranium 'Johnson's Blue'	610 mm, 2 ft	June/August
Iris 'Jane Phillips'	914 mm, 3 ft	June
Iris 'Harbor Blue'	914 mm, 3 ft	June
Iris 'Galilee'	914 mm, 3 ft	June
Rosmarinus 'Severn Seas'	610 mm, 2 ft	May/June
Salvia haematodes	1.1 m, 3 ft 6 in	June
Salvia nemorosa 'Superba'	762 mm, 2 ft 6 in	July/August
Campanula persicifolia 'Telham Beauty'	914 mm, 3 ft	June/August
Campanula poscharskyana	229 mm, 9 in	June/October
Scabiosa caucasica 'Clive Greaves'	610 mm, 2 ft	June/October

Delphinium belladonna 'Wendy'	1.1 m, 3 ft 6 in	July/August
Delphinium 'Blue Nile'	1.7 m, 5 ft 6 in	July/August
Delphinium 'Betty Hay'	1.7 m, 5 ft 6 in	July/August
Salvia uliginosa	1.4 m, 4 ft 6 in	August/October
Aster amellus 'King George'	762 mm, 2 ft 6 in	August/October
Aster × *frikartii* 'Mönch'	762 mm, 2 ft 6 in	August/October

Some of these can be planted in groups of from three to five of each plant to give a recurring rhythm of colour down the border. It is interesting to provide also for a 'continuo' of neutral colours out of which these firm assertive colours shall stand. For this purpose the following lilac/lavender flowers would be useful.

Nepeta × *gigantea* 'Six Hills Giant'	914 mm, 3 ft	June/September
Dianthus 'Lavender Clove'	381–457 mm, 15–18 in	June/July
Phlox 'Cool of the Evening'	914 mm–1.2 m, 3–4 ft	July/September
Campanula lactiflora 'Loddon Anna'	1.2–1.5 m, 4–5 ft	July–August
Delphinium 'Fanfare'	1.8 m, 6 ft	June/August
Salvia turkestanica	914 mm, 3 ft	July/August
Thalictrum delavayanum		
(*T. dipterocarpum*)	1.5 m, 5 ft	June/August
Lavandula 'Hidcote'	305–610 mm, 1–2 ft	July
Lavandula vera	610 mm, 2 ft	July
Phlox 'Toits de Paris'	914 mm, 3 ft	July/September

Grey-foliaged plants, some to stand at the front, others to penetrate into the mass of planting, would be:

Artemisia abrotanum	1.2 m, 4 ft	June/September
Ballota pseudodictamnus	610 mm, 2 ft	June/October; tender
Artemisia absinthium 'Lambrook Silver'	914 mm, 3 ft	June/October; tender
Santolina chamaecyparissus	305–457 mm, 12–18 in	Summer
Onopordon acanthium	1.5 m, 5 ft	July
(this is another punctuation, spike, plant)		

FRONT EDGING:

Nepeta × *faassenii* (*N. mussinii*)	305 mm, 12 in	May/September
Salvia lavandulifolia	229–305 mm, 9–12 in	June
Alchemilla mollis	229 mm, 9 in	June/September
Artemisa lanata	152 mm, 6 in	Summer; tender

Good plants for shade to use in a mixed border are *Euphorbia wulfenii*, perennial and evergreen, up to 1.1 m, 3 ft 6 in, with dark inky-green foliage and yellow flowers. If ever there was a plant for the dark this is one—with me it leans back into the shade of a yew tree, but it is accommodating enough to bear its flowers even better in full light. *Acanthus mollis*, 1.2 m, 4 ft, is upright and stately with hooded flowers appearing pale lilac on account of the bracts. *Hosta sieboldiana* is truly herbaceous, throwing up in June and July glaucous blue-grey foliage when once established, and tubular bell-shaped flowers in August; the best form is 'Elegans'. Much more use can be made of hellebores in shade and in positions facing north and west, in fact a collection of hellebores alone in a bed about 1.2 m, 4 ft, wide under a north-facing wall is a delight. They need a rich soil on the alkaline side of neutral, full of humus and with good water-holding capacity, but good drainage also. *Helleborus niger* is the Christmas rose, up to three white flowers on a stem at Christmastime, about 305 mm, 1 ft, high. *H. viridis*, about 305 mm, 1 ft, high, has half-drooping flowers made up of bright green petal-like sepals; it is a rare native but has been taken into nurserymen's catalogues, as also has *H. foetidus*, a stouter, taller plant, about 610 mm, 2 ft, high, with bell-shaped flowers in panicles; pale green with grey-purple rims, it has deeply cut dark green leaves. Another is *H. corsicus* (*H. lividus corsicus*), less hardy than the other two and needing a sheltered position. It grows to 610 mm, 2 ft, with glaucous, spiny leaves and grey-green flowers. Hellebores have been too much neglected; once seen they become indispensable plants, evergreen, shade-tolerant, perfect in positions looking to the north at the edge of a bed of shrubs. The firm called The Plantsmen of Holwell (Sherborne, Dorset), have made a speciality of hellebores and have many specially selected strains of *H. orientalis*, the Lenten rose.

Lilies of the valley—*muguets*, which are carried through the, for once, quiet streets of Paris on the first of May—are lovers of shade, preferably of the shade of high branches, and also of moist, humus-laden soils. They take a year or more to settle down after planting, but after that they spread persistently into gravel paths at the edge of borders. *Epimedium grandiflorum* is about 305 mm, 1 ft, high and has pink flowers in May, the foliage turning to red in the autumn. *Astrantia major*, 610 mm, 2 ft, has considerable quiet charm, needing to be studied to appreciate its greenish-white flowers 305 mm, 1 ft, high in June and July.

Some ferns tolerate shade well and give a pleasant softening to hard angles and dark corners. *Osmunda regalis*, the royal fern, is deciduous; its fronds will grow to 610 mm–1.8 m, 2–6 ft, tall and have a width of 305–914 mm, 1–3 ft. It needs a position where water is readily available at the roots. *Blechnum spicant*, the hard fern, is evergreen, and the fronds are of two different kinds; the fertile ones rise from the centre of the plant to a height of as much as 610 mm, 2 ft, while the outer fronds are shorter and become horizontal. This fern needs a peaty acid soil and resents being watered with hard tap water. *Phyllitis scolopendrium* is the hart's-tongue fern: it is also evergreen, and its long strap-like fronds, sometimes frilled, are familiar in cool, damp sunken lanes in the West Country and Ireland.

The more substantial climbing and wall shrubs, *Magnolia grandiflora*, *Wistaria* and others, have been included in foundation planting. For consideration now among the *Clematis*, with their very large coloured sepals, are 'Lasurstern', deep lavender-blue with yellow stamens, flowering in May and June; 'Henryi', very large creamy-white, flowering in May and June; and the popular 'Nelly Moser', pale mauve-pink with a crimson central bar. 'Ville de Lyon' is described as red but in fact it is, with me at any rate, well endowed with purple. *C. armandii*, evergreen with white flowers, needs a warm sunny wall; it tends to produce its flowers at the top of the plant unless the side growths are trained outwards. 'Virgin's Bower' is *C. montana*, the flowers of the variety 'Rubens' are pale pink, and the plant is quicker-growing even than the type. These *Clematis* are pre-eminently the plants for porches and arbours. Not unlike *Clematis* in some ways is the passion flower, *Passiflora caerulea*, the variety 'Constance Elliott' with ivory-white flowers being particularly beautiful. Passion flowers need a warm southern wall, preferably in a mild district. The native honeysuckle is *Lonicera periclymenum*, a deciduous climber with reddish-purple scented flowers in the latter part of the summer. An evergreen honeysuckle is *L. japonica* 'Halliana', exceedingly vigorous even on a northern aspect. *L. tragophylla* is not scented, but has large fawn-yellow flowers in June and July, and has the great virtue of flourishing in deep shade. Some of the vines have been considered in relation to pergolas, but not the old Virginia creeper, *Par-*

thenocissus quinquefolia, which can get to almost unimagined heights up unpromising brick walls. It takes at least two years to settle down, but when it has done this it begins to climb and cling in earnest.

Climbing roses which know their business and can get to 9.1 m, 30 ft, or more include the old 'Gloire de Dijon', with buff-coloured flattish flowers, and 'Madame Alfred Carrière', almost white. Both of these will do well on a north wall, and so also will 'Mermaid', single-flowered, primrose-yellow with shiny, evergreen-looking (but not quite) foliage. Nowadays there are many recurrent roses classified as being climbing, but few of them reach above 3 m, 10 ft; 'Altissimo' has large crimson single flowers, 'Schoolgirl' has double apricot-coloured flowers. Non-recurrent versions are 'Albertine', a very vigorous climber with salmon-pink flowers, sweetly scented, and 'Emily Gray', with deep chamois-yellow flowers and glossy dark green foliage.

The best climbing plants for deep shade are ivies, such as the common ivy, *Hedera helix*, or *H. colchica dentata*, with large leaves.

In spite of the great variety offered by bulb growers, it is surprising how seldom bulbous plants are included in planting plans. Daffodils for naturalizing and not too far away from the house, planted in drifts in grass, could be one or more of the enchanting *N. cyclamineus* hybrids: 'Charity May', all yellow; 'Dove Wings', with lemon-yellow cup and white perianth; and 'Jenny', whose crown is pale lemon-yellow when the flower opens, but soon turns to white to match the perianth. Taller ones to be seen from farther away, and still planted in drifts in grass, are 'Carlton', a good solid yellow; 'Polindra', with large lemon-yellow flowers; 'Beersheba', pure white; and 'Carbineer', yellow and orange. Among the crocuses are *C. chrysanthus* 'Blue Bird', 'Snow Bunting' and the bronze-yellow 'E. A. Bowles'. The small single tulips, *Tulipa praestans*, flower towards the end of March, and often bear at least two flowers to each stem, and can be naturalized, as also can *T. kauffmanniana* hybrids. The best tulips for planting close to the house are the lily-flowered ones, 'China Pink', 'White Triumphator', 'Golden Duchess', whose names explain their colours, and 'Aladdin', which is bright crimson. For tulips farther away from the house, some of the opulent Darwin hybrids are very impressive: 'Golden Springtime', a buff-yellow, and 'Holland's Glory', bright scarlet. The really unforgettable tulip is *T. fosteriana* 'Red Emperor', with flame-scarlet flowers opening flat in oriental ecstasy.

Scent near the house and under the windows can be brought in spring by wallflowers, winter pansies and, in a gentle subdued way, polyanthuses. In summer the best scent of all comes from the old tobacco plant, *Nicotiana affinis*, well supported in daytime by heliotrope ("Cherry Pie"), stocks for the early part of the summer, night-scented stocks and pansies.

The subject of ground cover has been written of with much insight and feeling by Graham Thomas in his *Plants for Ground-Cover*, which is the classic work on the subject. The concept is popular because it can greatly reduce time spent on weeding but it can be a disappointing exercise unless the plants used are themselves attractive and interesting.

In the open the best ground cover is grass, all the better if some of it, a wide band of uneven width perhaps, at one side, is kept longer than the main part of a lawn. In this longer grass can be planted small bulbs such as winter aconites, snowdrops, crocuses, dog's-tooth violets and small daffodils, but over areas where daffodils are planted the grass cannot be mown at all until the foliage has died down at the end of June, or the plants will be killed by defoliation.

Whole lawns were once made of camomile and thrashed to bring out the pleasant aromatic smell. It is a laborious process now because individual little plants have to be put in about 51 mm, 2 in, apart and the spaces between kept weeded by hand until the camomile grows together. The plant is *Anthemis nobilis*, of which there is a selected strain called 'Treneague', which is shorter growing than the common one and does not produce flowers.

For ground cover in the open, heather is often planted, the plants going in at 457 mm, 18 in, apart. Summer-flowering heathers are varieties of *Erica vagans*, the Cornish heath, *E. cinerea*, Scotch or bell heather, or *E. tetralix*, the cross-leaved heath; and *Calluna vulgaris*, ling or English heath. These all need acid peaty soils. Winter- and spring-flowering heaths such as *Erica carnea* and *E.* × *darleyensis* will succeed quite well on alkaline soil if it is well supplied with humus. I have an irrational prejudice against planting heathers inside a garden even if the garden is under a hillside covered with heather, for it always seems to me to be a plant needing limitless acres of freedom and ill at ease inside the garden enclosure, while to plant heather inside a garden which is miles away from naturally growing heather is a piece of ecological insensitiveness.

Little carpeting herbaceous plants of about 51 mm, 2 in, high for open situations are 'Creeping Jenny', *Lysimachia nummularia*, with small yellow flowers; bugle, *Ajuga reptans*, of which there are purple and white and green variegated versions; and the spitefully named *Cotula squalida*, also with very small green-yellow flowers. A small shrub 102 mm, 4 in, useful for being evergreen, is *Cotoneaster dammeri*, widespreading and with red berries. One of the most attractive and useful of all ground-cover plants is the wild strawberry, 'Fraise de Bois', *Fragaria vesca* 'Semperflorens', much too little seen. It will grow quite contentedly in moderate shade and the outer edges of woodlands. About 229 mm, 9 in, high, it bears delicious little-finger-nail sized strawberries and is triumphantly evergreen. In shade under trees the best plant is the Irish ivy, *Hedera helix* 'Hibernica', which has very large shiny green leaves making a beautiful rippling carpet, 305 mm, 1 ft, of light and shade in the woods, glinting in shafts of sunlight through the trees. There are many fancy ivies, variegated and small leaved, to touch the whimsical hearts of decorators and flower arrangers. The lesser periwinkle, *Vinca minor*, will reach to 203 mm, 8 in, and comes plain in green with blue flowers, or fancy with variegated foliage and sometimes also with white flowers. The larger plant, *V. major*, is much coarser, running a great deal to long untidy shoots. The little herbaceous plant sweet woodruff, *Asperula odorata*, 152 mm, 6 in, has white flowers and rich green-coloured leaves that are fragrant when they fade in the autumn.

I think that the compulsion to plant something wherever there is a bare piece of ground is sometimes to be resisted. In the woods it is natural and fitting to see the woodland floor brown with fallen leaves. In the open, brown earth seen from time to time and ready for planting is fecund and looks like business (but it is better to cover it with a layer of compost, peat or leaf soil to protect it from damage from hot sun or extreme cold).

Chapter 8

A Kitchen Garden

Self-sufficiency and independence in a garden extend naturally from collecting one's own rainwater and making compost to growing one's own fruit and vegetables. Some of the designs in Chapter 2 show spaces for these.

A kitchen garden, more than a garden of flowers, needs good conditions of shelter, aspect and light, fertility, water supply and drainage because most vegetables are sown or planted and harvested within the short space of a single summer.

Those who have seen small cottage gardens in the west country sloping sharply down to the Tamar or the Yealm will recognize immediately the perfect conditions—shelter on three sides gathering all the available sun, well drained, in a mild climate with black soil of perfect texture and fertility; none the less, vegetables and herbs can still be produced on much less promising pieces of ground provided that it is well prepared.

At the outset of the Second World War the then Ministry of Agriculture began its imaginative and successful "Dig for Victory" campaign directly encouraged by a number of exemplary leaflets. On the back of the first of these was printed:

> Every endeavour must be made to . . . produce the greatest volume of food of which this fertile Island is capable. . . .
>
> *Mr Winston Churchill*
> *in the House of Commons*
> *November 5th, 1940.*

In this same first leaflet a cropping plan was worked out to produce a sequence of vegetables for an average houehold. The plot measured 27.3 m by 9.1 m, 90 ft by 30 ft, 250 m², 300 sq. yds. This is the same size as the larger of the two model vegetable gardens laid out at the Royal Horticultural Society's gardens at Wisley in Surrey, and it is also the accepted size of an allotment garden. The cropping plan for both of these is similar and, if followed conscientiously, will produce a sound, relatively pest- and disease-free, if rather limited, supply of vegetables throughout most of the year. Since our national health was so good in war time, it is worth taking these as a basis for present-day vegetable growing. Epicures who are not content without asparagus, globe artichokes and seakale, which occupy the same ground for several years, or such rarefied delights as cardoons, chicory, Jerusalem artichokes, salsify, scorzonera, tomatoes, courgettes, cucumbers, green peppers and melons will need more ground and also a greenhouse and frames.

These ways of using glass to retain heat, whether from the sun or from electric or other heating inside, are some of the refinements of gardening and in making a plan for a kitchen garden space should if possible be allowed for them. Much entertainment and instruction and a fair amount of production also can be obtained from a greenhouse as small as 2.4 m by 1.8 m, 8 ft by 6 ft. A size of 3.7 m by 2.4 m, 12 ft by 8 ft, gives more scope, and what might be regarded as a full-sized amateur greenhouse 6.1 m by 3 m, 20 ft by 10 ft, makes it possible to produce substantial quantities of tomatoes, green peppers, etc. Span-roof greenhouses standing in the open usually run north and south: lean-to and three-quarter span greenhouses must face south.

Within the greenhouse compound space can be allowed for one or more frames, a space also for other stores, of glass, PVC or polythene used with cloches, a tool shed and a potting shed, preferably with the chill taken off by a single length of tubular electric heating, and certainly with electric light inside; and possibly a fruit store.

If fruit is to be grown it would be most convenient to keep all bush fruit together within a fruit cage for protection from birds; in here too could be grown apples and pears on dwarfing stocks as cordons, espaliers or dwarf pyramids, all three of which can be kept down to 1.8 m, 6 ft, not only to enable them to be cultivated inside the fruit cage but also because at this height they can be attended to, pruned and picked easily without ladders. Apples and pears are considered in Chapter 10. Other fruit grown on walls, usually fan-trained 6.1 m, 20 ft, apart, are peaches, nectarines, cherries (Morello cherries on north facing walls), plums and figs. In this kitchen garden area, space can be made for loam, which is brought in in thick turfs, stacked upside-down for from three to six months and then chopped down as required for potting; space also for bales of peat and a pen for litter, much referred to in old gardening books and very valuable to give protection against cold winters and excessive transpiration, working in the same way as cellular string vests in preserving micro-atmospheres. It can consist of dried autumn bracken or straw, or old leaves, and must be kept dry and loose, tossed with a pitch-fork to stop it bedding down and beginning to make compost, which is not wanted in this case. Space is also needed for compost bins for making humus as suggested in Appendix B, and alongside these a burning ground (away from the branches of trees), for swift disposal of coarse stems and branches which would take too long to be reduced in a compost heap, and some spare ground (see Postscript 1). This corner of the garden becomes as it were the power house. It will not be pretty but it may be possible to screen most of it from other parts of the garden, as is suggested in some of the specimen plans, but it is basic and essential, the private joy of gardeners who really mean business. The path leading to it should be firmly edged with concrete edging or wood boards and clear of overhanging branches.

An imaginative way with a small plot of land is to make it all into a decorative kitchen garden, after the manner of a French *potager*. Ways of doing this, indicated in Chapter 2, show that it is perfectly possible to make an attractive garden full of flowers with grass wide enough to sun-bathe on and a goldfish pool and fountain, wall-trained fruit trees on either side, and still produce enough vegetables to feed an ordinary household.

Chapter 9

Orchards

Fruit trees on dwarfing stocks trained as cordons, espaliers and dwarf pyramids can be controlled at 1.8 m, 6 ft, high and cultivated within a fruit cage. This is a course that will be followed by those who want good-quality fruit with a minimum of maintenance, because trees no more than 1.8 m, 6 ft, can be pruned, if necessary sprayed, and the fruit picked without recourse to more than a soapbox to stand on, whereas taller trees, large bushes and standards are difficult to reach up into and need ladders.

Apple and pear trees constitute a very large subject which can only be briefly summarized here. Those who wish to study it in depth could consult one of the specialized books listed in the Bibliography, page 147.

The spacings of apples and pear trees on dwarfing stocks are:

Cordons, 610 mm, 2 ft, apart.
Espaliers between 4.6 m and 6.1 m, 15 ft and 20 ft, depending on the variety and the stock upon which it has been budded.
Dwarf pyramids, 1.2 m, 4 ft, apart.

The following, not budded onto dwarfing stocks:

Bushes, 3.7–9.1 m, 12–30 ft, apart.
Standards, 9.1–12.2 m, 30–40 ft, apart.

Cordons need to be trained against a framework of usually three rows of wires at equal distances apart, finishing no more than 1.8 m, 6 ft, above ground if the trees are to be cultivated within a fruit enclosure of that height. If more than one row is to be cultivated the rows ought to be 1.8 m, 6 ft, apart. Espaliers are trained in the same way, and can look very attractive if planted alongside kitchen garden paths, although in such positions it may be impossible to give them the protection of a fruit net. Dwarf pyramids, bushes and standards all require stout stakes.

The selection of varieties of apples and pears is governed by personal preference, the season of maturity and the choice of pollinators to ensure fertilization of the blossom.

In the following varieties of apples, the letters A to D indicate the time of flowering of the blossom because each variety chosen must have at least one other variety flowering at about the same time to secure pollination. The months referred to are those in which the fruit is ripe for eating or cooking.

EATING APPLES
'James Grieve'. C. September to October. It should be eaten more or less off the tree because it does not store well. A recognized pollinator for 'Cox's Orange Pippin'.

106

'Ellison's Orange'. D. September to October. This is fairly self-fertile and if only one apple tree is to be planted it would be the best one to choose. Pollinated by 'Orleans Reinette', 'Duke of Devonshire' and the cooking apple 'Lane's Prince Albert'.

'Egremont Russet'. B. October to November. This apple is not only scab-resistant but of very good flavour, although it does not store well. Pollinated by 'Margil' and 'Ribston Pippin'.

'Margil'. B. October to January. Small pale yellow, of excellent flavour. Pollinates with 'Egremont Russet'.

'Blenheim Orange'. C. November to January. A dual-purpose apple, very good for both dessert and cooking. Stores well. Edward Bunyard wrote of it in 1933: '. . . the Blenheim flavour . . . a warm aroma which is to my taste the real apple gust; in fact, I take the Blenheim as a test case. The man who cannot appreciate a Blenheim has not come to years of gustatory discretion, he probably drinks sparkling Muscatelle.' 'Blenheim Orange' is one of the comparatively few varieties known as triploids, in which the arrangement of the chromosomes makes its own pollen useless for fertilizing other varieties. It therefore requires two diploid varieties flowering at the same time for pollination of its own blossom (two being required because while one of these auxiliaries will provide pollen for the 'Blenheim', the other auxiliary is needed to pollinate the first auxiliary, which 'Blenheim' cannot do). Two of those mentioned in this short list that will pollinate 'Blenheim' are 'James Grieve' and 'Ashmead's Kernel'. 'Blenheim' is suitable as standard, bush or espalier but not cordon or dwarf pyramid.

'Cox's Orange Pippin'. C. November to January. This is the best-known of all eating apples but it is by no means a universal choice. It is susceptible to both scab and canker and must have good deep soil, will not thrive on clay and also needs a warmer position than many other apples. It is pollinated by 'James Grieve' and 'Ashmead's Kernel'.

'Ribston Pippin'. B. November to January. A delicious apple, but another triploid, needing from this list both 'Egremont Russet' and 'Margil'.

'Ashmead's Kernel'. C. December to January. This is a scab-resistant apple of excellent flavour but not a heavy cropper. Pollinated by 'James Grieve' and 'Cox's Orange Pippin'.

'Orleans Reinette'. D. December to January. Possibly the best-flavoured apple. Crops well and stores well. Edward Bunyard (1933) wrote of it: 'Its brown red flesh and glowing gold . . . suggest that if Rembrandt had painted a fruit piece he would have chosen this apple. In the rich golden flesh there is a hint of the Ribston flavour, much of the Blenheim nuttiness and an admirable balance of acidity and sweetness which combine, in my opinion, to make the best apple grown in western Europe.' It is pollinated by 'Duke of Devonshire', 'Ellison's Orange' and the cooking apple 'Lane's Prince Albert'.

'Duke of Devonshire'. D. November to March. This is scab-resistant and of good flavour, cropping well and storing well. Pollinated by 'Ellison's Orange' and 'Orleans Reinette'.

COOKING APPLES

'Early Victoria'. C. July to August. To be cooked more or less off the tree as it does not store well. Pollinated by 'James Grieve', 'Ashmead's Kernel' and 'Cox's Orange Pippin', all dessert apples.

'Lord Derby'. E. November to January. Very large, cooks red, late flowering. Pollinated by 'Royal Jubilee'.

'Royal Jubilee'. E. October to December. A large apple with sub-acid flavour, crops well and stores well. Pollinated by 'Lord Derby'.

'Bramley's Seedling'. C. November to March. The best-known of all cooking apples, but it is another triploid and needs two pollinators, which could be 'Early Victoria' and the eaters 'James Grieve' or 'Ashmead's Kernel'.

'Lane's Prince Albert'. D. November to April. A very large apple, juicy and sharp, crops well and stores well. It is scab resistant. Pollinated by the eating apples 'Orleans Reinette', 'Ellison's Orange' and 'Duke of Devonshire'.

PEARS

Pears also are supplied by nurserymen trained as cordons, espaliers, dwarf pyramids, bushes or standards and are planted at the same distances apart as apples except for espaliers, which need be no farther apart than 4.6 m, 15 ft. Like apples, most pears require pollinators but the matter is more complicated in that there are incompatible groups. The following is a selection of eating pears.

'Jargonelle'. C. August. This earliest pear should be eaten more or less from the tree. It is a triploid and would be pollinated by 'Beurré Superfin', 'Joséphine de Malines' and 'Olivier de Serres'.

'Williams Bon Chrétien'. C. September. Pollinated by 'Olivier de Serres', 'Beurré Superfin'.

'Beurré Hardy'. D. October. Pollinated by 'Doyenné du Comice', 'Glou morceau' and 'Beurré Superfin'.

'Beurré Superfin'. C. October. According to Bunyard (1933) one of the half-dozen best pears. Pollinated by 'Joséphine de Malines' and 'Olivier de Serres'.

'Doyenné du Comice'. D. November. To pick in October and store. This is the pear of all pears. Pollinated by 'Beurré Hardy' and 'Glou morceau'.

'Glou morceau'. D. December to January. To pick in late October. Of good flavour, the best pollinator for 'Doyenné du Comice', itself pollinated by 'Doyenné du Comice' and also 'Beurré Hardy'.

'Joséphine de Malines'. C. December to January. Pollinated by 'Olivier de Serres'.

'Olivier de Serres'. C. February to March. Roundish pear perhaps best grown on a wall. Pollinated by 'Joséphine de Malines' and 'Beurré Superfin'.

Chapter 10

Fences and Gates

Besides defining boundaries, fences serve at least two other purposes—one to give physical protection from large animals and the other to provide degrees of privacy. What might be thought of as a classic fence to keep out cattle is the familiar post and rail, the perfect traditional country fence which can be of almost any height from about 1.1 m, 3 ft 6 in, up to 1.2 m, 4 ft, with three or four rails fixed to posts, usually 1.8 m, 6 ft, apart. The posts can be mortised to receive the rails or the rails can be butt-jointed and nailed to the posts. The rails are about 3.7 m, 12 ft, long spanning three posts. The posts are 76 mm by 102 mm, 3 in by 4 in, in section and the rails 38 mm by 88 mm, 1½ in by 3½ in. The tops of the posts must be weathered, that is, given a slope from front to back to allow rainwater to run off and not lie on the tops and rot them. The best and most durable material is oak or other hard wood such as sweet chestnut or western red cedar, but post and rail fences are now commonly made in soft wood, treated with creosote or Solignum or other preservative. Soft wood is not so long-lasting as oak, the posts tending to rot at ground level, but when this happens the life of the fence can be prolonged by fixing wood or concrete spurs at the base of the defective posts and bolting them through.

In modern jargon post and rail may be referred to as 'see-through' fences because they give no visual screening (but on that very account may be the best to choose when they allow a view through them into the country beyond). The chief of the other 'see-through' barriers are iron railings; the simplest of these are what were known as continuous wrought-iron fencing, or park fencing, ranging from 1 m, 3 ft 4 in, up to as much as 1.8 m, 6 ft, to keep out deer. There are also iron cattle hurdles usually in lengths of 1.8 m, 6 ft, which can be put together in any desired length.

Gardens generally call for more developed metal railings, often fences on top of low walls about 762 mm, 2 ft 6 in, high. These are more suited to gardens in towns, and even in villages, than to open country. Designs for these are very numerous; the most important quality they should have is that of massiveness and strength, which remind us once again that out of doors, in gardens and in the country also, the scale of such things as railings, fences and garden furniture is much larger and coarser in section than would be acceptable indoors—for instance elegant eighteenth-century dining-room chairs look entirely out of place outside on a garden terrace. This quality of strength is evident in the beautiful Spanish *rejas* used as grilles in front of windows and also at intervals in walls to let light into gardens and, incidentally, to throw shadows on to the pathway outside. The railings should always be dark in colour, black or what I believe is known as ordnance blue. There is scope for spearheads to be gilded but white painted railings, although well-intentioned, too often fail to please.

Fences that in addition to giving physical protection against smaller animals also provide a fair degree of visual screening are the white painted picket, or palisade, wooden fence; these are often made with rounded tops but are much more attractive when the tops are pointed. They look particularly charming on the boundaries of gardens giving onto a common. They can be supplied in pine wood as kits, to be assembled and painted white by the purchaser himself. These picket fences are usually best at a height not greater than 1.4 m, 4 ft 6 in, high. If white paling fence is required above this height it is better with perfectly flat, as though sawn off, tops and the pales closer together. Flat-top fences of this kind are being made in synthetic materials such as PVC, often unfortunately with small caps, arch-looking and out of scale, but apart from this the fact that they are a fake can be recognized from a quarter of a mile away.

In recent years a fashion grew up for what is sometimes known as ranch fencing—wide horizontal white planks fixed to white posts. It was taken up with such alacrity that it became a part of the inevitable furniture of every garage and as a result its coarse unimaginative character seems to have imprinted itself on the mind deeply enough to make it immediately repugnant in gardens—good as it probably is when applied to real ranches in the rolling prairies of the American continent. The most attractive of all the white painted fences is what I know as Cornish fencing, because I have seen it there and, in fact, had it copied. The slender upright wooden bars are set diagonally in the rails (Pl. 19).

Leaving now the 'see-through' or partly 'see-through' fences, by far the best solid visual barrier is that given by walls—brick, brick and flint, the natural stone of the locality, dry walls or cob walls by the sea, but for most people today these are too expensive, except for short runs, and usually in town gardens. Instead, close-boarded wooden paling fences are used, which can be of almost any height. The vertical palings overlap and give complete visual screening. They are fitted with horizontal gravel boards and fixed, traditionally, to oak posts, but often now concrete posts are used instead of oak, giving an institutional look to the fencing.

The least satisfactory is the cheap 'interplat' or 'interwoven' fencing made of soft woods treated with a preservative, too often fitted between posts too small in scale, often projecting above the line of the top rail and surmounted by feeble little timber caps. If really stringent economy dictates the necessity for using this type of fencing the projecting tops of the posts can be sawn off to a slope and a quick growing hedge planted on the sunny side to take over as soon as possible. The same principle can be applied to building developers' chain-link wire fencing by, in this case, planting privet in front of it to put on height as rapidly as possible and conceal the netting.

Mention of hedges is a reminder that in practically all cases the best barrier is a live hedge which, if properly pruned and looked after with supplies of fertilizer and water, is permanent and does not rot or get blown down.

Gates can often follow the pattern of fences, in the case of white-painted picket fences for instance and in the case of some railings. Here the quality of massiveness is important; thin flimsy wrought-iron or welded metal gates, now so commonly made and supplied, have a temporary, shanty-town suggestion about them. The commonest 'see-through' gate is an ordinary field gate 2.7 or 3 m, 9 or 10 ft, wide with or without a hand gate alongside it. Double hunting gates each 1.2 m, 4 ft, wide are also seen, and the advantage of these is that each gate is only half the length of a large field gate, putting less strain on hinges and fixings. Their appearance is attractive but a disadvantage is the fact that two gates instead of one have to be opened and secured to get a car through. Refined versions of field gates and hunting gates are seen in great variety, painted white.

Solid gates not only look out of place but in some way also suggest that inside there is something to hide, as though Sherlock Holmes and Watson might appear at any moment in a hansom to investigate a crime in Clapham or Wimbledon. Another point to remember about solid gates is that they present very considerable windage and when, after some years, the posts or the hinges sink and the central fixing becomes loose they can swing and batter dementingly in a gale.

When there is a landscape prospect beyond the garden a ha-ha gives the best of all possible worlds. Much was made of this in the eighteenth century, when it was probably first developed by Bridgeman. A ha-ha is constructed by making a vertical face on the home side retained by a wall of brick, concrete or stone or old railway sleepers, 1.2–1.5 m, 4–5 ft, high and from the base of the wall grading up the ground into the field, thereby making it impossible for cows or horses to jump out of the ditch up to the top of the wall. A diagram showing the construction of a ha-ha is shown in Appendix E. The ditch at the bottom will need to be drained; it can be given a gentle fall (but of course the top of the wall must remain level), and arranged to run into an outlet laid to lower ground or to a sump whose bottom is gravel or chalk. If this were not done the bottom of the ha-ha would partly fill up with water during the winter, possibly drown lambs and certainly become a stagnant ditch with no outlet. The charm of a ha-ha is that it gives an uninterrupted view into the landscape, creating the illusion that the garden stretches out indefinitely and the trees in the park are a part of the garden.

There are British Standards for fencing, noted in Appendix H.

Chapter 11

Ornament

One tends at first to shy away from ornaments through an instinctive feeling that the garden should be conceived as an integral whole and stand on its own feet for better or worse without gratuitous decoration. Nevertheless, statues, urns and vases have great value in providing contrast, that quickening juxtaposition of organic and inanimate.

There is a distinction between urns and vases. Urns were essentially lidded vessels containing ashes of the dead and were made of earthenware or metal, but in later years when used for decoration, tended to be broadly spherical with closed tops. In this form urns are valuable to accentuate the design, at the crossings of paths for instance or in positions where they close vistas.

By contrast vases are open-topped vessels first intended to hold water and wine and later used as decorations in their own right, although they really only come into their own when they hold plants whose stems and foliage sweep downwards, to make a figured pattern against their surface. Permanent plants for this purpose could be some of the ivies, what might be thought of as fancy kinds—'Glacier', with its silvered grey-white margined leaves, or 'Chicago', with dark green leaves spattered with bronze (more robust ivies like the Irish ivy would be too vigorous). Ivy would persist throughout a whole year and need minimal pruning and only initial tying down. For the summer only, vases can be planted with scented-leaf geraniums; *Pelargonium tomentosum*, whose large, hairy, friendly leaves smell strongly of peppermint when pressed, or *P.* 'Clorinda', which for a scented geranium has very large flowers, cerise in colour, and whose leaves have a typical rose-geranium scent when pinched.

The placing of urns and vases brings to mind again the contrast between height and space. Both of them can be stood on piers or plinths so that they are a good metre, rather more than 3 ft, above eye level. This same principle can be applied to statues, life-sized or above, on plinths; and also to herms, head and shoulder busts of human or god-like figures, usually of Hermes, upon tall plinths. Pools on terraces at ground level, even if they have shallow raised moulded copings, still contribute to the dimension of space; and terracotta or other ornamental pots at 457 mm, 18 in, will not compromise the contrast if they are placed to 'read' with the house. It would be hard to do without such plants as bay trees, or in the summer, orange trees in Versailles *caisses*, but these too should be placed near and within the influence of a house. It is the lower objects, such as sundials, bird-baths and, regrettably, staddle stones, that need the greatest care and consideration in their placing; they will compete less in their difficult dimensions if they 'read' with something taller—for example sundials against a tall yew hedge, instead of marooned in open space.

Some of these difficult middle-height elements can be turned through 90

16. Pergola at Les Bois de Moutiers, Normandy. The house was designed by Sir Edwin Lutyens, who also collaborated with Gertrude Jekyll. In the design of the garden the ascending short flights of steps alleviate the rather heavy-handed treatment characteristic of Lutyens's pergolas.

17. Pergola with tapering rounded columns at the Villa Musée, Île de France. This has an air of classic lightness lacking in that shown in plate 16.

18. 'Jack-and-Jill' walling in Cornwall.

19. 'Cornish' fencing with diagonally placed vertical rails, painted white.

20. Picket or palisade fence in white-painted wood.

21. Practical single hunting and handgate, painted white.

22. Simple white-painted double hunting gate.

23. A white obelisk; an example of the value of contrast between artefact and organic.

24. Bronze statue of Queen Victoria's dog Bosco at Frogmore.

25. Draped reclining figure by Henry Moore in a landscape designed by Lanning Roper.

26. Bronze horse by Elizabeth Frink, in a landscape.

27. Twinned elms near Chilton Foliat. The photograph was taken in spring, as the leaves began to unfold.

28 Radiating steps giving a generous spreading descent from the front courtyard to the garden at a lower level; Buckhurst Park.

29. More of a tunnel than a pleached alley of hornbeams. It runs along one end of a large *potager*, usefully productive and beautiful also with flowers, at Great Bedwyn.

30. Brick steps showing block construction, the riser being flush with the tread above; Great Bedwyn.

31. *Rosa filipes* 'Kiftsgate' and *Rosa brunonii* 'La Mortola' over the gateway at Croft Castle. Such a position is one of the best that could be chosen for these very vigorous roses. The fashion of making them grow into and through other trees dead or alive is silly and unfortunate. In this case the white and creamy-white flowers of these roses are seen to perfection against the stone walls.

32. 'March Sunshine' daffodils naturalized in grass in the garden described on pages 48 and 49.

degrees and put on walls. Sundials, for example, are very useful to fill in blank spaces between windows and can be much larger than they would be if standing on the ground. Wall fountains, arched jets of water pouring placidly from the twisted lips of grotesque masks, are more in scale with very small courtyards than conventional fountains at ground level.

There is a great variety of statues and smaller figures which, although made of concrete, are convincing copies of Florentine and other classical pieces, but the days when their originals were thrown off like sparks of renaissance genius are long past and today it would seem to be more fitting to look for artefacts of our own time. For those with substantial resources at their disposal the works of Henry Moore (see Pl. 25) and, in a different genre, of Elizabeth Frink (see Pl. 26), can be brought into a garden with immense significance.

The word pergola comes from the Latin through Italian and means a covered walk framed with growing plants. Pergolas are delicious in the hot climates of Mediterranean countries, to pace slowly along in a tussore suit and panama hat. The essentials of construction are a framework supported on piers, usually 2.4 m, 8 ft, high or more. In Italy these piers are generally round in section; one particularly attractive pergola at Amalfi has (or had) such pillars of rough rubble coarsely plastered over, tapering a little from bottom to top, perfectly plain, supporting a horizontal grid of poles. Sometimes these piers are much more elaborately designed in the form of classic Doric columns (they can now be bought ready-made in fibre glass). In this country some pergolas have received heavy-handed treatment, not least by Sir Edwin Lutyens, the piers square in section, not tapering, and sometimes even built with projecting courses of slate or tile at intervals, thereby destroying the whole sense of smooth ascent which such piers must surely have. A pergola of white classic columns could end appropriately in a peristyle of the same columns round a paved area with perhaps a compass-rose incised on it, but apart from this it seems to me that pergolas made today would be less obtrusive if they ran alongside a wall, that is, a single row of columns with the cross members bonded into the wall of the house, rather than left to go zig-zagging uncertainly across a garden showing off their horrid little thin York-stone courses.

In general I feel that the least should be made of the structure and the most of the plants. Pergolas were designed primarily for vines, to give textured, dappled shade in hot weather, and vines are still the most fitting plants. 'Golden Chasselas' and 'Madeleine Royale' will do very well, and in some years bear grapes which are beautiful to behold and give a great sense of mellow fruitfulness. Whether the grapes will ripen enough to make wine depends on how successfully wasps and mildew can be kept at bay and also on there being fairly continuous warm autumn sunshine. Another exceedingly decorative vine is *Vitis coignetiae*, which has truly enormous leaves as much as 305 mm, 1 ft, across that turn to a gorgeous coppery crimson in autumn. Apart from these, any climbing plants can be tied to the posts of a pergola but the essence of the process is that they should be vigorous enough to get to the top of the pillars and to be trained and tied horizontally along the supporting poles to make a true canopy. Roses which will only attain 3 m, 10 ft, with difficulty are unlikely to accomplish this, and I wonder also whether even taller climbing roses with their comparatively small flowers and small-scale foliage are really suited to pergolas. *Wistaria*, on the other hand, having much larger pinnate leaves and long racemes of flowers not unlike the shape of bunches of grapes hanging down, is very fitting. *Magnolia grandiflora* might also be a good plant to use but is better in really hot

113

climates where the close cover given by its large leaves would create quite deep but welcome shade.

The earliest treillage was probably a simple system of thin poles tied together with thongs to make squares and to which roses were trained, such as is seen in Luini's 'Virgin and Child in a Rose Bower' (early sixteenth century). When gardening became a fashionable form of art, trellis or treillage was very much taken up and often painted white. During the last century the lattice pattern was sometimes also made in iron, as in the aviary at Waddesdon Manor. I know of one instance where wooden treillage has been triumphantly used in recent years to make a rotunda at the end of a terrace. The wooden mesh, instead of being arranged in plain squares, has alternate double laths, giving it a 'tartan' pattern; it is secured to four-square trellis piers, the trellis work fixed to thick posts and surmounted by carved white-painted and gilded heads of heraldic beasts. Behind the mesh a beech hedge has been planted showing green or bronze behind the grid pattern in front of it.

There seems to be little reason for fixing trellis to the walls of a house to support climbing plants, something which can be done just as well by wires run through eyes held in the wall with rawlplugs. Unless it is made of cedar or some hard wood the trellis will need to be re-painted every three or four years, a process which may be impossible when it is covered with stems and foliage. Small pieces of trellis of a size possibly 610–914 mm by 1.8 m, about 2–3 ft by 6 ft high, bought separately for fixing alone against house walls for the training of one climbing rose are nothing short of ridiculous.

Four Postscripts

Postscripts

1. ON TAKING OVER AN EXISTING GARDEN

There are some obvious practical things to look to first before beginning to think of more attractive details of design and decoration. Among these are examination and repair of the fences and gates, making sure that the latter can be shut securely and will not blow open and bang and swing in gales. Then the internal lines of communication—a firm drive and courtyard properly drained, and firmly edged paths to essential working points, the kitchen garden, compost bins, tool shed and greenhouse; some of these may have to be visited in darkness in the winter, and sodden slippery turf possibly on a slant does not provide firm going. The clearance of overhanging branches, which can twitch off your cap or scratch your eyes as you blunder along in the dusk, must also be checked.

Adequate space is necessary, and may have to be provided, for at least two compost bins for recycling garden and household 'arisings' and, alongside, a burning ground clear of trees, for swift disposal of coarse matter unsuitable for composting. A weathercock here would be a well-mannered and justifiable ornament so that burning operations can be avoided when smoke would be carried over to neighbours. Here also should be spare ground, 25–42 m, 30–50 sq. yds, for the rescue of hyacinths, daffodils and tulips after they have served their gallant turns in bowls at Christmas. These will take a few years to revive, but after they have done so, can be planted out into the garden. Such a space would be useful for pricking out seedling wallflowers, Canterbury bells, fox-gloves, stocks and all the other biennial plants, of which the seed is offered with an *embarras de richesse* in seedsmen's catalogues, but the plants of which are generally available only as 'mixed' at garden centres and elsewhere. Such spare ground will be useful also for trying out at close quarters plants which have been admired at exhibitions and shows and compulsively ordered without proper thought of where they should go in the garden.

Next the state of the trees should be looked to. Important large trees, cedars and oaks among them, may need the attentions of a tree surgeon to remove damaged or infected branches, to strengthen forks with cables and to clear out the centres of trees which are becoming confused with too many branches. Large trees are precious and irreplaceable in a lifetime and should be taken care of. Some trees, old thorns and old apple trees for example, can become excessively twiggy in their middles and benefit from quite drastic pruning and thinning.

It is advisable to assess the efficiency of the water supply and drainage, making any necessary corrections.

The provision of shelter belts or simple screens of trees can be considered. Hedges should be cared for by clearing out the hedge bottoms, putting on a complete fertilizer when the ground is wet and warm and covering this with a mulch of animal manure if possible, or other bulk organic material, fertile peat or composted straw (see Appendix D). Evergreen hedges can be trimmed in August or September, but serious reshaping or shortening must only be done in spring. Thorn, beech and hornbeam hedges can be trimmed in the autumn.

The fertility of the garden generally will be reviewed. For this the purchase

117

of a soil testing kit is useful and it is also helpful to make contact with the Horticultural Adviser of the County Education Department to get the benefit of his local experience of growing conditions.

Having done all this it is good counsel to contain oneself in patience and live with a new garden for a whole year before making drastic alterations, both to assess the value of the existing arrangements of planting and also to discover where daffodils or other bulbs have been planted. It may be instructive to try to enter into the mind of the man who made the garden—even if he had a family of gnomes at the bottom he might also have had some ideas worth persevering with.

Large old greenhouses, even if partly dilapidated, may not be entirely beyond being brought back into some kind of service. If they can be made weather-proof and frost-proof by means of transparent polythene sheeting they could still be used as cold houses for peaches against walls or for fruit trees in pots. This is an unusual and attractive method of growing fruit in a small garden, and bushes established in pots can be bought from some nurserymen and placed on the terrace as pure decoration for most of the year. They require to be taken into shelter only in the very early spring until the fruit has developed. It may also be possible to bring back into use one end only of a large greenhouse by 'cannibalizing" parts of the rest of it and putting in an oil heater or electric fan blower simply to keep out the frost.

An anomalous tumble-down outhouse of stone or brick and flint abandoned by a previous owner can be made into a picturesque ruin by a little inspired knocking about here and there, clearing out its inside and planting ferns and deadly nightshade, and planting ivy on the outside for owls to roost in and hoot despairingly in autumn dusks.

2. A GARDEN ROOM

If it can be arranged either in the course of building a new house or by conversion of a room in an old house, a garden room is of great value and convenience, a room from which to go into the garden to work and to return to to change shoes, dry the dog after its walk and generally minimize the execrations of the janitress. In this room there would be a sink large enough to put a bucket into and deep enough to get the bucket under the taps. There should be one or more buckets and watercans for ordinary use and, if herbicides are used, one of each marked INFECT in purple underlined in red, because not all the waters in the rough, rude sea or all the perfumes of Arabia can remove all traces of modern selective weed-killers and, therefore, a separate bucket and can must be kept for their use.

A handbasin and a towel would be convenient. Here also would be kept wellington boots and a jack to pull them off with; also the small tools, such as secateurs and a jar of vaseline to keep them greased after they have been washed and dried; bird seed, chopped suet and nuts and, if necessary, fish food; labels also, indelible pencils, scissors, knives, flower vases, the garden notebook, seeds and string. There would be a lockable cupboard, high up and out of children's reach, for such poisons as the gardener's particular self-importance may cause him to feel entitled to use. The room could have also a cane chair of reasonable comfort out of range of the television and wireless and a spare basket for the dog and, not least, those individual essentials; for me, a pair of what I believe are known as industrial goggles, in which the 'glass' is a plastic, fitting very tightly round the sides. I have taken to these since twice walking into thorns on my blind side and injuring an eye which, although blind, is no less susceptible to pain than a sighted eye.

3. ROCK GARDENS

Conventional rock gardens of the 1920s in which hundreds of tons of water-worn limestone from Westmorland or the Cheddar Gorge were solemnly embedded on the sandy slopes of Surrey, may have been inspired in part by the grottoes of the eighteenth-century 'simple-lifers' who maintained personal hermits much as their descendants now fill their paddocks with bewildered zebras and giraffes: but today these rocks, ravished from their native gorge and mountainside, are incongruous to a degree beyond the accepted limits of contrast. A gardener who has an acre or so of land attached to his cottage on Pennine or Lakeland fells or the slopes of the Mendips can with minor excavation here, and building up there, make for himself a perfectly legitimate and acceptable rock garden in tune with the surroundings, providing that sharp drainage, high rainfall, pure air and exposure to sunlight that alpine plants require. In other parts of the country the desire to cultivate alpine and rock plants is far better satisfied by what a friend described as his RWR—rock garden without rocks. In this case there were three tiers retained by peat blocks built and bonded like a dry-stone wall. The first layer was about 305 mm, 1 ft, above the surrounding ground, the next 610 mm, 2 ft, and the highest 914 mm–1.2 m, 3–4 ft. Sharp drainage material similar to that described by Valerie Finnis[1] was filled in and alpine plants put in in accordance with the sharpness of the drainage which they require, with due regard to the *dicta* magisterially laid down by Reginald Farrer in *The English Rock Garden* (2 vols, T. C. and E. C. Jack, 1918). Peat blocks are generally supplied about 305 mm by 114 mm by 114 mm, 12 in by 4½ in by 4½ in, in size, and usually hard and dry when received. They must be soaked thoroughly before a start is made on building them into the walls, laying them flat on their bed and lengthwise into the soil behind them. The lowest course should be sunk a little into the ground to avoid slipping, and succeeding courses slightly recessed to prevent drying out and separation from the soil behind the wall.

4. SWIMMING-POOLS

A croquet lawn seems to be a natural part of an English garden, suggesting the unhurried grace of garden parties; so also to a degree do grass lawn tennis courts whose netting enclosures and supporting posts can be taken away. Hard courts and swimming-pools, however, are very different; they belong to the self-conscious world of Outdoor Life and Leisure. In climates where the sun shines for most of the year, these are acceptable in gardens which have been designed and planted to match—no trees near enough to drop their leaves in the water, and use of bright contrasting colours to live up to the perpetual glare. But in our softer-toned landscape, swimming-pools are intractable elements in design. Their hard rectangular shapes and glittering chromium hand-rails are startling enough in the summer, and when fitted with their winter covers they look like draped furniture in a seaside hotel out of season, and a contemplative gardener

[1] See page 22.

will want to keep his swimming-pool away from a main prospect and as far as possible out of sight altogether. Ways of doing this are suggested in Figures 3, 8, 12, 13, 18 and 21.

Pools for use in private gardens can be of almost any size and shape, apart from those made with a synthetic prefabricated lining of fixed size. A useful pool can be as small as 6.1 m by 3.7 m, 20 ft by 12 ft, with a depth of 2 m, about 6 ft 6 in. What might be called a family size may be in the region of 11 m by 5 m, about 36 ft by 16 ft 5 in, with a depth of 2 m, about 6 ft 6 in.

The depth is an important consideration in the interests of safety. To take one example, the Amateur Swimming Association advises that to dive from a spring board fixed 1 m, about 39 in, above water level the depth of water should be 3 m, 9 ft 10 in, and that this depth should be maintained forward for a distance of 5.3 m, about 17 ft 4 in, and sideways for a width of 2.2 m, about 7 ft 2 in. Mr G. D. Oakley of Penguin Swimming Pools has written to me a very helpful letter on a practical approach to this matter of depth, as follows:

> In this country laid-down standards for diving depths apply to school and other such pools. These state a water depth of 9 ft 10½ in for a one-metre spring board. This is, obviously, impracticable for a garden pool which normally varies in length between 30 ft and 40 ft. Thinking in terms of garden pools, if one is plunging off the edge of the pool then it would be quite difficult to hit the bottom if there was a 6 ft depth. When one has a small board this, obviously, should not be too springy or danger increases, not only of hitting the bottom through being able to get too much lift off the board but through being able to spring too far forward and ending in shallow water. Probably the ideal depth, if one is to be practical, would be 8 ft. However, if you have a 36-ft pool, to have a shallow end of, say, 3 ft and a deep end of 8 ft is not very practical because the slope on the floor is far too steep. It is also too short a length to go from, say, 3 ft to 4 ft 6 in and then break away quickly into the deeper area. This break-away point causes a danger in that people are just about to get out of their depths and then slide rapidly into the deep or, alternatively, if they dive a little too far forward they can hit the transition point unexpectedly.
>
> After many years of experience we compromise in most cases by having a deep point of 7 ft to 7 ft 6 in set on average 8 ft from the end of the pool.
>
> One point which is terribly dangerous is to break away suddenly into a 'hopper' from any depth where a non-swimmer is comfortably within his depth one minute and then on the 45° slope the next. Equally dangerous are ledges around the side of a pool.

It is rare nowadays for garden pools to be made of reinforced concrete placed between shuttering; instead, some form of block construction is more usual. A reinforced concrete floor slab is usually put in first and the walls built up with some form of concrete blocks vibrated and reinforced with metal rods. Another very satisfactory method is the pneumatic application of liquid concrete by a process often known as Gunite. In this case the reinforcement is fixed first to make a cage into which the concrete is pumped under considerable pressure. In any case, provision has to be made to relieve or dispose of pressure of water from under the pool—if this were not done it is quite possible for rising water to be able to push the whole pool a few feet up out of the ground. The usual method is to have a hydrostatic relief valve in the bottom of the pool. This will admit ground water into the pool when the latter is empty. Other methods are also to provide for adequate under-floor drainage.

When the main construction is finished, the pool is usually lined with two or three coats of cement 'rendering'. The last coat often has marble chippings and marble dust mixed in with the mortar, and is later rubbed down to give a smooth finish.

Many swimming-pool makers consider that we should be compelled to have pools of a postcard, Mediterranean-that-never-was blue. This they achieve by using a mosaic tile strip at the water line, which alone is quite enough to colour the whole pool. This may be very good in California, but it does not go with our gentle gradations of cloud and shade. It is far more attractive not to apply any colour whatever, but to allow the water to take soft aquamarine colours from the sky.

Filtration is necessary to remove solid particles of pollen, fibres from bathing dresses, general dust and leaves. This is carried out by a recirculating system: an electrically driven pump draws water both from the bottom of the pool and also from skimmer fittings at the sides. These skimmers draw a volume of water over efficient little weirs and remove much of the floating matter. Water from the skimmers and from the bottom is then passed through a filter which may be of diatomaceous earth, in which case it will have to be flushed to waste from time to time and replaced, or through sand which does not have to be replaced but still needs to be back-washed periodically to wash out the impurities. Provision therefore must be made for the water resulting from these back-washing operations to be disposed of, usually to a sump. Solid matter and leaves which sink to the bottom can be drawn up by a water vacuum-cleaner moved over the floor on a long handle. In large plants chlorination is carried out by the direct injection of chlorine gas into the circulating system. In small garden pools a solution, usually of sodium hypochlorite, is injected. There are also now available capsules which can be suspended in the pool and provide slow release of chlorine into the water.

Heating, very desirable in Britain, is incorporated with the circulating filtration system and can be by gas, electricity or oil. An effective heating system should be capable of providing a temperature lift of 9 deg. C, 16.2 deg. F, in reasonably still air conditions (a full north-easter will countervail the best laid schemes), within twelve hours or so; for this reason it is practical to fit an oversize heating plant to get the temperature up quickly—it costs no more to gain 9 deg. C, 16.2 deg. F, in twelve hours than in forty-eight hours.

Before work begins it is advisable to agree to a timetable. The filtration equipment at least, with all its connecting pipes, should be installed and the electrical supply tested and approved by the local authority, before the lining of the pool is begun, and this lining should not be started until the coping has been fixed. As soon as the lining is finished, that is within a few hours, the filling of the pool must begin and be finished as soon as possible in order to 'cure' the rendering and prevent its cracking. Then just as soon as the pool is filled to skimmer level the filtration plant must be set going. If this is not done there will be a high-water mark which will be difficult to get rid of later, and also fallen leaves and other debris may stain the bottom. This is of cardinal importance and should be insisted upon.

Appendix A

WATER SUPPLY

In the case of what have been referred to as primary sources—wells, ponds, streams or bore holes—delivery of water to the points of irrigation is most conveniently done directly by a mechanically driven, usually electric, pump, whether of submersible or dry motor type. Delivery of water can also be effected by pumping first to a staging tank, which acts as a reservoir and static tank, from which water is pumped on to final delivery points. Such a tank is necessary to collect rainwater from a roof, unless this water is conducted directly into a pond or stream. The amount of water falling on a roof may be surprising; even a modest-sized house about 18.3 m by 9.1 m, 60 ft by 30 ft, with a roof area of 167.2 m², 200 sq. yds, and an average annual rainfall of 762 mm, 30 in, would collect in a year over 127,247 litres, 28,000 gallons. This is enough to put the equivalent of 152 mm, 6 in, of rain over 836 m², nearly 1,000 sq yds. To hold this amount of water at one time would need a tank 9.1 m by 9.1 m by 1.5 m deep, 30 ft by 30 ft by 5 ft—the equivalent of a shallow swimming-pool, and much more than would be needed in a small to medium sized garden. A smaller tank measuring 6.1 m by 8.5 m by 1.2 m deep, 20 ft by 28 ft by 4 ft, would hold over 63,189 litres, 13,900 gallons, which is enough to supply 152 mm, 6 in, of rainwater over 418 m², 500 sq. yds. This area and this volume of water may constitute a useful module for calculating water need. It could be made up of 250.8 m², 300 sq. yds, of kitchen garden, the accepted size of an allotment garden, plus 167.2 m², 200 sq. yds, of flowers and grass (a tenth of an acre is 484 sq. yds).

Whatever may be the ultimate disposal of water from a roof, it is useful to arrange for down pipes to run first into waterbutts and to overflow from these into the tank or pond. Waterbutts usually hold about 181.8 litres, 40 gallons, and are useful to dip watercans into for supplies of soft water at atmospheric temperature, which is much more congenial to freshly planted vegetables and other crops than a cold douche of hard water from the main. A static tank or reservoir is also useful for storage of water which can only be delivered either intermittently, as in the case of some wells which may dry up and need to regenerate after a certain amount of pumping, or when the supply is small as, for instance, from a ram.

Where there is a stream which is not subject to marked fluctuations in level, and in which a dam can be made, it is usually possible to raise water by means of a hydraulic ram, a device which, although it only raises a low percentage—something in the region of 10 per cent of the water passing through it—none the less does this continually day and night, and needs no petrol or electricity, operating simply by the pressure developed from the velocity of water passing through it.

In order to operate a Hydram[1] a minimum working fall of the order of 914 mm, 3 ft, is required, plus a reliable flow of driving water in keeping with the size of ram. The driving water is conveyed to the ram through a drive pipe of specific size and length, and the water expended from the ram must be able to run freely to waste downstream.

The smallest ram will raise about 909.2 litres, 200 gallons, in twenty-four hours to a height of 6.1 m, 20 ft, with only 914 mm, 3 ft, fall, and a much larger one will raise 8,182.8 litres, 1,800 gallons, in the same time. With a greater working fall, the ram will raise similar quantities to heights well in excess of 6.1 m, 20 ft.

The figure of 909.2 litres, 200 gallons, a day may not sound very impressive, but in the six winter months alone, during which time probably no irrigation water would be

[1] The trade name of the type investigated, see list of suppliers, page 144.

required and consequently no water taken from the storage tank, 163,656 litres, 36,000 gallons, could be raised and stored, more than enough to put 305 mm, 12 in, of rain-water in the six months April to September, on to the putative 418 m², 500 sq yds, more than double what could be required.

Static water tanks are also useful safeguards against fire in isolated places, and now can be made without the expense of concrete, by lining an excavated area with a synthetic waterproof membrane such as butyl rubber, which has a long life and does not deteriorate on exposure to sunlight as membranes of other materials may do. The makers [1] supply detailed directions for finishing the excavated surface on which the membrane is to be laid, and also specify the bank-gradients to be observed for different soils. They also give directions for the securing and finishing of the edges. It is an advantage if small shallow tanks can be kept covered to keep out light, which promotes the growth of algae.

The following short table indicates volumes of water over certain areas:

Rainfall		Area Covered		Volume of Water (approx.)	
mm	*inches*	*Metric*	*Imperial*	*litres*	*gallons*
25	1 ⎫	4046.9 m²	1 acre	⎧ 102,738.5	22,600
152	6 ⎭			⎩ 616,431	135,600
25	1 ⎫	404.69 m²	484 sq. yds	⎧ 10,273.9	2,260
152	6 ⎭			⎩ 61,643.1	13,560
25	1	0.84 m²	1 sq. yd	20.9	4.6

An average watercan holds about 9 litres, 2 gallons, therefore two canfuls per 0.84 m², 1 sq. yd, of ground would be needed to put on the approximate equivalent of 25 mm, 1 in, of rain.

0.02 m,³ 1 cubic foot, of water = 28.32 litres, 6.23 gallons.

If water is to be conveyed by means of a hose from a main supply, it is necessary first to determine the requirements of the sprinkler or nozzle, then to calculate the loss of pressure from friction in the delivery hose, and relate these two factors to the pressure at the tap from the main. In the case of a widely used (Hozelock) oscillating sprinkler, a pressure of 3 kg/cm², 43 lb. per square inch (psi) is needed at the sprinkler with a volume of 18.2 litres, 4 gallons, per minute. The table on page 127 indicates loss of head (or pressure) due to internal friction. To assume in this case that the sprinkler is to be fed through 30.5 m, 100 ft, of 19 mm, ¾ in, hose at 18.2 litres, 4 gallons, per minute, the loss of head due to internal friction will be in the region of 3 m (0.3 kg/cm²), 10 ft (4.3 psi); probably more, because hose generally causes more internal friction than smooth pipe. The requirement, therefore, at the tap to work the sprinkler will be 3 kg/cm², 43 psi, plus loss of pressure in the hose, total 3.3 kg/cm², 47.3 psi.

The term 'head' will be explained later, but the conversion rates for head and kilos per square cm, pounds per square inch, are:

> 1 ft head equals 0.03 kg/cm²—0.43 psi
> 10 ft head equals 0.3 kg/cm²—4.3 psi
> 2.31 ft head equals 0.07 kg/cm²—1 psi

The internal diameter of the hose used is an important matter to be taken into consideration. A 19 mm, ¾ in, hose is usually satisfactory for distances of between 30.5 m and 61 m, 100 and 200 ft, but if the delivery run is longer it is better to use 25 mm, 1 in, size to avoid excessive loss of pressure at the nozzle due to friction in the pipe. For these volumes a 13 mm, ½ in, hose is much too small. It is widely marketed, but only really suitable for small rates of flow, 2.3 litres to 4.5 litres, ½ to 1 gallon, per minutes in short lengths, which may be appropriate for small gardens. A maker of sprinklers told me that it is impossible to calculate the internal pipe friction of 13 mm, ½ in, old, possibly rather kinky, hose. The best that he could do was to hazard a guess

[1] See Appendix J.

that the loss of head due to internal pipe friction is not less than 22.9 m, 75 ft head, 2.3 kg/cm², 32 psi, at 13.6 litres, 3 gallons, per minute.

It will be evident that instead of mains pressure through a tap electric pumps can be used to deliver water to points of irrigation from wells, ponds, streams and tanks. In nearly all cases the most satisfactory kind is an electrically driven submersible pump, the motor being entirely waterproofed and installed below water level. With this there are no priming problems, no difficulty with condensation in the motor and seldom any danger from frost; and it is almost completely silent running. What are known as dry-motor or surface centrifugal pumps can be used instead, but they must be installed where the motor is adequately ventilated to prevent overheating, not in a chamber below ground where dampness—if not actual flooding—might destroy the electric motor and other gear.

The output of a pump is stated as litres/gallons per minute against a given head. This head, expressed in metres or feet, is the resistance which the pump has to overcome to work a sprinkler or a fountain jet at its designed maximum performance. It is referred to as "total head from all causes", and is made up of gravity, and friction within both the suction and delivery pipes or hoses. Head due to gravity is approximately equal to the difference in level between the collecting and delivery points in the case of irrigation, and between the collecting point and the top of the jet in the case of a fountain. When the pump is installed above its collecting source, as may occur with a dry-motor pump in a garage or room of a house above a pool on a terrace, head due to static lift of water from the source to the pump must be added. (Some pumps are capable only of limited suctional lifts, and this requirement must be confirmed.)

When installed in a cellar at a lower level than the water in the pool dry-motor pumps have the benefit of flooded suction, and do not need priming, but for those above water level provision must be made either to keep the pump primed, or to have a means of priming it by hand. In the first case a foot-valve is fitted in the strainer at the end of the suction pipe; this is a one-way valve and works well until a piece of grit lodges in it to prevent it shutting properly, with the result that the suction pipe will empty and the pump must be reprimed, which may be an awkward procedure.

A better arrangement is to fit a special, and easily accessible, priming tank above the level of the pump in such a way that it is easy to fill from a watercan, or a hose and funnel. A non-return valve is necessary in the suction pipe below the connection to the tank, so that water added for priming cannot run away out of the suction pipe, and a controllable valve should also be fitted in the delivery pipe as close as possible to the pump, to prevent water siphoning back; this valve, which can be of wheel type, will in any case be useful for regulating the amount of water being delivered, and consequently the height of the jet or the power at the point of irrigation. Centrifugal pumps can quite safely be throttled back, so that they give only 25 per cent of their maximum delivery.

The table overleaf indicates rates of flow required to give jets of different heights through various nozzle sizes.

The table on page 127 indicates the approximate loss of head due to internal pipe friction, in pipes of different internal diameters and at different rates of flow. The figures are those generally applied in commercial practice, and in some cases are rather higher than would be experienced in new, smooth, non-ferrous pipes in good condition.

To take two examples:

1. To give a jet of 3 m, 10 ft, through a 6 mm, ¼ in, nozzle at 13.8 litres, 3.03 gallons, per minute, a pressure of 0.3 kg/cm², 4.3 psi, or 3 m, 10 ft, head is required. In the case of a submersible pump in the pool, the vertical head is 3 m, 10 ft (the height of the jet) and there are no significant friction losses. So a submersible pump capable of delivering 13.6–18.1 litres, 3–4 gallons, per minute against the total head of 3 m, 10 ft, is what is needed.

125

LITRES/GALLONS PER MINUTE DISCHARGED FROM JETS

NOZZLE SIZE	HEIGHT OF JETS			
	1.5 metres 5 feet	3.0 metres 10 feet	4.6 metres 15 feet	6.1 metres 20 feet
3 mm ⅛ in	2.4 litres 0.537 gallons	3.4 litres 0.758 gallons	4.2 litres 0.929 gallons	4.9 litres 1.07 gallons
4.7 mm ³⁄₁₆ in	5.5 litres 1.21 gallons	7.8 litres 1.71 gallons	9.5 litres 2.09 gallons	10.9 litres 2.41 gallons
6 mm ¼ in	9.8 litres 2.15 gallons	13.8 litres 3.03 gallons	16.9 litres 3.72 gallons	19.5 litres 4.29 gallons
8 mm ⁵⁄₁₆ in	15.3 litres 3.36 gallons	21.5 litres 4.74 gallons	26.4 litres 5.81 gallons	30.4 litres 6.70 gallons
10 mm ⅜ in	21.9 litres 4.83 gallons	31.0 litres 6.82 gallons	38.0 litres 8.36 gallons	43.9 litres 9.66 gallons
11 mm ⁷⁄₁₆ in	29.9 litres 6.58 gallons	42.3 litres 9.30 gallons	51.8 litres 11.4 gallons	59.1 litres 13.0 gallons
13 mm ½ in	38.9 litres 8.57 gallons	55.0 litres 12.1 gallons	67.3 litres 14.8 gallons	78.2 litres 17.2 gallons
16 mm ⅝ in	60.9 litres 13.4 gallons	85.9 litres 18.9 gallons	105.5 litres 23.2 gallons	121.8 litres 26.8 gallons
19 mm ¾ in	87.7 litres 19.3 gallons	124.1 litres 27.3 gallons	151.8 litres 33.4 gallons	175.5 litres 38.6 gallons
22 mm ⅞ in	119.5 litres 26.3 gallons	168.6 litres 37.1 gallons	206.8 litres 45.5 gallons	239.1 litres 52.6 gallons
25 mm 1 in	156.4 litres 34.4 gallons	220.5 litres 48.5 gallons	270.0 litres 59.4 gallons	311.8 litres 68.6 gallons

If, on the other hand, a dry-motor pump is used in, say, a barn 15.2 m, 50 ft, away from the pool and 1.5 m, 5 ft, above it, the calculation is more elaborate, thus:

Friction loss in 30.5 m, 100 ft (suction and delivery added together) of 19 mm, ¾ in, pipe at 13.6 litres, 3 gallons, per minute, is 1.5 m, 5 ft. The gravity head is made up of a suction lift of 1.5 m, 5 ft, and the height of the jet, 3 m, 10 ft, making 4.6 m, 15 ft. This is added to the 1.8 m, 6 ft, frictional loss to give a 6.4 m, 21 ft, loss of head from all causes. Here a pump to deliver 13.6 litres, 3 gallons per minute against a total head of 6.4 m, 21 ft, is needed, and one also capable of a suction lift of 1.5 m, 5 ft.

2. A much larger scheme might require a jet of 6.1 m, 20 ft, through a 25 mm, 1 in, nozzle, and call for, say, 318.2 litres, 70 gallons per minute, therefore a submersible pump capable of delivering this against a head of 6.1 m, 20 ft, is needed. But a dry-motor pump, say 30.5 m, 100 ft, away and 3 m, 10 ft, above water level, would need to overcome a gravity head of 9.1 m, 30 ft (6.1 m, 20 ft, for the jet, 3 m, 10 ft, for suction lift) and a friction loss equivalent to 2.4 m, 8 ft, head incurred by 61 m, 200 ft (30.5 m, 100 ft, each way) of 63 mm, 2½ in, pipe in which the friction loss at 318.2 litres, 70 gallons, per minute is equivalent to 1.2 m, 4 ft, per 30.5 m, 100 ft. The total head, therefore, from all causes is 11.6 m, 38 ft, so the pump chosen would have to deliver 318.2 litres, 70 gallons, a minute against a total head of 11.6–12.2 m, 38–40 ft.

Litres/Gallons per Minute	Pipe Size	Frictional Loss in metal pipe per 20 metres/100 feet *
9.1 litres 2 gallons	13 mm ½ in	9.1 metres or more 30 feet or more
9.1 litres 2 gallons	19 mm ¾ in	1.2 metres 4 feet
13.6 litres 3 gallons	19 mm ¾ in	1.5 metres 5 feet
18.2 litres 4 gallons	19 mm ¾ in	3 metres 10 feet
18.2 litres 4 gallons	25 mm 1 in	762 mm 2½ feet
22.7 litres 5 gallons	25 mm 1 in	914 mm 3 feet
45.5 litres 10 gallons	25 mm 1 in	3 metres 10 feet
45.5 litres 10 gallons	38 mm 1½ in	610 mm 2 feet
227.3 litres 50 gallons	51 mm 2 in	3 metres 10 feet
227.3 litres 50 gallons	76 mm 3 in	457 mm 1½ feet
318.2 litres 70 gallons	76 mm 3 in	762 mm 2½ feet

* Resistance through hose is likely to be greater.

Away from a terrace and farther out in the garden, a slab of rock with water just dripping from it can be effective, although usually a cascade needs to be assertive. The higher the waterfall the greater the depth of water needed over the weir sill, because the falling water is subjected to the acceleration of gravity and so the sheet gets thinner and thinner until it breaks into 'lace' and then mist. For small falls a depth of at least 13 mm, ½ in, of water over the sill is usually desirable. This requires about 45.5 litres, 10 gallons, per minute per 305 mm, 1 ft, width: a depth of 19 mm, ¾ in, needs about twice as much flow as 13 mm, ½ in, and 25 mm, 1 in, about four times as much. Avoid a round-nosed outer edge to the weir sill; make its surface smooth and sloping forward a little, and give it a sharp edge; this is to throw the water clear of the edge and prevent it dribbling down the wall.

Pipes going through walls and floors should be fitted with 'puddle-flanges'. These are collars attached to the pipes which, when cemented into the walls, help to prevent leaks through the masonry along the outsides of the pipes. Pipes going through plastic liners need pairs of flanges, surfaced with rubber sheeting to cushion their sharp edges, and must be assembled with the plastic sheet as a 'sandwich-filling' between them. Because of the frailty of the sheeting it is wise to nest the lower flange in concrete to give it support and avoid stresses.

To top-up the pool against evaporation loss, automatic valve gear can be provided, but it is usually adequate to use the garden hose occasionally to do it by hand. Equally, automatic equipment can be installed to sense the force of the wind and to turn down the high jets if it gets too strong. This can be an advantage especially in a municipal setting where the public may protest if they get splashed by the fountain.

Appendices

In this country the normal mains electricity supply to private houses is 230–250 volts single-phase AC, which is perfectly suitable to drive small motors up to 3-horsepower. Industrial and other premises are supplied with electricity at 400–440 volts 3-phase AC, and this type would be necessary for motors of over 3-horsepower. Motors must be provided with switch gear to start and stop them. Advice on the type of gear should be obtained from an electrical engineer experienced in water supply. It is a wise precaution to have the whole installation checked and approved for safety by the electricity undertaking, particularly where there are children, and where cables and mains voltages are led to submersible pumps.

Appendix B

MAKING COMPOST

The importance of making compost to produce humus is stressed in the section on soil in Chapter 1. To do it one or more bins are needed. For small gardens these can be 1 m by 1 m by 1 m high, about a 3 ft cube, so that each bin can be filled reasonably quickly, because in small gardens it is seldom possible to fill a bin in one day, and perhaps not even in a week, but the more quickly it can be filled and topped off with a layer of soil the more quickly material can be subjected to the rise in temperature at one time. Bins are made of solid material such as wood, concrete or straw bales and not of open mesh wire-netting, which gives too much ventilation and prevents the necessary temperatures being reached at the outside edges. It is absolutely essential that there should be no bottom and that the waste material as filled in should rest on the soil. A sloping top of iron or asbestos will stop the pile from being wetted by rain.

The first filling should be of coarse material such as thick cabbage stalks, thin twigs, etc., to allow of access of air from the bottom. Upon this lower ventilating layer vegetable material and household waste are put in to a depth of 152 mm, 6 in, and can include lawn mowings, weeds, nettles, cabbage leaves, tea leaves, orange peel, banana skins, fish bones, meat trimmings, and, in small quantities only, sawdust, shavings, shredded paper and chopped straw. When the layer has reached 152 mm, 6 in, an activator is needed. This can be a thin covering of animal manure, urine or a seaweed product such as Marinure. The activating layer, whatever it may be, is dusted over with soil and ground limestone. The process is then repeated until the bin is filled.

Aeration all through the heap is necessary and can be effected by pushing a crowbar down in the middle and just inside each of the four corners and swaying it a little from side to side to leave temporary funnels about 152 mm, 6 in, in diameter.

In two to three days the temperature will rise to nearly 65.5° C, 150° F. During the course of the process the temperature fluctuates in accordance with the rate of decomposition and in so doing allows different bacteria and fungi to play their parts.

Three weeks after the first filling the contents must be turned: the upper layer, which will not by then be much decomposed, into the centre where the heat is and the sides from outside to inside. Six weeks after this the contents should be turned again. By now the material will be dark in colour and finer in particle size. The ripening process now begins, and continues for about six weeks after the second turn, i.e. three to four months after beginning the process. The compost should now be nearly all humus, and a sign that it is 'done' is an invasion of small red worms from the soil beneath.

The quality of the compost will depend on what materials go into it; for instance, Raymond P. Poincelot, in *The Biochemistry and Methodology of Composting*, gives a table showing that grass clippings alone yielded 2.41 per cent by dry weight of nitrogen only and no phosphorus and no potassium; but grass clippings and weeds together gave 2.03 per cent nitrogen, 1.09 per cent phosphorus, 2.03 per cent potassium. So the more varied the materials that can be put in, the more complete as a fertilizer the humus will be.

Appendix C

TECHNIQUES OF PLANTING

Container-grown plants can be put in at any time of the year except in frost, provided that they are properly looked after, particularly in dry weather. The ground will have to be prepared for them in the same way as it would be for plants moved with bare roots. Nurserymen usually advise that deciduous trees and shrubs may be put in at any time between November and March in open weather, and it is remarkable how many plants survive under this rule of thumb. Most nurserymen also concur in the view that evergreens ought to be transplanted in October, or in March and April, for the reason that evergreens do not have an automatic dormant season in the way that deciduous plants do, although their growth is still slowed down and finally stopped at soil temperatures below about 5.6° C, 42° F. According to Hall[1] the active growth of plants is virtually suspended when earth temperatures are between 4.4° and 7.2° C, 40°–45° F. The killing of plants during frost is due chiefly to low temperatures at the roots, preventing the absorption of water to compensate for the drying effect of frost, and to cold winds.

This suggests that whenever it is practicable, planting should be done when the soil in the district concerned is at a temperature of over 5.6° C, 42° F, so that the root-hairs in their new environment can quickly establish biological contact with the soil. Records show that the mean soil temperature at Kew is above 5.6° C, 42° F, in October and November, and then drops below this until March, when it regains 5.6° C, 42° F, and is well above this from April until November. At Aberdeen the October average is 9.6° C, 49.3° F, November 6.2° C, 43.1° F, but 5.6° C, 42° F, is not exceeded until May, at 9.6° C, 49.3° F. By contrast, the mean soil temperatures at Plymouth are above 5.6° C, 42° F in every month.

It seems then that whenever it is possible to override the nurserymen's convenience, even deciduous plants are much better put in during November, or failing that in March or April, depending upon its being possible to give proper care, watering and screening from drying winds, to spring-planted material. Even those planted in the autumn could suffer from continued frost or cold winds round their stems or leaves if evergreen, and this can be substantially mitigated if a litter of dried bracken, large leaves, loose straw, etc. is put around them to reduce dangerous transpiration.

In preparing the ground for planting herbaceous material, roses and shrubs a cultivated depth of topsoil of 305–457 mm, 12–18 in, is needed. This is prepared by bastard trenching to the required depth, and incorporating compost or other organic material, animal manure, composted peat or composted straw.

Plants in hedges have to subsist unnaturally close together and they suffer also from lack of rain, which tends to bounce off the top of a hedge instead of getting to the roots. Hedge-lines therefore must be thoroughly prepared by taking out trenches at least 610 mm, 2 ft, wide and the same depth. The bottom of the trench is broken up and a good layer of animal manure put in and covered with soil before the plants are put in. The distances apart are indicated in Chapter 3.

Trees require what are known as tree-pits to be excavated, usually 610 mm by 610 mm by 610 mm, 2 ft by 2 ft by 2 ft, deep, and correspondingly larger in the case of trees with more widely spreading roots. The procedure is to excavate the soil from its pit, and if the soil at the bottom is of a free-draining character, simply to break this up with a pick, and then replace the excavated soil with a 76 mm, 3 in, layer of animal

[1] Sir A. D. Hall, *The Soil*, 4th edn 1931, John Murray.

manure or compost just below the position where the roots will be when the tree is planted. If the soil in which the tree-pit is excavated is retentive, it will be necessary to lay a length of drain from the bottom of the pit to an outlet to lower ground if this can be done. If the surrounding levels are such that it cannot be done, it will be advisable either to abandon the planting of the tree in that place, or to raise the tree-pit by first making a mound, or perhaps even building a brick or stone retaining wall around it. Before planting, a stake is put in, usually 1.8. m, 6 ft, above ground, and 610–914 mm, 2–3 ft, in the ground. The tree is then planted, the soil being consolidated every 76–102 mm, 3–4 in, by treading, and secured with two ties to the stake. The ground at the base of the tree is then tidied over, and if the soil temperature is 7.2° C, 45° F, or above, or if the soil temperature is lower, mulching will simply keep in cold conditions, and is a bad practice.

Evergreens, although usually small when they arrive from the nursery, will one day grow into tall trees and it is a mistake, when confronted with a plant only 610 mm, 2 ft, high to slip it unceremoniously into the ground. Proper planting positions, even tree-pits with all the benefits of drainage at the bottom, a thin layer of animal manure, good topsoil for filling, a stake in exposed positions, should be prepared. Camellias, azaleas, rhododendrons and other evergreen calcifuges should not be planted in limy soil, but in soil with a pH between 5.5 and 6.0 (see page 22). Camellia plants are as hardy as the common laurel; it is only the flower-buds that are vulnerable to early winter frost (it is said that if camellia buds survive until Christmas they will endure hard frosts later), but the flowers themselves can always be spoiled by biting winds and frost—particularly if exposed to early morning sunshine after a frost: this is the reason for planting them on north- or north-west-facing walls, or in woods and with a high top-cover of old oaks and pines.

All evergreens except holly, which should be planted in May only, are much better if planted in October while the soil is warm, so that their roots can start working and be ready to push up moisture to replace transpiration in the drying winds of March.

It is impossible to give a general recommendation for the distances apart of trees because so much depends on what they are required for. Most often they should not be planted so close that their branches touch in maturity but there are many exceptions to this, for example when a group of trees is planted close enough together to form a composite head in later years.

In planting shrubs regard must be had to their various ultimate overall widths, given in some nurserymen's catalogues. It is reasonable to make a compromise between the spread of the plants when first bought and their ultimate spread, calculated on a five-year expectation of width. For example, *Skimmia japonica*, supplied at a width of 305–457 mm, 12–18 in, and having an ultimate spread of perhaps 1.4 m, 4 ft 6 in, would be planted 914 mm, 3 ft, apart or possibly a little less.

Herbaceous plants can, for convenience, be averaged at 3 per 0.8. m², 3 per sq. yd, but there will be considerable variations depending on the size of the plant concerned. Delphiniums, for instance, should be at least 914 mm, 3 ft, apart, whereas small front-row edging plants such as *Campanula poscharskyana* would be 7–9 per 0.8 m², 7–9 per sq. yd.

Suggested densities of other plants are: seasonal bedding material (wallflowers, forget-me-nots, polyanthuses, petunias, tobacco plants, heliotropes, stocks), 305 mm, 1 ft, apart, 9 per 0.8 m², 9 per sq. yd; tulips 152 mm, 6 in, apart, 36 per 0.8m², 36 per sq. yd, or 229 mm, 9 in, apart, 16 per 0.8 m², 16 per sq. yd.

Daffodils for naturalizing are calculated at 229 mm, 9 in apart—but rolled out and planted where they stop (after a few obvious corrections), so that few are exactly 229 mm, 9 in, apart, and the whole 'drift' is irregular in outline. They should have 76 mm 3 in, of soil above their noses. Snowdrops, aconites, scillas and similar small bulbs are planted 25–76 mm, 1–3 in, apart and 102 mm, 4 in, deep; except cyclamens, which are planted only 51–76 mm, 2–3 in, deep and 305 mm, 12 in, apart.

Madonna lilies, *Lilium candidum*, are planted with the tops just showing above ground, in limy soil in full sun, in August.

Appendices

Lilium regale is planted in November in rich leaf-soil, a little acid, 76 mm, 3 in, deep.

'Crown Imperials'—*Fritillaria imperialis*— are planted 152–203 mm, 6–8 in, deep in August in rich soil.

Crinums are planted in spring 229 mm, 9 in, deep in warm positions, and at least 762 mm, 2 ft 6 in, apart.

Flag irises need a good dressing of lime. Lupins prefer an acid soil.

Phlox and peonies like some light shade for a part of the day.

Appendix D

PLEACHED TREES

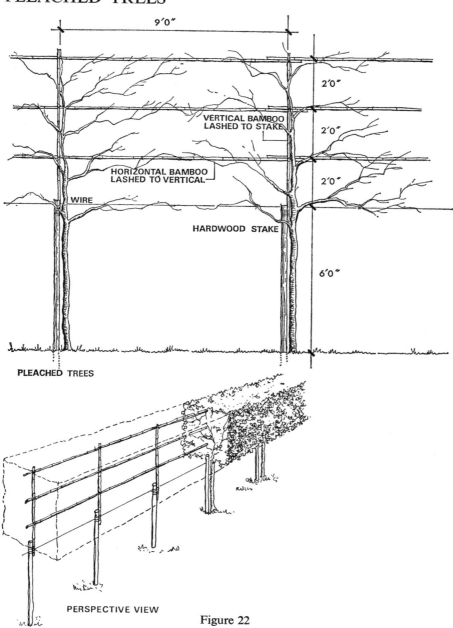

9'0"

2'0"

VERTICAL BAMBOO
LASHED TO STAKE

2'0"

HORIZONTAL BAMBOO
LASHED TO VERTICAL

2'0"

WIRE

HARDWOOD STAKE

6'0"

PLEACHED TREES

PERSPECTIVE VIEW

Figure 22

When it has grown into maturity, a line of pleached trees appears like a continuous box on stilts (see Pl. 4). It has been called an aerial hedge, and consists usually of 1.8 m, 6 ft, of clear stem (the stilts), surmounted by the continuous box of branches and leaves, again 1.8 m, 6 ft, high and about 1.8–3 m, 6–10 ft, wide depending on the training.

The most commonly pleached trees are limes; hornbeams are also used. In either case, standard trees with clear stems of 1.8 m, 6 ft, high, are planted 2.7 m, 9 ft, apart, sometimes in a double row to make a pleached alley. The trees are very firmly staked, preferably to chestnut stakes, which need not extend more than 1.8 m, 6 ft, above ground. To each stake is then lashed a very stout bamboo projecting for 1.8 m, 6 ft, above the top of the chestnut stake; three rows of stout horizontal bamboos are then lashed to the vertical ones to give the framework to which the growths of the trees are tied, and trimmed at least every other year.

The bamboos are exceedingly long-lasting but there may come a time when the chestnut stakes have rotted; then the bamboos can be fixed to the developing framework of lime or hornbeam.

Appendix E

DRAINAGE PLAN

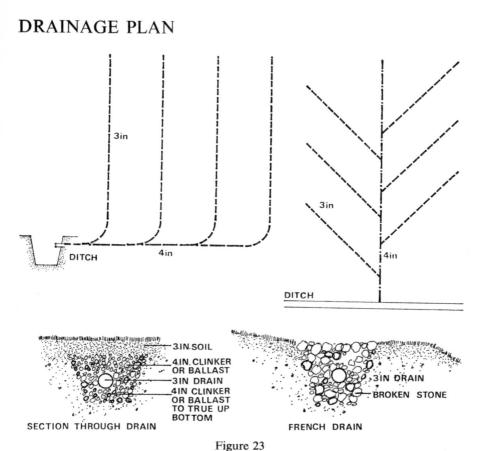

Figure 23

These drawings indicate two different ways of arranging undersoil drainage and a section of a French Drain described in Chapter 1.

Appendix F

HA-HA

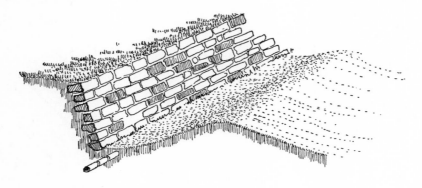

SECTION THROUGH HA-HA

Figure 24

The drawing shows the construction of a sunk fence, or ha-ha, permitting unrestricted views over the country beyond a garden and eliminating the necessity for a fence or a hedge.

Appendix G

CATTLE GRID PLAN

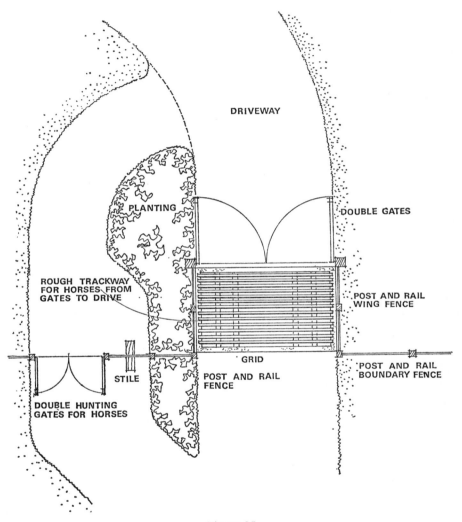

DRIVEWAY

DOUBLE GATES

PLANTING

ROUGH TRACKWAY
FOR HORSES FROM
GATES TO DRIVE

POST AND RAIL
WING FENCE

GRID

POST AND RAIL
BOUNDARY FENCE

STILE

POST AND RAIL
FENCE

DOUBLE HUNTING
GATES FOR HORSES

Figure 25

The drawing shows the design and indicates the construction of a cattle grid used in country districts to prevent horses, cattle and sheep from entering a drive without the necessity of shutting gates. To one side there is access over an ordinary drive for horses or for other livestock when they may need to enter the property. Here gates are provided and normally kept shut.

Appendix H

BRITISH STANDARDS IN NURSERY AND HORTICULTURAL PRACTICE

Gardeners, in common with others at the receiving end of production and distribution, will find the British Standards a reliable guide to normal acceptable quality. In their own words the British Standards Institution's main function is to 'draw up voluntary standards and codes of practice by agreement among all the interests concerned—manufacturing, using, professional and distributive—and to promote their adoption'.

The Institution, which dates from 1901, is financed by subscriptions from firms, trade associations, local authorities, professional institutions and other interested bodies, by a government grant and by sale of its publications. It produced the first standards for horticulture, including landscape work, in 1965.

Among those standards which may be of direct interest to gardeners are:

BS 3936, *Nursery Stock*. Part I, *Trees and Shrubs*, which after giving definitions of different types and shapes of trees and shrubs provides a table that includes normal retail sizes at which trees and shrubs are usually obtainable. To take three examples, *Magnolia* × *soulangiana*, 457–914 mm, 18 in–3 ft, lilacs 610 mm–1.2 m, 2–4 ft, *Viburnum tinus* (laurustinus), 305–457 mm, 1 ft–18 in. It is often possible to find larger plants than the sizes given if the purchaser has the time and the knowledge of where to look for them, or has a tame consultant whose business it is to know where he can put his hands on above-average specimens, but to an average gardener, advance knowledge that these are the usual sizes may prevent disappointment when the plants arrive.

BS 3936, *Nursery Stock*. Part 2, *Roses*, from which a purchaser can learn that good plants should have a minimum of two shoots arising directly from the union or one shoot which branches not more than 64 mm, $2\frac{1}{2}$ in, above the union, that there should be a minimum of three major roots, and that root growth shall arise within 64 mm, $2\frac{1}{2}$ in, of the base of the union.

BS 3936, *Nursery Stock*. Part 7, *Bedding plants grown in boxes or trays*, in which—after the statement that the plants should be true to name, have been pricked out, and be growing in a weed-free, disease-free, pest-free compost—reference is made to the maximum desirable number of different plants in each box offered for sale. The most valuable part of this British Standard is the stipulation that plants grown in boxes or trays shall not be offered for sale before certain dates, depending on the region. For instance, petunias should not be offered for sale before early May in the London area, mid-May in Birmingham, and late May in Aberdeen. Therefore a retailer who displays boxes of petunias for sale in London in mid-April is not complying with this British Standard; the purchaser should recognize this and also that by buying them at that time for planting in the open ground he is incurring a risk of losing them all through a late frost.

BS 3936, *Nursery Stock*. Part 9, *Bulbs, Corms and Tubers*, which chiefly gives information on minimum sizes of different bulbs.

BS 3969, *Turf*, which gives a list of common botanical names of desirable and undesirable grasses, of perennial weeds, soil conditions, dimensions of turfs, etc., but no descriptions or drawings to enable the grasses or weeds to be identified.

BS 4156, *Peat*, giving the desiderata for pH, moisture content, ash, particle size and yield.

BS 3975, *Glossary for Landscape Work*. Part 4, *Plant Description*, and BS 3975,

138

Glossary for Landscape Work. Part 5, *Horticultural, arboricultural and forestry practice*, will give the private gardener a working knowledge of the technical terms of the nursery-man and the jargon of the landscape contractor, and reveal to him the meaning of such words as bulb, calcicole, calcifuge, corm, fasciation, fastigiate, feathered, panning, pleaching, rhizome, stratification, tuber, vernalization.

There are three other British Standards largely concerned with skilled operations, but an acquaintance with the recommendations made in the Standards will assist the owner of a garden to keep a knowledgeable eye on work in progress.

BS 4428, *Recommendations for General Landscape Operations excluding hard surfaces*, deals with the practical operations of, for instance, spreading top soil, drainage, seeding, turfing and planting.

BS 3998, *Recommendations for tree work*, gives useful information on pruning and training, and the good cautionary advice: 'When it is known that the death of a tree has been caused by the honey fungus, *Armillaria mellea*, it is essential that the stump and roots should be removed and burned.' It also gives precise instructions for feeding trees of mature size. This is most important and too often neglected. Proper fertilizing of old trees will preserve their vigour and shape past maturity, and it will also encourage rapid growth of younger trees.

BS 4043, *Recommendations for transplanting semi-mature trees*. This gives information on the whole process, from the preparation by root pruning, which must be done at a sufficient interval before extraction to allow for development of a new fibrous root system, methods of extraction, loading and transporting, to replanting and securing.

British Standards on nursery and horticultural practice give specifications for the following:

BS 1722, Part 7, definitive sizes for the timbers and the kinds of timbers recommended for post-and-rail fences.

BS 1722, Part 5, close-boarded fences including oak pale fences.

BS 1722, Part 11, woven wood (interplat) fences.

BS 1722, Part 6, wooden palisade fences.

BS 1722, Part 4, cleft chestnut pale fences.

BS 1722, Part 8, mild steel or wrought iron continuous bar fences.

BS 3798 coping units for unreinforced cast concrete, unreinforced cast stone, natural stone and slate.

BS 585 contains the specification for wood stairs and within it the formula for the relation of tread or 'going' to riser, as follows:

2 R plus G equals 575 mm to 630 mm

where R equals rise and G equals 'going'

Translated to inches, 575 mm equals $22\frac{5}{8}$ in, 630 mm equals $24\frac{4}{5}$ in, so in Imperial terms the formula would read:

Twice the rise plus the 'going' equals 23–25 in

A full list of British Standards is available from the BSI Sales Office, 101–113 Pentonville Road, London N.1.

Appendix I

METRICATION

As mentioned in the Introduction, both metric and Imperial dimensions are given because we have already entered the period of change-over to full metrication with the adoption in this country of the Système International d'Unités (SI), yet it may be assumed that for a number of years many people will find it easier to visualize dimensions in the old terms.

Throughout the book decimal places are not used for millimetres, which have been rounded up to the higher figure when the decimal is 0.5 mm or above. In the case of metres, the second decimal place is approximated upwards when it is 0.05 or above; thus 5.67 m is expressed as 5.7 m, 5.63 m is expressed as 5.6 m. In practice it will probably be found that dimensions will be rounded off to a convenient figure—for example, already a paving slab measuring 3 ft by 2 ft is no longer made at that size and offered as 914.4 mm by 609.6 mm, but instead is manufactured at the new rounded-off size of 900 mm by 600 mm. This process may take a little time to settle into common usage.

Under the SI system there are six base units, of which in this book we are concerned with four: metre (m), kilogramme (kg), second (s), kelvin (K). (The others are ampère (a) and candela (cd).) The general recommendation for the use of SI units is that prefixes representing 10 raised to a power which is a multiple or sub-multiple of 3 are particularly preferred. This is to avoid the danger of confusion that might arise where two different multiples closely related in value are used in the same context. This means that for most technological purposes the use of the millimetre is preferred to the use of the centimetre.

The base unit for length is the metre (m). The recommended multiple is the kilometre (km), or 10^3 m, and a recommended sub-multiple the millimetre, or 10^{-3} m.

For the area the base unit is the square metre (m^2), the multiple the square kilometre (km^2) and a recommended sub-multiple the square millimetre (mm^2).

For volume the base unit is the cubic metre (m^3). A sub-multiple is the cubic millimetre; the litre and millilitre may also be used.

For mass (weight) the base unit is the kilogramme; a preferred sub-multiple is the gramme.

The unit of power derived from base units is the watt (W).

METRIC CONVERSION TABLES
LENGTH CONVERSION FACTORS

Metric	Inches	Feet	Yard
1 mm	0.039	0.003	—
1 cm	0.393	0.032	0.011
1 m	39.37	3.280	1.093

Inches	mm	m	Feet	mm	m
$\frac{1}{8}$	3.175		1	304.8	0.305
$\frac{1}{4}$	6.350		2	609.6	0.610
$\frac{3}{8}$	9.525		3	914.4	0.914
$\frac{1}{2}$	12.70		4		1.219
$\frac{5}{8}$	15.87		5		1.524
$\frac{3}{4}$	19.05		6		1.829
$\frac{7}{8}$	22.22		7		2.134

Inches	mm	m	Feet	mm	m
1	25.40		8		2.438
2	50.80		9		2.743
3	76.20		10		3.048
4	101.6		11		3.353
5	127.0		12		3.658
6	152.4		13		3.962
7	177.8		14		4.267
8	203.2		15		4.572
9	228.6		16		4.877
10	254.0	0.254	17		5.182
11	279.4	0.279	18		5.486
12	304.8	0.305	19		5.791
18	457.2	0.457	20		6.096
			30		9.144
			40		12.19
			50		15.24

AREA CONVERSION FACTORS

Metric	Sq. inches	Sq. feet	Sq. yards
1 mm²	—	—	—
1 cm²	0.155	0.001	—
1 m²	1550	10.76	1.196

Sq. inches	mm²	m²
1	645.2	
2	1290	
3	1936	
4	2581	
5	3226	
6	3871	
7	4516	
8	5161	
9	5806	
10	6452	
11	7097	
12	7742	0.007
18	—	0.012
144 (1 sq. foot)		0.093

1 sq. yard (1296 sq. ins)	0.836 square metres or m²
1 acre (4840 sq. yds)	⎧ 4046.86 square metres or m² ⎨ 0.4047 hectares ⎩ 0.0040 square kilometres or km²

VOLUME CONVERSION FACTORS

Metric	Pints	Gallons
1 millilitre	0.0017	0.0002
1 litre	1.7598	0.220
1 cubic metre	1759.8	219.9

Imperial	Millilitres	Litres	m³
½ pint	284.0	0.284	
1 pint	568.0	0.568	
1 quart	1136	1.136	
½ gallon	2273	2.273	
1 gallon	4546	4.546	
1 bushel		36.37	0.036
1 cubic foot		28.32	0.283
1 cubic yard (21 bushels)		764.5	0.764

MASS CONVERSION FACTORS

Metric	Oz.	lb.
1 gramme	0.035	0.0022
1 kilogramme	35.26	2.205

Imperial	g	kg
1 ounce	28.34	0.028
1 lb.	453.6	0.454
7 lb.	3175	3.175
14 lb.	—	6.350
28 lb.	—	12.70
56 lb.	—	25.40
1 cwt	—	50.80
1 ton	—	1016

POWER CONVERSION FACTOR

(1 Watt = 0.00134 horsepower)

Horsepower	Watts
$\frac{1}{32}$	23.30
$\frac{1}{16}$	46.60
$\frac{1}{8}$	93.91
$\frac{1}{4}$	186.4
$\frac{1}{2}$	372.8
$\frac{3}{4}$	559.2
1	745.7
2	1491
3	2237
4	2982
5	3728

VOLUME—RATE OF FLOW

Gallons per minute	Litres per second	Litres per minute	Litres per hour	m^3 per hour	Gallons per hour
1	0.075	4.55	272.7	0.273	60
2	0.151	9.09	545.5	0.545	120
3	0.227	13.64	818.3	0.818	180
4	0.303	18.18	1091	1.091	240
5	0.378	22.73	1363	1.363	300
6	0.454	27.27	1636	1.636	360
7	0.530	31.82	1909	1.909	420
8	0.606	36.37	2182	2.182	480
9	0.681	40.91	2454	2.454	540
10	0.759	45.46	2727	2.727	600
11	0.833	50.00	3000	3.000	660
12	0.909	54.55	3273	3.273	720
13	0.985	59.10	3545	3.545	780
14	1.060	63.64	3818	3.818	840
15	1.135	68.10	4091	4.091	900
16	1.212	72.74	4364	4.364	960
17	1.288	77.28	4636	4.636	1020
18	1.363	81.83	4909	4.909	1080
19	1.438	86.38	5182	5.182	1140
20	1.515	90.92	5455	5.455	1200

PRESSURE

lb. per square inch	*kilogrammes per square centimetre*
1	0.07
2	0.14
3	0.21
4	0.28
5	0.35
6	0.42
7	0.49
8	0.56
9	0.63
10	0.70
20	1.40
30	2.11
43	3.02
50	3.51
100	7.03

TEMPERATURE

°F	°C
0	−17.78
4	−15.56
8	−13.33
12	−11.11
16	−8.89
20	−6.67
24	−4.44
28	−2.22
32	0.00
36	2.22
40	4.44
44	6.67
48	8.89
52	11.11
56	13.33
60	15.56
64	17.78
68	20.00
72	22.22
76	24.44
80	26.67
84	28.89
88	31.11
92	33.33
100	37.78
212	100.00

Miscellaneous Dimensions

At the time of going to press no decision has been made on metrication for the following:

Lawn tennis court: playing area 78 ft by 36 ft, 23.8 m by 10.98 m.
Approved overall area 120 ft by 60 ft, 36.6 m by 18.3 m.

A reasonable practical overall size for a grass tennis court is 108 ft by 54 ft, 33 m by 16.5 m.

for a croquet lawn: 35 yds by 28 yds, 32 m by 25.6 m.

for a bowling green: either 40 yds by 40 yds, 36.6 m. by 36.6 m or 42 yds by 42 yds, 38.4 m by 38.4 m.

Appendix J

(a) SHORT LIST OF SUPPLIERS

PLANTS

Garden centres can supply many plants usually of excellent quality, especially when container grown, but their range is often limited. In the light of experience in replying to correspondence arising out of articles I have been surprised to find how little known some of the major and specialist nurseries are. Because of this I give a short list.

SPECIALIST NURSERIES

General: trees, shrubs, herbaceous plants, roses, fruit trees:

Jackmans Nursery Ltd,
Woking,
Surrey.

Hillier & Sons,
Winchester.

John Scott & Co.,
Merriott,
Somerset.

Sunningdale Nursery Ltd,
Windlesham,
Surrey.

Notcutts Nursery Ltd,
Woodbridge,
Suffolk.

Rose Specialists:

John Mattock Ltd,
Nuneham Courtenay,
Oxford.

Fruit-tree Specialists:

Thomas Rivers & Son Ltd,
The Nursery,
Sawbridgeworth,
Herts.

Unusual Plants:

The Plantsmen,
Buckshaw Gardens,
Holwell,
Sherborne,
Dorset.

Bulbs:

P. De Jager & Sons,
Marden,
Kent.

Walter Blom Ltd,
Leavesden,
Watford,
Herts.

Peter Nyssen Ltd,
Railway Road,
Urmston,
Manchester.

Small Bulbs:

Broadleigh Gardens,
Barr House,
Bishops Hull,
Taunton,
Somerset.

J. A. Mars,
Haslemere,
Surrey.

Water Plants:

Perry's Hardy Plant Farm,
Enfield,
Middlesex.

Herbs:

E. & A. Evetts,
Ashfields Herb Nursery,
Hinstock,
Market Drayton,
Shropshire.

BUTYL RUBBER MEMBRANE

Gordon Low Prefabrications Ltd,
88 Place Road,
Cowes,
Isle of Wight.

GARDEN ORNAMENTS

Anthony Mawley Ltd,
PO Box 75,
London, SW1X 0LD

Chilstone Garden Ornaments,
Great Linford Manor,
Newport Pagnell,
Bucks.

Iudex Limited,
The Manor,
East Haddon,
Northampton, NN6 8BU

144

HOSES, SPRINKLERS, ETC.

Hozelock Limited,
Haddenham,
Aylesbury,
Bucks.

SWIMMING-POOLS

Bishop Swimming Pools Ltd,
Beechwood House,
Taplow,
Maidenhead,
Berkshire.

Penguin Swimming Pools Ltd,
Five Tree Works,
Bakers Lane,
Galleywood,
Chelmsford,
Essex, CM2 8LD.

WATER RAM (Hydram)

John Blake Limited,
PO Box 43,
Royal Works,
Accrington,
Lancashire.

WATER SUPPLY ENGINEERS

Guthrie Allsebrook & Co. Ltd,
Artesian Works,
Crown Street,
Reading,
Berkshire.

PROFESSIONAL BODIES AND TRADE ASSOCIATIONS

The British Association of Landscape
Industries, Honorary Secretary:
J. E. Parnham,
North Lane Gardens,
Leeds 8.

The British Association of Sportsground
and Landscape Contractors,
87 London Road,
Croydon, CR0 2RF.

The British Standards Institution,
2 Park Street,
London, W1Y 4AA.

The Cement & Concrete Association,
52 Grosvenor Gardens,
London, SW1.

The Garden History Society,
Honorary Secretary:
Mrs Mavis Batey,
12 Charlbury Road,
Oxford.

Membership Secretary:
Miss J. Lee,
24 Woodlands,
North Side,
London, SW4 0RJ.

The Horticultural Trades Association,
18 Westcote Road,
Reading, Berkshire.

The Institute of Landscape Architects,
12 Carlton House Terrace,
London, SW1.

John Innes Institute,
Colney Lane,
Norwich, NOR 7OF.

The Royal Horticultural Society,
Vincent Square,
Westminster,
London, SW1.

The Swimming Pool & Allied Trades
Association,
87 London Road,
Croydon, CR0 2RF.

Bibliography

I have divided the list of books into two. In Part I are those most directly related to the practical side of design and construction; those in Part II are for more general reading round the subject of gardens in general.

The dates of publication where given are those of my own copies. There may be earlier or later editions of some of the books.

PART ONE

Allen of Hurtwood, Lady, and Jellicoe, Susan, 1956. *The New Small Garden.* Architectural Press.

Anderson, E. B., 1961. *Camellias.* Blandford Press.

Anderson, E. B., Fish, Margery, Balfour, A. P., Wallis, Michael, Finnis, Valerie, illus. Nicholson, B. E., 1963. *The Oxford Book of Garden Flowers.* Oxford University Press.

Arnold-Forster, W., 1948. *Shrubs for the Milder Counties.* Country Life.

Bagenal, N. B., 1939. *Fruit Growing.* Ward Lock.

Beadle, Dave, 1972. *Concrete Round the House* (pamphlet). Cement & Concrete Association.

Bean, W. J., 1929–33. *Trees and Shrubs Hardy in the British Isles*, 3 vols. John Murray. 1945. *Wall Shrubs and Hardy Climbers.* Putnam.

Beazley, Elisabeth, 1962. *Design and Detail of the Space Between Buildings.* The Architectural Press.

Brett, W. S., 1957. *Planning Your Garden.* Ward Lock.

Bruce, M. E., 1967. *Common-sense Compost Making.* Faber & Faber.

Bunyard, E. A., 1920. *A Handbook of Hardy Fruits, Apples and Pears.* John Murray. 1925. *A Handbook of Hardy Fruits, Stone and Bush Fruits, Nuts, etc.* John Murray.

Church, Thomas, D., 1955. *Gardens are for People.* Rheinhold Publishing Corporation, New York, U.S.A.

Clapham, A.R., Tutin, T.G., and Warburg, E. F., 1959. *Excursion Flora of the British Isles*, Cambridge University Press.

Clark, H. F., 1948. *The English Landscape Garden.* Pleiades.

Colvin, Brenda, and Tyrwhitt, Jacqueline, illus. Badmin, S. R., 1949. *Trees for Town and Country.* Percy Lund Humphries.

Crowe, Sylvia, 1971. *Garden Design.* Country Life.

Dutton, Ralph, 1950. *The English Garden.* Batsford.

Fish, Margery, 1964. *Gardening in the Shade.* Collingridge.

Franck, Nicolette, 1968. *Concrete and Gardens* (pamphlet). Cement & Concrete Association.
1972. *Concrete in Garden Making* (pamphlet). Cement & Concrete Association.

Fraser, H., 1966. *The Gardener's Guide to Pruning.* Collingridge.

Hadfield, Miles, 1957. *British Trees.* J. M. Dent.

Hervey, George F., and Hems, Jack, 1958. *The Book of the Garden Pond.* Stanley Paul.

Hillier's *Manual of Trees and Shrubs*, 1971. Hillier & Sons, Winchester.

Howard, Sir Albert, 1940. *An Agricultural Testament.* Oxford University Press.

Howard, Alexander L., 1949. *Trees in Britain and Their Timbers.* Country Life.

Ingram, Collingwood, 1948. *Ornamental Cherries.* Country Life.

Jackson, Robert, 1946. *Gardening on Chalk and Lime Soil.* Williams & Norgate.
Jekyll, Gertrude, 1899. *Wood and Garden.* Longmans Green & Co.
    1901. *Wall and Water Gardens.* Country Life—George Newnes.
Jekyll, Gertrude, and Hussey, Christopher, 1927. *Garden Ornament.* Country Life.
Jellicoe, Geoffrey, 1960. *Studies in Landscape Design.* Oxford University Press.
Jellicoe, Susan and Geoffrey, *Modern Private Gardens.* Abelard-Schuman.

Le Sueur, A. D. C., 1949. *The Care and Repair of Ornamental Trees,* Country Life.
    1951. *Hedges, Shelter Belts and Screens.* Country Life.
Lloyd, Christopher, 1970. *The Well-Tempered Garden.* Collins.

Macself, A. J., 1952. *Ferns for Garden and Greenhouse.* Collingridge.
Makins, F. K., 1946. *British Trees in Winter.* J. M. Dent.
    1952. *The Identification of Trees and Shrubs.* J. M. Dent.
Manley, Gordon, 1971. *Climate and the British Scene.* Collins.
Meteorological Office, 1960. *Averages of Earth Temperature for the British Isles* (booklet). H.M.S.O.
    1963. *Averages of British Sunshine* (booklet). H.M.S.O.
    1969. *Averages of Temperature* (booklet), H.M.S.O.
    1970. *Averages of Rainfall* (booklet). H.M.S.O.
    1973. *Tables of Temperature, Relative Humidity and Precipitation for the World. Part III, Europe and the Atlantic Ocean North of 35° N.* H.M.S.O.
Miller, Gault S., and Synge, Patrick, M., 1971. *The Dictionary of Roses.* The Royal Horticultural Society and The Royal National Rose Society.
Ministry of Agriculture, Fisheries and Food, 1970. *Modern Farming and the Soil.* H.M.S.O.

Nicholson, H. H., 1942. *The Principles of Field Drainage.* Cambridge University Press.

Page, Russell, 1962. *The Education of a Gardener.* Collins.
Pauli, F. W., 1967. *Soil Fertility.* Adam Hilger.
Perry, Francis, 1947. *Water Gardening.* Country Life.
    1957. *Collins' Guide to Border Plants.* Collins.
Pirone, P. P., 1959. *Tree Maintenance.* New York, Oxford University Press.
Poincelot, Raymond P., 1972. *The Biochemistry and Methodology of Composting* (leaflet). Connecticut Agricultural Experiment Station, New Haven, U.S.A.

Roper, Lanning, 1957. *Successful Town Gardening.* Country Life.
Royal Horticultural Society, The, 1941. *The Vegetable Garden Displayed.* The Royal Horticultural Society.
    1951-6. *Dictionary of Gardening,* 4 vols. and supplement. Oxford, The Clarendon Press.
    1962. *Some Good Garden Plants.* The Royal Horticultural Society.
    1967. *Rhododendron Handbook, Part I, Species, Part II, Hybrids.* The Royal Horticultural Society.
    1968. *The Fruit Garden Displayed.* The Royal Horticultural Society.
Russell, Sir John E., 1971. *The World of the Soil.* Collins.

Street, Frederick, 1958. *Hardy Rhododendrons.* Collins.
Sutton & Sons, 1902. *The Culture of Vegetables and Flowers.* Simpkin, Marshall, Hamilton, Kent & Co.
Synge, Patrick M., 1971. *Guide to Bulbs.* Collins.

Thomas, Graham Stuart, 1955. *The Old Shrub Roses.* Phoenix House.
    1962. *Shrub Roses of Today.* Phoenix House.
    1970. *Plants for Ground-Cover.* J. M. Dent.
Triggs, H. Inigo, 1913. *Garden Craft in Europe.* Batsford.

Whitehead, Stanley B., 1954. *Fruit from Trained Trees.* J. M. Dent.

Yates, Robert C., 1952. *A Handbook of Curves and Their Properties.* J. W. Edwards, Ann Arbor, U.S.A.

Bibliography

PART TWO

Books of more discursive interest

Ary, S., and Gregory, M., illus. Nicholson, B. E., 1962. *The Oxford Book of Wild Flowers*. Oxford University Press.

Blunt, Wilfred, 1950. *The Art of Botanical Illustration*. Collins.

Bowles, E. A., 1972. *My Garden in Autumn and Winter*. David & Charles.
1972. *My Garden in Spring*. David & Charles.
1972. *My Garden in Summer*. David & Charles.

Bunyard, E. A., 1933. *The Anatomy of Dessert*. Chatto & Windus.
1936. *Old Garden Roses*. Country Life.

Crowe, Sylvia, and Miller, Zvi, ed., 1964. *Shaping Tomorrow's Landscape*, 2 vols. Djambatan, Amsterdam.

Edlin, A. L., 1972. *Trees, Woods and Man*. Collins.

Evelyn John, [1664] 1726. *Silva*, with notes by A. Hunter, M.D., F.R.S. Ward, York (for Dodesley, Pall Mall).

Fairbrother, Nan, 1956. *Men and Gardens*, Hogarth Press.
New Lives New Landscapes, Architectural Press.

Farrer, Reginald, 1918. *The English Rock Garden*. 2 vols, T. C. & E. C. Jack.

Forestry Commission Booklet No. 18, 1966. *Forestry in the Landscape* by Sylvia Crowe, H.M.S.O.

Forestry Commission Booklet No. 20, 1968. *Know your Broadleaves* by Herbert L. Edlin. H.M.S.O.

Forestry Commission Booklet No. 33, 1972. *Conifers in the British Isles* by A. F. Mitchell, H.M.S.O.

Forestry Commission Bulletin No. 30, 1957. *Exotic Forest Trees in Britain*, H.M.S.O.

Gerard, John, *Herball 1636*, ed. Marcus Woodward. Gerald Howe, 1927.

Hadfield, Miles, 1960. *Gardening in Britain*. Hutchinson.

Hampton, F. A., 1925. *The Scent of Flowers and Leaves*. Dulau.

Hanmer, Sir Thomas, *The Garden Book 1659*. Gerald Howe, 1933.

Hatfield, Audrey Wynne, 1969. *How to Enjoy Your Weeds*. Frederick Muller.

Hill, Jason, 1932. *The Curious Gardener*. Faber & Faber.

Hoskins, W. G., 1967. *Fieldwork in Local History*. Faber & Faber.

Hussey, Christopher, 1967. *The Picturesque*. Frank Cass.

Huxley, A. J., 1962. *Garden Terms Simplified*. W. H. & L. Collingridge.

Hyams, Edward, 1971. *A History of Gardens and Gardening*, J. M. Dent.
ed., 1953. *Vineyards in England*. Faber & Faber.

Jones, Barbara, 1953. *Follies and Grottoes*. Constable.

Keeble, Sir Frederick, 1939. *Science Lends a Hand in the Garden*. Putnam.

Knight, R. P., 1795. *The Landscape, A Didactic Poem in three books*. London, W. Bulmer; republished by Gregg International, 1972.

Lousley, J. E., 1950. *Wild Flowers of Chalk and Limestone*. Collins.

Mack, Maynard, 1969. *The Garden and the City*. Oxford University Press.

Macleod, Dawn, 1968. *A Book of Herbs*. Duckworth.

McLintock, David, 1966. *Companion to Flowers*. Bell.

Malins, Edward, 1966. *English Landscaping and Literature*. Oxford University Press.

Masefield, G. B., Wallis, M., Harrison, S. G. and Nicholson, B. E., 1969. *The Oxford Book of Food Plants*. Oxford University Press.

Mason, W., 1783. *The English Garden. A poem in four books*, A. Ward, York; republished by Gregg International, 1971.

Masson, Georgina, 1961. *Italian Gardens*, Thames & Hudson.

Maxwell, Sir Herbert, 1923. *Flowers, A Garden Notebook*. Maclehose Jackson, Glasgow.

Mellanby, Kenneth, 1967. *Pesticides and Pollution*. Collins.

Ministry of Agriculture, Fisheries and Food, 1967. *Horticulture in Britain, Part I, Vegetables*. H.M.S.O.
1970. *Horticulture in Britain, Part II, Fruit and Flowers*. H.M.S.O.

North, Pamela, 1967. *Poisonous Plants*. Blandford Press.

Parkinson, John, 1629. *Paradisi in Sole Paradisus Terrestris*.

Pemberton, the Rev. J. H., 1920. *Roses, their History, Development and Cultivation*. Longmans Green.

Philbrick, Helen, and Gregg, Richard, B., 1967. *Companion Plants*. Stuart & Watkins.

Price, Uvedale, 1794. *Essays on the Picturesque*; edition of 1810 republished by Gregg International, 1972.

Proctor, Michael, and Yeo, Peter, 1973. *The Pollination of Flowers*. Collins.

Raven, John, 1971. *A Botanist's Garden*, Collins.

Robinson, W., 1901. *English Flower Gardens*. John Murray.

Rohde, Eleanour Sinclair, 1948. *The Scented Garden*. The Medici Society.

Royal Horticultural Society, The, 1973. *Fruit Present and Future*. The Royal Horticultural Society.
Year Books—Rhododendrons and Camellias, 1971; *Lilies*, 1971; *Daffodils and Tulips*, 1970, 1971.

Sitwell, Sir George, 1909. *On the Making of Gardens*. Reissued by Gerald Duckworth, 1970.

Sitwell, Sacheverell, 1939. *Old Fashioned Flowers*, Country Life.

Smith, A. W., ed. Stearn, W. T., 1972. *A Gardener's Dictionary of Plant Names*. Cassell.

Taylor, Geoffrey, 1952. *The Victorian Flower Garden*. Skeffington.

Taylor, George M., 1948. *The Little Garden*. Collins.

Villiers-Stuart, C. M., 1913. *Gardens of the Great Mughals*. A. & C. Black.
1936. *Spanish Gardens*. Batsford.

Wood, Denis, 1970. *Terrace and Courtyard Gardens*. David & Charles.
and Crosby, Kate, 1975. *Grow It and Cook It*. Faber & Faber.

Woodbridge, Kenneth, 1970. *Landscape and Antiquity*. Oxford, The Clarendon Press.

Index

150